"This is a really important book addressing the fundamental question of how younger evangelicals read the Bible and engage with deeper questions of faith. It is thorough and convincing, allowing participants' voices to be heard alongside Perrin's intelligent analysis of their engagement. It is a compelling read, and, given that this is a largely missing demographic from our churches, I commend it to all church leaders, especially those who seek to engage with this generation."

—**Mark Tanner**, Warden, Cranmer Hall, Durham University

"The importance of young evangelicals in the leadership of church and society, both present and future, should not be underestimated and consequently what they actually believe is of both academic and pastoral concern. Ruth Perrin's ground-breaking research gives both new data and insightful interpretation to help us all in this task."

—**David Wilkinson**, Principal, St. John's College; Professor of Theology and Religion, Durham University

The Bible Reading of Young Evangelicals

The Bible Reading of Young Evangelicals

An Exploration of the Ordinary Hermeneutics
and Faith of Generation Y

Ruth H. Perrin

FOREWORD BY
James S. Bielo

PICKWICK *Publications* · Eugene, Oregon

THE BIBLE READING OF YOUNG EVANGELICALS
An Exploration of the Ordinary Hermeneutics and Faith of Generation Y

Pickwick Publications
An Imprint of Wipf and Stock Publishers
199 W. 8th Ave., Suite 3
Eugene, OR 97401

www.wipfandstock.com

PAPERBACK ISBN: 978-1-4982-9342-6
HARDCOVER ISBN: 978-1-4982-9344-0
EBOOK ISBN: 978-1-4982-9343-3

Cataloguing-in-Publication data:

Names: Perrin, Ruth H. | foreword by Bielo, James S.

Title: The Bible reading of young evangelicals : an exploration of the ordinary hermeneutics and faith of generation y / Ruth H. Perrin, with a foreword by James S. Bielo

Description: Eugene, OR: Pickwick Publications, 2016 | Includes bibliographical references.

Identifiers: ISBN 978-1-4982-9342-6 (paperback) | ISBN 978-1-4982-9344-0 (hardcover) | ISBN 978-1-4982-9343-3 (ebook)

Subjects: LSCH: Bible—Criticism, interpretations, etc. | Bible—Reading | Bible—Hermeneutics | Bible—Reader response criticism.

Classification: BS476 P27 2016 (print) | BS511.3 (ebook)

Manufactured in the U.S.A.   09/29/16

This book is dedicated to the remarkable emerging adults I have been privileged to know and work with. Their faith and courage continues to inspire me.

Contents

Foreword

How do Christians read the Bible? This is a serious question with far-reaching implications: sociological, cultural, theological, political, personal. To put the question more precisely: how do *ordinary* Christians *actually* read the Bible? That is, when people of faith without formal training in ancient languages, hermeneutics, or textual criticism sit down with scriptural texts, how do they understand them and what do they have to say about them?

Of course, what evangelical Christians call "the Bible" is actually a collection of sixty-six different books, written across a period of multiple centuries by different authors and ranging across genres and styles. Northrop Fry described the Bible as "a mosaic: a pattern of commandments, aphorisms, epigrams, proverbs, parables, riddle, periscopes, parallel couplets, formulaic phrases, folktales, oracles, epiphanies, *Gattungen, Logia,* bits of occasional verse, marginal glosses, legends, snippets from historical documents, laws, letters, sermons, hymns, ecstatic visions, rituals, fables, genealogical lists, and so on almost indefinitely."[1] Really, the act of reading Scripture could be considered overwhelming, even immobilizing. Perhaps it is the height of futility? Or, perhaps, daring?

Foolish or fearless, ordinary Christians do read the Bible. Millions do, every day, and again the next. And so, serious questions demand serious answers. As scholars in the social sciences and humanities, when we want to engage a question such as this—how *do* Christians read the Bible?—we are confronted with a decision of method. Quantitative measures are helpful, but eventually they raise more questions than they answer. Questionnaires can tell you how often the Bible is read, where, among who, which texts are favored, how people characterize their approach to Scripture, and so on, but even the most finely and cleverly crafted survey instrument cannot

1. Frye, Northrup, *The Great Code: The Bible and Literature* (New York: Harcourt Brace, 1981).

observe how people struggle to make sense of the text and what emerges from that struggle. For this, we need qualitative research that embraces the complexity, the creativity, and the messiness of modern readers grappling with ancient words in specific cultural contexts during particular socio-historical moments.

Enter Ruth Perrin's marvelous new book. Strictly speaking, this is a book about "ordinary biblicism" among young adult British evangelicals. It results from Perrin's research with focus groups of readers in three English congregations. But really, it exceeds this modest description. It is a systematic and insightful contribution to comparative scholarship in the social life of scriptures.

First and foremost, readers have been given a gift: a model for what it means to do rigorous, well-crafted qualitative work. With any qualitative project, there are numerous questions of research design to consider, numerous choices to make, numerous ways in which the project can go right or wrong. Perrin has made one good choice after another, orchestrating a project that is elegant and compelling. Readers in the process of designing their own project will benefit greatly from the clarity and transparency with which she invites us into the fieldwork process.

Of course, many readers will not be holding this book as researchers plotting a project, but as scholars, citizens, and/or believers genuinely wanting insight into the question of how Christians read the Bible. They will also benefit. Perrin marshals her data to address numerous questions about these British evangelicals. We learn about the difference between popular and authorized readings. Following scholars like Brian Malley and Andrew Village, Perrin shows how easy categories like "biblical literalism" fail to capture the diversity of interpretive practices among Christians who all affirm scriptural inerrancy. We learn how reading is a social, collaborative process, best understood in the context of group discussion. We learn about how factors of gender and age intersect to shape how individuals read the same text differently. And, to my mind one of the book's most distinctive contributions, we learn how Bible reading is deeply affective, not merely cognitive. When these British evangelicals read Scripture, they do so through the experiential and emotional registers of their lifeworld, not merely a set of easily definable intellectual dispositions.

More than the sum of its individual findings, Perrin's work will be a lasting contribution to multiple fields of inquiry. Scholars working in comparative areas like the ethnography of reading and the sociology of evangelicalism will find fresh insight in these chapters. Scholars interested in the movements and contours of contemporary British religion will read this book productively alongside recent works like Anna Strhan's *Aliens and*

Strangers? and Matthew Engelke's *God's Agents*. This book poses a particular promise for the budding field of ethnographic theology. Writing as an insider to the British evangelical community, Perrin presents her research and the lives of her readers with the eye of a diligent analyst seeking to make trustworthy claims and the heart of a fellow traveller seeking to make the trail more visible. Ethnographic theology is about expressing, generating, and realizing theological knowledge through the research process. Still young, the field is long on ambition and theoretical sophistication, but short on well-designed, rigorous qualitative fieldwork. Perrin's work will inspire and educate her colleagues.

How *do* Christians read the Bible? No book, sociological or theological, will really answer this question. But, good books, generative books, will help reveal what is really entailed in asking and addressing this question. Good books excavate the question, sharing the forms of foolishness, fearlessness, curiosity, creativity, doubting, and faithfulness discovered in the process. The book you are holding is just such a read.

James S. Bielo

Miami University

Preface

MANY HAVE ATTEMPTED TO teach the Bible to young people. Some of us have done it for a long time. Many of us have also wondered what effect our preaching, teaching, and mentoring has actually had; what we have intentionally (or unintentionally) modelled?

This book, and the research on which it is based, came out of personal curiosity about how I, and many others, had influenced the Bible reading of those we have tried to help. Rather than anecdote and supposition I wanted rigorous evidence: What happens when young adults are given a Bible passage? How do they make sense of it? What is important to them and why? The findings have subsequently shaped my own preaching and teaching. My hope is that they might also help others reflect on their own attempts to teach Scripture in a faithful and life giving way, particularly to those who are in the early days of their faith journey.

Acknowledgments

I WOULD LIKE TO acknowledge the encouragement and support that made this book possible. In particular, Mathew Guest and Richard Briggs at the University of Durham who supervised the PhD on which it is based.

Likewise I would like to thank "Sarah," "Will," "Ken," and their congregations for their willingness to participate in the research. Similar thanks go to the leadership of "Hope Community" who permitted me to run pilot studies.

Finally, I would like to thank the friends, family, and colleagues who have supported and encouraged me to pursue this study and its subsequent publication; the Bible Society for their financial assistance; James Bielo for his foreword; and the editorial team at Pickwick Publications.

1

Introduction

Background to the Project

Rationale for the Research

THIS PROJECT WAS BORN out of fifteen years of ministry with young British evangelical Christians. To date there has been little empirical research into this group and so this research set out to explore four areas of their faith.

- Firstly, how it develops as they progress through the liminal period of their twenties.

- Secondly, since Evangelicals emphasize the Bible as central to their faith and yet there is considerable evidence of declining biblical literacy, it aimed to explore their biblical engagement and hermeneutic processes.[1]

- A third priority was to examine differences across the spectrum of British evangelicalism; to explore how far young evangelicals conform to the doctrinal positions of their churches and the extent to which trans-denominationalism is creating a more eclectic form of evangelical spirituality.[2]

- Finally, having previously undertaken research into gender-related issues I wanted to examine how far attitudes to gender influenced behaviour and biblical engagement.

These sociological, theological and hermeneutical questions are interrelated and are woven throughout this book, providing nuanced evidence

1. Field, "Is the Bible becoming a closed book?," 503–528.
2. McGuire, *The Social Context*, 290- 293.

1

and fresh insight into contemporary British evangelicalism and the faith of young adults in that context.

Researcher Context

With the advent of liberationist and feminist research methodologies, it has become standard practice for sociologists of religion to declare their understood biases and personal agendas. I am a charismatic evangelical, biblical feminist and a non-ordained minister. However, I grew up within Reformed evangelicalism and have been involved in a range of national and international evangelical organizations. I have friends and colleagues from across the world and have been fascinated by the differences in global evangelicalism. Within the UK I have attended Baptist, Anglican, and New Churches, have friends and colleagues from Methodist, Brethren, Pentecostal, and Reformed traditions and have often found myself translating across denominational boundaries. I am an insider researcher, with the advantages and limitations that brings. However, I am not blind to the limitations of my chosen tradition, nor entirely unsympathetic towards others I do not belong to. In fact, my diverse background facilitated this research. The church leaders invited to participate were personal friends and colleagues, and our shared concerns motivated their cooperation. Inevitably, as an insider researcher there were dynamics that I was normalized to, however it also allowed me to understand references and responses that an outsider might have misunderstood. I have therefore endeavoured to be both objective and respectful towards the range of beliefs and traditions among those participating.

Who Is This Book For?

This book is adapted from a doctoral thesis and aimed at two audiences. Firstly, the academy; those interested in the fields of the sociological study of evangelicalism and of emerging adulthood. It adds to a growing body of work in both fields. However, it is also aimed at those in the church who wish to reflect on their own ministry, Bible teaching and its impact on younger generations. The first chapter provides definitions which will help in understanding specific terminology and highlight related work. The second, a methodology chapter, introduces the participating churches and focus groups. Chapters 3 and 4 consider in detail the ordinary readings and interpretative methods of the young adults involved, comparing them with scholarly analyzes and wider evangelical trends. Chapters 5 to 7 reflect on three of the theological distinctives which divide British evangelicals: attitudes towards the supernatural, acts of violence attributed to God, and issues around gender. Each considers current debates before presenting the response of the readers. Chapter 8 examines group dynamics and chapter 9 draws some conclusions. My hope is that it will stimulate discussion, reflection, and thoughtful engagement with both the faith of contemporary young adults and how they read the Bible.

Situating the Research

Although this project has clear overlaps with the field of practical theology it has not primarily focussed on transforming practice or creating ministerial outcomes. It is a study in biblical hermeneutics or "ordinary biblicism" and the sociology of evangelicalism with particular reference to emerging adults. To situate the project, some terms first need to be defined and the literature in those fields considered. They are: "contemporary British evangelicalism," "emerging adulthood," and "ordinary biblicism."

Defining Evangelicalism

As philosophers and linguists have long told us, words do not have clear meanings. We interpret them in their context and from our own perspective.[3] This means that, for those belonging to a certain group, a word may carry one set of meanings, yet for an outsider or academic it may mean something entirely different. This is particularly pertinent when labelling religious groups. Words can simply be descriptive yet perceived as positive or pejorative. Likewise, an individual's self-described faith might be linguistically inconsistent with an academic description. Ammerman notes, in her work on Fundamentalism, that self-identification is not entirely reliable.[4] Similarly, Guest discovered confusion and the contesting of labels within a single English church congregation.[5] Religious and theological labels amongst ordinary church goers can often be vague.[6] Thus, asking someone to define their Christian tradition may or may not be a helpful indicator of their doctrine and religious praxis. "Evangelical," as a descriptor of a type of Protestant Christian spirituality, is a good example. Despite its linguistic

---

3. Clines, *The Bible and the Modern World*, 6.

4. Ammerman, *Bible Believers*, 4.

5. Guest et al., *Congregational Studies*, 75.

6. Village, *The Bible and Lay People*, 1–2.

root (*evangel* meaning good news), its definition has always been contested. Lord Shaftesbury in the eighteenth century wrote, "I know what constituted an Evangelical in former times, I have no clear notion what constitutes one now."[7] Scholarly work distinguishing between evangelicalism and fundamentalism is discussed in chapter 3, but essentially evangelical describes a set of core theological positions summarized by Bebbington: "*Conversionism*, the belief that lives need to be changed; *activism*, the expression of the gospel in effort, *biblicism*, a particular regard for the Bible; and what may be called *crucicentrism*, a stress on the sacrifice of Christ on the cross. Today they form a quadrilateral of priorities."[8]

Critiques of this quadrilateral include arguments for a prioritized version, the addition of revivalism, christocentricity (a prioritization of Christ over other members of the Trinity), and the addition of expectation of a transformed life.[9] Larsen has a five-point description and Warner adds faith not works and trans-denominationalism, describing "twin and rival axes" within British evangelicalism. One axis he describes as conversionist-activist, the other biblicist-crucicentrist.[10]

Some of these suggestions are helpful. Certainly evangelicals expect a transformed life. However, it could be argued that this expectation falls within a prioritization of crucicentrism—the ongoing transformational power of the cross in the life of the believer. Likewise, an emphasis on faith not works is directly theologically related to conversionism, it need not be a discrete fifth category. With regard to christocentrism, charismatic evangelicals strongly emphasize the Holy Spirit and some prioritize "the father heart of God."[11] Similarly, trans-denominationalism is not universal; some conservative evangelicals and parts of the New Frontiers network discourage movement to other evangelical churches.[12]

Warner's dichotomous axes are insightful, but they are based on Bebbington and do not account for all evangelical groupings. Particularly among younger evangelicals, resources and teaching from both axes are adopted. Those Pally calls "the new evangelicals" might be described as biblicist-activists. Inspired by biblical themes of justice and mercy, they are

7. Bebbington, *Evangelicalism*, 1–2.

8. Ibid., *Evangelicalism*, 3.

9. Barclay reorders them: biblicism, crucicentrism, conversionism, activism. *Evangelicalism*, 10; McGrath, *Evangelicalism*, 51; Calver and Warner, *Together we stand*, 98.

10. Larsen, "Defining Evangelicalism," 1–14; Warner, *Reinventing English Evangelicalism*, 18–20.

11. McClung, *The Father Heart of God;* Dawson, lastdaysministries.org; Bickle, mikebickle.org.

12. Robbins and Kay, "Evangelicals and the Charismatic Movement," 140.

concerned to communicate the love of Christ through social justice and societal transformation rather than through traditional conversionism. Indeed, many evangelicals have adapted and modified position and praxis since Warner's model was published. Ultimately, none of these alternatives significantly undermine Bebbington's model. Since his axes are not fixed points, it allows for sufficient flexibility to accommodate most evangelical groupings and remains the most helpful summary to date. Bearing all this in mind I shall continue to use it, assuming that those I am describing assert faith not works and expect a transformed life but may prioritize the four qualities differently.

Despite certain groups mentioned above, one of the reasons clear definitions within British evangelicalism are so difficult to formulate is the increasing trend towards trans-denominationalism.[13] Anecdotal evidence that denominational loyalty is in decline is confirmed by the 2013 Evangelical Alliance survey which reports that only 8 percent of respondents considered denomination a very important factor when considering which church to attend.[14] A more transient lifestyle means it is typical for individuals to belong to a number of denominations.[15] For example, a significant number of Baptists have been drawn to the New Frontiers network and many charismatic Anglicans now lead New Churches.[16] Increasing social mobility, the "haemorrhaging" of young and middle-class worshippers to "fashionable congregations in city suburbs," and the development of New Church streams with aggressive church planting policies are significant.[17] These, combined with the internet and media-driven culture of conferences and publications have given individuals access to global teaching and worship, transforming church attendance habits.[18]

Inevitably, as people move from church to church they carry with them a mixture of theological positions, stylistic preferences and diverse influences; thus, although people tend to do this within a limited range of denominations, few evangelical congregations can be defined as "pure" anything. Often only the leadership are consciously aware of the doctrinal positions with which a certain church is associated. In a simultaneously globalized and individualistic society, while denominational heritage still

13. Richter, "Denominational Cultures," 169.

14. Smith, 21st Century Evangelicals, 22.

15. 90 percent of 50 young women surveyed belonged to two or more denominations. Perrin, "Biblical Role Models."

16. Kay, Apostolic Networks,70; Scotland, Charismatics, 302.

17. Guest, Congregational Studies, 75; Chambers, "The Effects of Evangelical Renewal," 61.

18. Warner, Reinventing English Evangelicalism, 67–68.

has influence, a hybridization of doctrine and praxis appears routine, with many Christians unconsciously adopting theological positions from eclectic sources.[19] Therefore, even if it is possible to label a particular evangelical church, this by no means ensures that its members hold the same beliefs.[20] It is likely that they would fit within a theological range, but denominational labels are less significant than shared Christian identity. In a post-Christian culture like contemporary Britain, believers tend to be more aware of stylistic than denominational or theological differences and may well look for a church based on individual preferences such as worship style, the needs of their children, social compatibility or geographical convenience.[21]

In reality, this is nothing new. Since the Reformation, Protestant groups have been separating, redefining, and influencing each other's spiritual practice. Mennonite influence on the Anglican John Wesley is a good example and, in 1851, nineteen evangelical denominations were identified in England and Wales.[22] Celtic, Brethren, and Quaker spirituality have influenced other Protestant traditions, and Pentecostalism has had influence far wider than its actual membership. Bebbington describes evangelical Christianity as an ongoing kaleidoscope.[23] Its ability to engage with contemporary culture and adapt to the demands of each subsequent generation are arguably one of its greatest strengths. Nonetheless, this makes the task of defining any particular group a taxing one. For some believers, evangelical is a description they embrace whole-heartedly. For others it is an adjective, a descriptor of the sort of Anglican, Methodist, or charismatic they are. Yet, for many it has become pejorative, synonymous with a hardline absolutism that disregards other types of Christian spirituality. However, this is often a caricature, since churches that hold to Bebbington's quadrilateral are so diverse. Regardless of how assertive or diplomatic they are, or how open or closed to ecumenism, some hold firmly to the label, while others are reluctant but maintain the core values. Evangelicals are typically pragmatic: if dropping a culturally incomprehensible label, while holding to their values, achieves their purpose of communicating the gospel to contemporary society, many are happy to do so. Indeed, of the four churches involved in this study, two used the label evangelical, one has publicly modified it to "Bible teaching church" (but still uses evangelical as a self-descriptor amongst its

19. Richter, "Denominational Cultures," 170–72.

20. Guest, *Congregational Studies*, 82.

21. Richter, "Denominational Cultures," 170.

22. Wolffe, *The Expansion of Evangelicalism*, 218.

23. Bebbington, *Evangelicalism*, 270.

established congregation) and one was reluctant to use the language at all (although its leader accepted that they were "evangelicals really").

Contemporary British Evangelicalism

Contemporary British evangelicalism has a complex and distinct history, rooted in attempts to redress theological liberalism in the traditional denominations and historical-criticism in the academy.[24] Wright describes it as the child of British Puritanism and German Pietism, stressing serious theological and biblical enquiry with an emphasis on personal relationship with God.[25] Although it has overlaps with global evangelicalism, it has taken a unique path that is influenced by, but does not always parallel, its transatlantic cousin. The theological diversity within British evangelicalism means: "There is no British, still less any European, evangelical theology, if by that is meant an identifiable, commonly held and distinctive position; instead there is an ongoing conversation, returning often to central themes, but in different ways."[26]

A number of taxonomies have been proposed to describe these diverse groupings. Wright adopts Fackre's categorisation of: fundamentalist, old, new, justice and peace, charismatic, and ecumenical evangelicals.[27] Warner also creates six categories: neo-fundamentalist, neo-conservative, moderate conservative, Lausanne mainstream (engaged) evangelicals, reconstructed evangelicals, and radical evangelicals.[28] However, none of these models manage to capture the subgroupings, alliances and fractures that mark the ever evolving face of British evangelicalism.[29] They may describe a snapshot in time, but are outdated as new churches, partnerships, or conflicts emerge.

Writing in the mid-1990s, Wright argued that evangelicalism was not disappearing but mutating.[30] Warner, published in 2007, suggested that it was becoming increasingly polarized and anticipated both ends of the spectrum abandoning the label in order to avoid association with each other.[31] Bebbington is less pessimistic, seeing British evangelicalism as eclectic but

---

24. Bebbington, *Evangelicalism*, 181–228.

25. Wright, *The Radical Evangelical*, 3.

26. Greggs, *New Perspectives*, 5.

27. Wright, *Radical Evangelical*, 6.

28. Warner, *Evangelicalism*, 229–30.

29. Evangelicals appear to be unaware of tribal labels. Holmes, "Evangelical Theology," 33.

30. Wright, *Radical Evangelical*, 1.

31. Warner, *Evangelicalism*, 241.

acknowledging that any former unity has been broken.[32] Indeed, the decline in membership of the Evangelical Alliance suggests that British evangelicals no longer see their common heritage as enough to theologically unite them. Instead, Ward argues that they have become tribal, although "intermarriage, trade and exchange between the tribes is considerable."[33] Perhaps then, it is most helpful to see British evangelicals as an extended (and complex) family whose relationships ebb and flow, ranging from fierce disagreement to intentional solidarity, but none the less grounded in the same essential DNA of Bebbington's quadrilateral.

Studies of British Evangelicalism

Touching on the field of congregational studies the present work follows in the tradition of qualitative research, exploring the theological variations, behaviours and beliefs of evangelicals. The field of evangelical ethnographic study is extensive and well established in the United States.[34] A growing body of British research in the last decade includes the work of Aune, Guest, Rogers, Cartledge, and Strhan.[35] This project is informed by, but not entirely comparable with any of these works. Some ethnographic observation was undertaken to assist in understanding context, but it is not primarily an ethnographic study. It is an examination of a particular age group across a number of evangelical congregations, and is comparative in nature. Thus, rather than trying to build a full picture of these communities, the project focuses on the way their emerging adults behaved in corporate Bible study.

Defining Emerging Adulthood

Given the age-related focus of this project, developmental research is pertinent and some further definitions are required.

---

32. Bebbington, "Evangelical Trends," 104.

33. Ward, "The Tribes of Evangelicalism," 19–34; Wright, *Radical Evangelical*, 9.

34. E.g., Ammerman, *Bible Believers*; Wuthnow et al., *I Come Away Stronger*; Bartkowski, "Beyond Biblical Literalism," 259–72; Crapanzano, *Serving the Word*; Friend-Harding, *The Book of Jerry Falwell*; Malley, *How the Bible Works*.

35. Aune, "Marriage," 638–57; Guest, *Evangelical Identity*; Rogers, "Ordinary Biblical Hermeneutics; Cartledge, *Testimony in the Spirit*; Strhan, "Discipleship and Desire".

Faith Development Models

It is widely recognized that in late adolescence/early adulthood cognitive transitions take place.[36] These are related to maturation in brain structure and include synaptic pruning (the selective elimination of unnecessary neuronal connections), myelination of the prefrontal cortex (which optimizes the transmission of electrical signals around the central nervous system), and changes in the limbic system.[37] Changes in the prefrontal cortex cause the subsequent development of executive functions. These make cognitive processing more efficient, allow for the suppression of distractions while increasing working memory and the capacity for abstract thinking. Thus the age period is highly significant in developing conceptual frameworks and advanced reasoning ability about abstract and complex subjects—such as ultimate concerns including religious belief.[38]

There is also a growing body of literature around changes in religiosity during this life stage (much of which comes from the United States). These often differentiate between religious practices and religious beliefs and focus on the transition away from the childhood home into independent living which many young adults in developed societies undertake. Much of the evidence suggests that, despite significant life changes and the opportunity to explore wider religious concepts, spiritual and religious beliefs tend to remain stable.[39] However, religious practices such as attending church and praying decline.[40] Nonetheless, it is widely recognized that this life stage is particularly significant to identity formation and meaning making, thus exposure to and exploration of religious faith can be a significant part of this developmental task.[41]

Models to explain faith development originate with James Fowler,[42] who used the developmental stages mapped out by Levinson.[43] Fowler argued that between the ages of seventeen and twenty-two faith typically moves from a non-reflective and conformist stage (largely determined by others) to "individuative-reflective" faith; an individualistic stage with the

36. Luna et al., "Maturation of Cognitive Processes," 1357–72.

37. McNamara, "Religiosity and Spirituality," 312.

38. Levenson, "Religious Development," 147, 312.

39. Astin and Astin, *Spirituality in College Students*; Lefkowitz, "Things Have Gotten Better," 40–63; Guest, *University Experience*.

40. Koening, "Stability and Change," 532–43; Stopp and Lefkowitz, "Longitudinal Changes," 23–38.

41. Reynolds, "Friendship Networks," 383–98.

42. Fowler, *Stages of Faith*, 241–45.

43. Levinson, *Seasons of a Man's Life*.

loci of authority moving to the self.[44] Criticisms of Fowler argue that his model is falsely universalizing, hierarchical, and gendered and that it promotes rationalism and theological liberalism over other forms of knowledge and spirituality. However, in a western context, Astley acknowledges that the experiences of many do resonate with Fowler's descriptions.[45] Feminist alternatives also perceive this age span as particularly significant.[46] Similarly, *The Critical Years*, written in 1986, argued for the late teens and early twenties being a significant period in establishing a life pattern.[47] However, current work suggests that economic and sociological changes have had an influence so significant on the development of the current young adult generation as to render earlier models outdated.

The work of Arnett, *Emerging Adulthood*, has led to a growing field of academic study. He argues that the lifestyle and expectations of young adults are radically different to those of previous generations and thus the developmental process has extended to at least twenty-five.[48] Economic factors have altered employment patterns; extended periods of education (and the associated debt), combined with changing patterns of sexual behaviour and marriage, mean that young adults do not expect to settle down by their mid-twenties.[49] Instead they are expected to negotiate a "self-biography," gathering experiences and defining themselves without an established cultural model.[50] Wuthnow concurs, arguing that the statistical midpoint of adulthood in America is now forty-nine and that, since parents are living longer, young adults demonstrate a longer psychological dependence on them. Thus, many complete what were typically considered the early "tasks of adulthood" in their thirties rather than twenties, and some never marry, establish a career, buy a house, or raise a family.[51]

Perspectives on emerging adults vary. Some commentators are highly critical of "Generation Me," understanding them as self-indulgent narcissists.[52] Others note the disturbing levels of anxiety and mental health

44. Fowler, *Stages of Faith*, 112.

45. Astley, "Insights from Faith Development," 126.

46. Loevinger, *Ego Development*; Field-Belenky, *Women's Ways of Knowing*; Harris, "Completion and Faith Development"; Gilligan, "Remapping Development," 37–53; Liebert, "Seasons and Stages," 19–44.

47. Parks, *The Critical Years*.

48. Arnett, *Emerging Adulthood*.

49. Beck, *Individualization*, 32–72; Bogle, *Hooking Up*; Beaujouan, "Cohabitation and Marriage."

50. Beck, *Individualization*, 3.

51. Wuthnow, *After the Baby Boomers*, 10–11.

52. E.g., Twenge, *Generation Me*; Bauerlein, *The Dumbest Generation*.

problems faced by those whose future is so uncertain.[53] Beck and Arnett are more optimistic, describing emerging adults as "altruistic individualists," while Wuthnow suggests that advances in travel and technology have raised awareness and concern for global issues.[54] By contrast, Smith paints a depressing picture of a highly individualistic, sexually promiscuous, socially, politically, and ethically disengaged generation whose consumerism, and drug and alcohol misuse are the result of endemic boredom.[55] However this generation are viewed, "emerging adulthood" refers to an extended developmental period from eighteen to twenty-five, which may actually last for most of an individual's twenties. As Douglas describes,

> Adulthood is seen by many contemporary young people as a peril to be avoided, the end of independence. For them, the new stage of emerging adulthood represents unprecedented freedom to explore—education, love, work, and fun—and to gain a broad range of life experiences. It is also a time for self-focus, with few ties or daily obligations to others. It is, in short, an in-between time, full of possibilities and high hopes. However, this time of exploration is also a time of instability.[56]

Arnett argues that the tasks of establishing individualized patterns of work, love, and worldview in order to formulate identity are the tasks of this extended period.[57] Like earlier developmental models, it has been criticized for its western, socioeconomic limitations and a more nuanced six paths into adulthood has been described by Osgood.[58] But Arnett's model provides a helpful framework for this project, since the majority of participants fit the appropriate socioeconomic grouping and are experiencing an extended period of independence, development and uncertainty in their twenties.

---

53. Beck, *Individualization*, 7.

54. Ibid., 27; Arnett, "The Dangers of Generational Myth Making," 17–20; Wuthnow, *After the Baby Boomers*, 44.

55. Smith, *Lost in Transition*.

56. Douglas, "From Duty of Desire," 108.

57. Arnett, "Emerging Adulthood," 469–80.

58. Hendry and Kloep, "Redressing the Emperor"; Osgood et al., "Six Paths to Adulthood," 320–47.

Generation Theory

Rooted in the work of Mannheim, the idea of distinct age related generations is also pertinent to this study.[59] It describes, "A unique type of social
location based on the dynamic interplay between being born in a particular
year with the socio-political events that occur throughout the life course of
the birth cohort, particularly when the cohort comes of age."[60] Sears and
Marshal describe, "Groups of people who travel together through time and
share a unique perspective that shapes their cultural understanding and
civic roles."[61] Estler considers that "a particular view of social reality [is] reflected in each generation's unique personality and shared identity."[62] Generational models have become lucrative in America, providing theoretical
explanations and expectations of the attributes of subsequent generations.[63]
Copeland's 1991 work, *Generation X: Tales for an Accelerated Culture,* influenced popular culture in the UK and the language of generations is used in
both academic and popular vocabulary as a way of distinguishing between
groups born within a certain time span. Although exact boundaries are contested, broadly accepted descriptions are: "Baby Boomers" (born from the
end of the 2 World War until 1960), "Generation X" (born between 1961
and 1980)[64] and "Generation Y" or "Millennials" (born between 1981 and
2000).[65]

Generational theories are not without their critics. Twenty-year periods (based on average length of female fertility) are broad; it is more than
feasible for a parent and child to belong to the same generation. Wuthnow
is sceptical that current events have shaped generations in the same way
that the 2 World War or great depression did.[66] Likewise, the boundaries are
somewhat arbitrary, and transitions in worldview are far more gradual and
less delineated than such models accommodate for. The term "generations"
also is used to describe kinship descent, cohort, life stage and historical period.[67] Thus, cohort has been suggested as a more specific and appropriate
term to describe a group growing up together.[68] With regard to generational

59. Mannheim, "The Problem of Generations," 276–320.

60. McMullin et al., "Generational Affinities," 299.

61. Sears, "Generational Influences," 199.

62. Esler, *Generations in History.*

63. Howe and Strauss, *Generations.*

64. Collins-Mayo and Dandelion, *Religion and Youth,* 7.

65. Lawrence, "Engaging Gen Y," 5.

66. Wuthnow, *After the Baby Boomers,* 5

67. Kertzer, "Generation as a Sociological Problem," 125–49.

68. Ryder, "The Cohort," 843–61.

attributes, Hoover is scathing about the mythical status afforded Millennials while others demonstrate that the experiences of American Black, Hispanic, Indigenous, and LGBT students do not fit the generalizations about their generation and that events affect people in the same generation differently.[69]

Recognizing these valid limitations, this project is situated within a body of literature which often uses "Generation Y" or "Millennials" to describe those under investigation. In order to situate this work clearly, I shall also use this terminology. However, I shall also use the term cohort to describe each of the three age-related sets of focus groups.[70] While they might belong to the same sociological generation, the formative experiences and life-stages of those currently aged between eighteen and thirty-three are diverse. Since the majority of participants have tertiary education, the cohorts are structured on periods of length approximate to university education, i.e., four years. This is an appropriate length of time for participants to have had similar political, economic and social experiences and to have undertaken similar developmental changes. Part of the purpose of the project is to observe what difference, if any, progression through the developmental stage of emerging adulthood makes to theological engagement and Bible reading practices; thus it is hoped that the comparisons of age-related cohorts within a single generation will introduce more nuanced data into the body of literature on Generation Y.

Contemporary Studies on the Faith of Emerging Adults

Within the current body of work on the faith of today's emerging adults, the extensive longitudinal work of Smith in the United States has led him to describe the *de facto* religion of American teenagers as "Moralistic Therapeutic Deism."[71] "We have come to believe that a significant part of 'Christianity' in the USA is actually only tenuously Christian in any sense that is seriously connected to the actual Christian tradition, but has rather substantially morphed into Christianity's misbegotten step-cousin: Christian—MTD."[72] Smith and others suggest that even those who describe themselves as Christian amongst Generation Y do not necessarily hold to orthodox theological beliefs but show an eclectic form of quasi-Christian spirituality.[73] Flory

69. Hoover, "The Millennial Muddle"; Bonner et al., *Diverse Millennial Students*; Vaidhyanathan, "Generational Myth."

70. Ryder, "The Cohort," 843.

71. Smith, *Lost in Transition*; Smith, *Souls in Transition*.

72. Smith, "Moralistic Therapeutic Deism," 41–46.

73. E.g., Mason, "The Spirituality of Young Australians," 55–62; Tacey, "What spirituality means," 67–71.

and Miller describe religious attitudes among western emerging adults as optional rather than an obligation, tolerant of the beliefs of others, and a spiritual journey rather than a set of propositional beliefs. Experience and internal authority are more important than external religious structures, and key priorities are authenticity of religious community and the pursuit of justice. Thus, emerging adults are likely to create eclectic, personalized, spiritual hybrids.[74] Researchers in the UK describe a happy-midi-narrative in which spirituality is of value if it contributes to personal happiness.[75] Generation Y seems to be a memory-less generation who are largely de-churched and do not know traditional Christian values and narratives.[76] However, for the minority who have it, Christian faith appears to be more important in their self-identification than it was in previous generations.[77]

It is clear that the attitudes and behaviour of practising evangelical emerging adults are increasingly removed from their secular peers, with many reporting experiences of bullying or ridicule for their churchgoing.[78] Irby identifies evangelical dating habits as being at odds with the wider culture of hooking up, while Guest describes the social isolation of Christian students who do not wish to participate in British drinking culture.[79] British evangelicals may well be "caught between differing moral terrains," but they also demonstrate shifting attitudes on ethical and moral issues.[80] Christian students are more conservative than their secular peers, but less conservative than the wider adult church.[81] Considerable research has explored the effects of liberal higher education on the faith of American Christians.[82] (General findings have proved inconclusive, although evangelical and black Protestants appear to be among those least influenced[83] and in the UK academic studies are reported to make little difference to the faith of most British emerging adults.[84])

74. Florey and Miller, "Expressive Communalism," 10.

75. Nash et al., *The Faith of Generation Y*, 18.

76. Ibid., 23.

77. Ibid., 15; Rainer and Rainer, *The Millennials*, 246–50; Ryan, "Islam Does Not Change," 446–60.

78. Savage et al., *Generation Y*, 14.

79. Irby, "Dating in Light of Christ," 260–83; Guest, *University Experience*, 119.

80. Strhan, "Discipleship and Desire," 16.

81. Guest, *University Experience*, 101–2.

82 E.g., Pascarella and Terenzini, *How College Affects Students;* Uecker et al., "Losing My Religion," 667–92; Bryant and Astin, "Spiritual Struggle," 1–27; Mayrl and Oeur, "Religion and Higher Education," 260–75; Reimer, "Higher Education," 398–408.

83. Hill, "Faith and Understanding," 543–546; Smith, *Souls in Transition*, 281.

84. Guest, *University Experience*, 104.

By contrast there is a small but growing body of academic work exploring the Christian faith of British emerging adults. Between 1993 and 2001, there were fifteen popular Christian publications[85] but a limited number of scholarly studies exist. These include work by Collins-Mayo, Lawrence, and Savage.[86] *Religion and Youth* presents snapshots of international findings, and much needed empirical data is provided by Aune, Guest, and Strhan.[87] My own contribution is a chapter in *The Faith of Women and Girls*.[88] However, there is, in general, a lack of empirical work on the Christian faith of emerging adults in the UK, and I am unaware of any comparable Bible reading projects or explorations of evangelical orthodoxy.

Defining Ordinary Biblicism

The final area that needs definition is that of "ordinary Bible reading." Ordinary theology is a relatively recent field emerging from the discipline of practical theology. It is multi-disciplinary, relying on qualitative research methods plus theological and social scientific expertise. Critics and proponents recognize that defining "ordinary" is not straightforward. Astley explains:

> Ordinary Christian Theology is my phrase for the theology and theologizing of Christians who have received little or no theological education of a scholarly, academic or systematic kind. "Ordinary," in this context, implies non-scholarly and non-academic; it fits the dictionary definition that refers to an "ordinary person" as one who is without exceptional experience or expert knowledge.[89]

The study of how non-academically trained individuals and groups understand their faith is a growing field. It is described by De Wit as "one of the biggest embarrassments and gaps in modern biblical scholarship."[90] Rogers comments that it is "surprising how little empirical research has been done, as yet, on the hermeneutics of ordinary Christians, particularly

---

85. Hilborn and Bird, *God and the Generations*, 7.

86. Collins-Mayo, *Generation Y*; Lawrence, "Engaging Gen Y"; Savage, *Making Sense of Generation Y*.

87. Aune, "Postfeminist Partnership"; Guest, *University Experience*; Strhan, "Practising the Space Between," 225–39.

88. Perrin, "Searching for Sisters".

89. Astley, *Ordinary Theology*, 102.

90. De Wit, *Eyes of Another*, 10.

in the UK."[91] Similarly, Village observes "a dearth of empirical studies on how people who have no theological training relate to the Bible."[92]

The practice of "giving voice" to ordinary Christians is still very much a marginal field of research, but it has considerable overlap with liberationist methodologies. West, argues that ordinary readers are the marginalized poor from the southern hemisphere, describing "all readers who read the Bible in an untrained or pre-critical way," as opposed to critical readers "who have been trained in the use of the tools and resources of biblical scholarship."[93] De Wit suggests that genuine ordinary reading is existential rather than analytical in nature, i.e. an individual or group looks instinctively for an insight from the text for their situation.[94] To assume that this is not the case for western Christians is to assume, incorrectly, that western academic traditions and practices have been adopted by all churches or that all western Christians are highly educated. Randall notes differences between British and American evangelicalism, suggesting the British have sought to distance themselves from a fundamentalist, anti-intellectual stance.[95] Warner, on the other hand, describes some sections of British evangelicalism as making little reference to the Bible, demonstrating impatience with critical reflection and having an instinctive anti-intellectualism.[96] Malley concludes that despite a majority engaging with historical-critical methodology at some level, all "evangelical Bible reading is driven by the search for relevance." Thus it could be argued that all (or at least much) evangelical reading is ordinary reading.[97]

However, a legitimate question, within the highly literate world of British evangelicalism, is how ordinary any group or individual may be? Cartledge observed in his study of Hockney Pentecostal Church that many lay members of the congregation had undertaken informal theological study and thus "their theology cannot be regarded as necessarily naive or simplistic."[98] The churches participating in this study were in university towns and had a high level of tertiary education amongst members. Many participants demonstrated considerable theological interest, citing books

91. Rogers, "Ordinary Biblical Hermeneutics," 17.

92. Village, "Biblical Interpretative Horizons," 159.

93. Dube and West, "Reading With," 7.

94. De Wit, *Eyes of Another*, 8–9.

95. Randall, *Educating Evangelicalism*, 9.

96. Warner, *Reinventing English Evangelicalism*.

97. Malley, *How the Bible Works*, 119.

98. Cartledge, *Testimony in the Spirit*, 16.

they had read, informal theological courses they had attended and groups they had belonged to. These are highly educated ordinary readers.

Grenz and Olson categorized faith in terms of: folk, lay, ministerial, professional, and academic.[99] Their model is somewhat pejorative towards the first and last categories but helpful in considering a spectrum. Thomson includes parish clergy in his definition of ordinary readers arguing that "their theological reflections are predominantly occasionalistic, informal and rooted in ordinary life."[100] Astley also describes a spectrum of ordinary theologizing and Village notes that some academic hermeneutic traditions are used within evangelical preaching and thus accepted as ordinary in those churches.[101] Indeed, much ordinary British evangelicalism is eclectic, absorbing (often indiscriminately) readings from a wide variety of theological positions.[102] It is difficult therefore to define what an ordinary biblical reader might look like. West however, is correct in noting that there is a difference between those in the western world who have access to such theological resources, and those in the developing world who do not.[103] Perhaps it might be helpful to view ordinary as a culturally relative term, distinguished according to the background and opportunities of any given group. Having said all this, the term "ordinary," used to describe those who are not theologically "exceptional" (i.e. ordained, trained as church leaders or with formal academic qualification in biblical scholarship), is still helpful and will be adopted to describe what the Bible reading of young British evangelicals looks like.

Situating This Project within Research into Biblicism

Using Bielo's definition of biblicism as "a working analytical framework intended to facilitate comparative research on how Christians interact with their sacred texts," [104] this project overlaps with a number of empirical Bible projects.

Quantitative projects on attitudes towards the Bible among the general population include the, now dated, work of Clines, Field's summary of surveys from 1948 to 2013, Brierley's ongoing research, and the Bible

99. Grenz and Olsen, *Who Needs Theology?* 27–33.
100. Thomson, "Phronesis and Sophia," 133–46.
101. Astley, *Ordinary Theology*, 57–58, 86; Village, *The Bible and Lay People*, 26.
102. Ward and Campbell, "Ordinary Theology as Narrative," 226–42.
103. West, *The Academy of the Poor*, 11.
104. Bielo, *The Social Life of Scriptures*, 2.

Society surveys in 1997, 2004, and 2008.[105] Further work on attitudes to the Bible includes Buckler and Astley, Fisher et al., and Francis.[106] More specific investigations into the practices of Bible college students and pastoral practitioners concluded that their use of the Bible was largely pragmatic, aimed at reinforcing existing beliefs and practices and for the "purposes of comfort or challenge without imposing hermeneutic controls."[107]

Data from observations of general trends and clergy practise is useful; however, it does not present the practices of ordinary believing readers. The aim of this project was not to gather widespread quantitative data, nor views on the Bible in general. It focussed not on "correct," idealized, or abstract answers but on the ways in which conscious and unconscious assumptions and attitudes outworked as young evangelicals read the Bible in a group setting. Interviews with clergy provided an insight into how far their perceptions of Bible reading among their young adult congregations were accurate, but much of their enthusiasm to participate was so that they could identify ordinary reading habits.

Also of significance in the field of ordinary Bible reading is the Contextual Bible Study (CBS) Movement. CBS intentionally incorporates ordinary reading with historical-critical reflection, prioritizing folk-consciousness responses to biblical texts it aims to use the Bible as an agent of change in marginalized communities.[108] It is a growing field both of biblical engagement and of research.[109] The publications of the Sheffield Urban Unit explore how creative interpretations of New Testament narratives have been appropriated to enrich and explore pastoral practice.[110] However, the Practice Interpretation series primarily includes work by clergy and scholars rather than by ordinary readers.

The most developed British CBS project, *The Word in Place: Reading the New Testament in Contemporary Contexts,* uses Lucan texts to explore their experience of location in the light of the Gospel. CBS intentionally aims to give language to the experiences of participants, selecting texts as

---

105. Clines, *The Bible and the Modern World*; Field, "Is the Bible Becoming a Closed Book?"; Brierley, *Quantitative Study*; Brierly, *Pulling out of the Nose Dive; UKCH Religious Trends;* Bible Society, "Taking the Pulse."

106. Buckler and Astley, "Learning and Believing," 396–416; Fisher et al., "A Survey of Bible Reading," 417–23; Francis, "The Pews Talk Back," 161–86.

107. Walton, "Using the Bible," 133–51; Dickson, *The Use of the Bible in Pastoral Practice.*

108. Lawrence, *The Word in Place,* 23.

109. E.g., Segovia and Tolbert, *Reading from this Place*; Peden, "Contextual Bible Study," 15–18; Ekblad, *Reading the Bible with the Damned.*

110. Vincent, *Stilling the Storm*; Vincent, *Acts in Practise.*

a catalyst around a particular issue. By contrast, this project's texts were selected to provoke theological reflection and examine reading patterns. Personal experience was neither encouraged nor discouraged. Indeed, one research question centred on how far (without prompting) the participants would appropriate the text or relate personal experience to it? Likewise, the explicit aim of CBS is to instigate change. This project did not set out to alter the praxis of participants. It may have done (people reported feeling inspired or challenged), but it was not intentionally interventionist. Thus, its underlying ethos is different to CBS.

Beyond the field of CBS there are a small number of explorations of group Bible reading. Bielo states, "a significant and surprising lacuna persists—an in-depth, comparative analysis of that most pervasive of social institutions in evangelical Life: group Bible study."[111] In the United States, his work on the readings of a Lutheran men's Bible study is notable.[112] The large scale work *Through the Eyes of Another* engaged small groups from multiple countries in reading John 4, subsequently sharing their readings with a group from a different cultural background. It aimed to encourage understanding, widen readings and have a transformational impact. In this, it is closer to CBS.[113] Mark Allan Powell's creation of "Narrative Criticism" (exploring "expected" and "unexpected" readings) in *Chasing the Eastern Star* compares the interpretative strategies of clergy and laity, concluding that formal theological education fundamentally altered the way in which clergy read the Bible.[114]

In Britain, Andrew Village compared readings of Mark 9:14–29 across the Church of England using textual and authorial horizons as markers to locate types of readers.[115] Although quantitative, his findings are pertinent since they are comparative and overlap with this project. Distinctly different in his methodology, Andrew Todd used discourse analysis to study the reading of rural Anglican Bible study groups.[116] Finally, although citing his work as a Bible reading project, Andrew Rogers's comparison of the hermeneutics of two evangelical churches is far more wide ranging.[117] He provides a wider ethnography, observing services, worship, sermons and personal biblicism through interviews and questionnaires as well as through small

111. Bielo, *Words upon the Word*, 3.

112. Bielo, "On the Failure of Meaning," 1–21.

113. De Wit, *Through the Eyes of Another.*

114. Powell, *Chasing the Eastern Star*, 30–52.

115. Village, *The Bible and Lay People.*

116. Todd, "Talk, Dynamics and Theological Practice."

117. Rogers, *Ordinary Biblical Hermeneutics.*

group Bible studies. His work is similar to Malley's study of Creekside Baptist in the United States.[118] The comparative nature of Rogers's work makes it significant, since two of the churches involved in this project have theological parallels with Holder Evangelical and The Fellowship. However, practical constraints mean that this project is more narrowly focussed on a textual examination within specific sub-groups of each congregation.

Despite being informed by a wide body of cross disciplinary literature, this project establishes a new methodology and area of research. Having an age related emphasis, using a qualitative, fixed-text, focus group methodology and being comparative both across the British evangelical spectrum and a demographic generation make it entirely unique.

118. Malley, *How the Bible Works.*

2

Research Methodology

Introduction

IN ORDER TO OBSERVE the ordinary Bible engagement of evangelical emerging adults and focus on comparative questions (age, gender, theological, and interpretative differences) there were various methodological considerations. Qualitative research that observed the discussion, interests, behaviour, and interpretative processes of participants appeared most appropriate.

Ordinary theology embraces respectful listening, affirming value in people's self-described faith and allowing them to explore beliefs that are not necessarily fully formulated.[1] Therefore, focus groups were adopted, since they allow the exploration of attitudes, beliefs, experiences and reactions in ways other methodologies cannot, allowing participants "to generate their own questions, frames and concepts and to pursue their own priorities on their own terms, in their own vocabulary."[2]

Since this was a comparative study, focus groups provided data on social interaction within institutions and on the various dimensions of that process (E.g., joking, teasing, and arguing).[3] Fish argues that interpretative practices are communal property, proceeding from the interpretative community to which an individual belongs.[4] "Readers read the way they do because of their participation in defined communities of practice. Such communities operate on common procedures for engaging with the text, sharing hermeneutic assumptions, interpretative strategies and performative

---

1. Astley, *Ordinary Theology*, 147, 103–4.
2. Barbour and Kitzinger, *Developing Focus Group Research*, 5.
3. Kitzinger, "Introducing Focus Groups," 299–302.
4. Fish, *Is there a Text?* 14.

styles."[5] Thus it seemed likely that multiple focus groups from each congregation would illustrate normal and atypical interpretative practices and theological values within their community. Focus groups are also useful in navigating power differences between leaders and congregants, potentially building bridges by providing leaders with feedback on the language, thinking and experiences of ordinary believers.[6] They may therefore provide a helpful diagnostic tool, uncovering new insights or unanticipated issues that can be used to modify training or educative processes.[7]

Due to the comparative ethos of the study it was also necessary to approach a number of congregations rather than carry out an ethnographic study of any one church. The value of case studies in both initiating and refining theories is well documented and, since this project is unique and part of an emerging field, to examine a few cases in close detail seemed more appropriate that attempting a large-scale survey.[8] This methodology, combined with the diversity of the participating churches, provides a rich and complex picture of ordinary evangelical Bible reading.

Participating Evangelical Churches

Five churches were initially approached through my existing relationship networks. They were selected because they had a sizeable cohort of emerging adults and were evangelical in their ethos. One was used for pilot studies, another was unable to participate within the necessary time frame and the other three became full participants. They were all situated in university cities across England and led by non-ordained individuals.

All three churches were independent and demonstrated characteristic evangelical emphases of conversionism, activism, crucicentrism, and biblicism.[9] Their practices included Sunday services, mid-week small groups, and an emphasis on personal Bible study. All of them were members of the Evangelical Alliance, belonged to a variety of additional networks and were enthusiastic about the project. Each has been given a pseudonymous name intended to evoke their ethos and values. Their leaders and all participants have also been anonymized.

---

5. Bielo, *Words upon the Word*, 13.

6. Morgan and Krueger, "When to Use Focus Groups," 15–16.

7. Hennink, *International Focus Group Research*, 10–11.

8. Flyvbjerg, "Five Misunderstandings," 420–34.

9. Bebbington, *Evangelicalism*, 3

Trinity Church

Trinity Church was planted in 2003. It is an independent evangelical church with links to the FIEC, Proclamation Trust, and a conservative evangelical regional training partnership.[10] Its leader Will described its theology as, "gently Reformed or Calvinist." In our interviews he emphasized a continuist doctrine of charismatic gifts, although admitted the use of tongues or prophecy was irregular and something the leaders were unsure how to encourage.[11] He explained that the complementarian policy of the church meant that women could not be elders or preach (except occasionally in partnership with their husbands). Will was confident that women felt empowered, despite the church's theological position, although at the time of the project the staff team of ten contained only one woman: the administrator.

The congregation has two hundred adult members, the majority of whom are under thirty-five. 85 percent of the congregation already have or are studying for a degree, and 80 percent are incomers to the city. It has a growing number of young families, and about 25 percent of its congregation are international students, refugees or asylum seekers. The church places a high emphasis on conversionism; the services I attended repeatedly addressed issues of sharing faith with non-believers. It was also explicit in explaining the doctrine of penal substitutionary atonement, challenged non-believers to convert and advertised a variety of evangelistic meetings and courses such as *Christianity Explored*.[12]

Trinity Church holds morning and evening services each Sunday in a local secondary school. Refreshments and social time, available before and after services, are well attended with a lively buzz of conversation. It prides itself on being friendly, and it advertized opportunities for communal meals and informal theological discussion in the pub.

On the day I visited, worship was led by a band but was somewhat reserved and relatively formal in style, with a mixture of hymns and modern songs from charismatic traditions. It also included a Bible story and song time for young children (of whom there were a large number), and an open question and answer time following the sermon. On this occasion,

10. The Fellowship of Independent Evangelical Churches (FIEC) was founded in 1922. The Proclamation Trust was established in 1981 to encourage conservative, expository teaching.

11. "Continuism" rejects the doctrine of cessationism (which claims charismata have ceased). Grudem, www.challies.com, accessed April 22, 2015.

12. A ten-week course presenting a Reformed perspective on the Christian faith for seekers.

questions focussed on depression. Will explained that they aimed for their Bible teaching to be "intelligent but not intellectual" and that they mixed topical, doctrinal, and systematic expository preaching. Personal Bible reading was encouraged but, in reaction to what Will described as "conservative legalism," this was not a hard line. It was evident that being relevant, gracious and appropriate to their demographic were high priorities for Trinity Church and that they saw themselves a "gentle" or "left-leaning" Reformed church rather than a hard line, conservative one.

Central Chapel

Central Chapel was founded in the nineteenth century. It is an independent evangelical church with Brethren roots that appointed its first salaried elder in the 1980s and has subsequently modernized by appointing a salaried staff team. Its leadership team has seven members and Ken, one of the senior leaders was my point of contact.

In many ways, Central Chapel is a remarkable evangelical community. Over the past few years, it has changed its policy on female leadership, moving from a complementarian position to an egalitarian one. It now has one female leader and regular women preachers, although Ken noted that it will take time for the gender balance to become equal.

Central Chapel has links with local evangelical and national Brethren organizations. Its theological breadth is illustrated by its relationships with the conservative Keswick Convention, mainstream Spring Harvest and charismatic Soul Survivor conferences.[13] The church has between five and six hundred attendees most weeks, ranging from young families to elderly members. Ken noted a dip in numbers among those aged in their forties and fifties but described a considerable number of internationals (mostly Chinese students). It too has a strong conversionist ethos: one service I attended summarized a sermon series that had encouraged members to be proactive in evangelizing. There were also interviews with overseas missionaries, and the church had produced its own evangelistic small group materials. Ken described their attitude towards the Bible in terms of "wanting God to speak to us" and explained that they alternated topical preaching and systematic exposition at their morning and evening services, aiming to cover

---

13. Running since 1978 the Keswick Convention is a conservative evangelical conference. Spring Harvest holidays were established in 1979. They combine evangelical Bible teaching with charismatic worship. Soul Survivor is a large charismatic youth conference which 25,000 attended in 2015. www.eauk.org, Accessed 13 September 2016.

the whole biblical canon every ten years. The services I attended, similar to Trinity Church, included sung worship led by a band and used a mixture of hymns and charismatic songs. The congregation were also reserved during this worship; Ken explained that they were hoping to become more overtly charismatic with time, but that the breadth of personal spiritualities (from Reformed to "gently charismatic") among the congregation made them look more theologically conservative than they were.

New Life

New Life was planted in the early 1990s and belongs to the Pioneer Network.[14] It is charismatic and egalitarian in its leadership: its senior leader being a woman, Sarah. It has a membership of two hundred, of whom eighty are undergraduates. It also has about sixty young children and is oriented around the needs of young adults and families (only three individuals are older than their mid-forties). It is led by an oversight team of three women and two men with two distinct congregations (one for families and one for undergraduates), which both have their own leadership teams.

The church is structured around "Missional Communities" and places a high emphasis on conversion, encouraging members to be proactive in sharing their faith by inviting non-believers into relationship with other members of the church community.[15] Theologically it leans towards open theism and intentionally emphasizes the love and acceptance of God, since the leaders perceive the stereotype of an angry God has alienated people from the Christian faith. New Life is linked to Fusion, the 24/7 prayer network, and charismatic conferences such as New Wine, Soul Survivor, Momentum, and Greenbelt.[16] It uses resources produced by Holy Trinity Brompton (HTB), such as the Alpha course.[17]

14. Kay, *Apostolic Networks*, 122–24.

15. The Missional Community movement began in 1994. It encourages informal groups which focus on mission to others with similar backgrounds and interests.

16. Established in 1997, Fusion is a charismatic student movement. 24/7 prayer network is an international, interdenominational movement of prayer, mission and justice across 100 nations. Established in 1989, New Wine is a network of Charismatic churches. Its conferences were attended by 26,000 in 2014; Momentum developed out of the Soul Survivor movement and runs a five day conference for students and young adults; Greenbelt is an annual arts, faith and justice festival. It has evangelical roots but now describes itself as standing for an "inclusive and progressive Christian faith." www.greenbelt.org.uk, Accessed 16 June 2014.

17. HTB has produced resources on marriage, parenting and a variety of other lifestyle issues. It runs national conferences on leadership and charismatic worship. www.htb.org.uk, Accessed 16 June 2014.

With regard to worship, New Life encourages the use of tongues and prophecy in its meetings. One of the services I attended had extensive periods of worship both before and after the sermon. This was led by a small group of musicians and was informal, flexible, and encouraged spontaneous contributions (of which there were several) from the congregation. There were few chairs; the majority of the young adults sat on cushions on the floor, and it was common for them to pray for each other during the worship. The morning service was different: led by a band, it was a celebration of the adoption and birth of children. An emphasis on accessibility for the children meant the service was somewhat chaotic. The regular members appeared to enjoy this, but visitors (of whom there were many) seemed to find it awkward. There was a short talk followed by a time of writing a letter to a child we wished to encourage.

Sarah explained that relevance to people's lives was a key priority, and thus Bible teaching tended to emphasize discipleship and lived faith. Sermon series alternated topical and systematic themes, and preaching was delivered by a group of eight to ten individuals of both genders, based on their teaching gift. Sarah ran a preaching course to help individuals develop that gift, and was concerned with biblical literacy levels. She had used a number of techniques to encourage Bible reading in the congregation. These included tweeting and texting verses to the whole community and using the Bible Society "You've got time" programme.[18] She also described encouraging "Jewish murmuring" and "Lectio Divina" practices.[19] Sarah described the church as post-modern, using multimedia and creative formats to encourage those who were more visual or imaginative. She explained that there were members who would describe themselves as post-evangelical, but this was not the position of the leadership. She was, however, reluctant to use any theological labels as she considered them unhelpful for most people.

In Summary

To have such a diversity of churches participating was an enormous asset to the project since they represent a significant portion of the breadth within British evangelicalism. They all reflect Bebbington's quadrilateral although they express those values in various ways with differing priorities. In terms

18. A series of podcasts designed to enable individuals to listen to the entire New Testament in forty days. www.biblesociety.org.uk/you've got time. Accessed 16 October 2016.

19. Repeating Bible verses over and over again to oneself (Jewish Murmuring) and Benedictine meditative techniques (Lectio Divina).

of evangelical taxonomies, Warner's model is moderately helpful, although these congregations only approximately fit his categories. Trinity Church overlaps between "neo-conservative" and "moderate conservative" evangelicalism. Central Chapel fits "engaged evangelical" but individuals expressed views that fit within the "neo-conservative" and "reconstructed evangelical" categories. New Life is the clearest, being "radical evangelical."[20] However, it is noteworthy that both Central Chapel and Trinity Church expressed a sense of their own ongoing evolution towards a moderate charismatic spirituality. Their worship style illustrates what Tomlinson calls the "charismaticization" of the British church, the "way in which mainstream evangelical churches have come to absorb and imbibe aspects of charismatic culture."[21] Much of this influence has come from attendance at conferences such as Spring Harvest, but even conservative churches are demonstrating extended periods of continuous sung worship led by worship bands. Alternatively, Sarah was particularly concerned with encouraging biblical engagement within the creative and experiential spirituality of New Life and developing preachers who focussed on historical context and literary style as well as application. These are practices often associated with more conservative evangelicals rather than some forms of charismatic or Pentecostal hermeneutics.[22] Overall then, even among these three churches, the continually developing kaleidoscope of evangelical spirituality is evident.

Methodology

Choice of Participating Churches

In terms of recruitment, church leaders were initially approached with an introductory letter followed by an email and phone call. Two of the churches required further letters of explanation to be sent to their eldership teams, while the leader of the third agreed to participate with no wider reference. All of the churches were enthusiastic about the rationale of the research and appeared to view it as a form of consultation on the biblical engagement of their emerging adults. It was agreed that, respecting the confidentiality of participants, leaders would be given feedback from the findings on their groups and a copy of the final doctoral thesis. The leaders of my own church

---

20. Warner, *Reinventing English Evangelicalism*, 229–30.
21. Scotland, "Evangelicalism and the Charismatic Movement," 296–97.
22. Stibbe, "This is That," 181–93; Martin, "Pentecostal Hermeneutics," 1–9.

also agreed to allow me to run pilot groups among our own emerging adults; it is here referred to as Hope Community Church.[23]

Choice of Focus Groups

Focus groups are, by their nature, artificial and thus unusual in studying religious belief.[24] However, since the majority of evangelical churches operate small groups of some sort, and group Bible study is common practice, focus groups appeared likely to be a familiar environment for participants. Bielo notes that evangelical groups "move with ease among topics as diverse as theological doctrines, hermeneutics, moral questions, politics, social mores, history, current events, congregational concerns and personal experiences."[25] Since observing hermeneutic processes was a priority, having a group work together on a text seemed more likely to reveal how points of view are constructed and expressed than collecting the perceptions in one-to-one interviews would.

After running four pilot groups, I concluded that using further groups from Hope Community Church was unwise. Despite the valuable data gathered and the advantage of knowing participants, I felt that, as a Bible teacher within the community, my ability to sufficiently distance myself would be difficult and that the balance of power leant too strongly towards the researcher.[26] Several pilot group members expressed anxiety that they were being tested by the church leadership in some way. Although I was able to allay such fears, the potential for focus groups to cause anxiety and even conflict within the congregation (over who had and had not been included) meant that using alternative churches where I had no previous relationships was ethically preferable.

Focus group numbers of between of five and eight were used since this is a typical-sized Bible study group and allows people space to participate while not causing them to feel unduly pressured to contribute.[27] The groups were mixed in gender in order to replicate the majority of evangelical small groups and to facilitate the observation of gender interaction. Single-gender

23. Hope Community Church is part of the Ichthus network. It is evangelical, charismatic, and egalitarian in its practices. Kay, *Apostolic Networks*, 111–20.

24. Recent examples include: Ryan, "Islam Does Not Change"; Gallagher, "Defining Spiritual Growth," 232–61; Miles, "Overcoming the Challenges," 199–226.

25. Bielo, *Words upon the Word*, 4

26. Finlay, "Negotiating the Swamp," 220; Kitzinger, *Developing Focus Group Research*, 18.

27. It is also the appropriate size for a focus group. Powell and Single, "Focus Groups," 499–504.

groups would have made an interesting comparison but, in order to make the project manageable, this was not pursued at this time.

Since ordinary practices were central to the study it was important that participants had not undertaken formal academic theological study. It was hoped that they would better represent the wider body of the church than those who were aware of hermeneutic methodologies. One option would have been to use existing small groups from the churches. However, since a key research question was to observe age-related patterns and consider developmental issues, creating artificial groups around age cohorts was deemed preferable.[28] These cohorts were undergraduate aged (eighteen to twenty-two), mid-twenties (twenty-three to twenty-six), and rising thirties (twenty-seven to thirty-two).

Finding churches with sufficient numbers to produce the required focus groups meant using churches in university towns and subsequently almost all the participants had tertiary levels of education.[29] These findings are therefore limited to predominantly middle class, university educated individuals. However, this demographic is fairly representative of British evangelicalism. Further comparative work with other socioeconomic groups would be valuable.

Choice of Biblical Texts

Focus group methodology suggests some form of group exercise to galvanise discussion and the biblical text performed this function.[30] However, consideration of which passages to use to best facilitate data on my key questions was important. A number of factors were considered as follows.

Relative Familiarity with the Text

It was decided to use texts which were unfamiliar in order to elicit naïve rather than strongly socialized responses. Although Christians repeatedly read the Bible and so entirely naïve responses are unlikely, a recitation of sermons or previous Bible studies was not of particular interest. Instead, the

---

28. Kitzinger identifies both encouraging and inhibiting factors in using existing groups. "The Methodology of Focus Groups," 105.

29. Debate exists as to whether homogeneity or diversity creates most productive focus group data. Homogeneity was desirable on this occasion. Morgan, *Focus Groups*, 20.

30. Kitzinger, "The Methodology of Focus Groups," 106.

priority was to investigate processes of interpretation and examination of unfamiliar texts was deemed most likely to reveal those.

Type of Biblical Literature

The option of using different types of biblical literature (e.g., prophetic, poetic, legal, or epistles) as a comparison of hermeneutic processes was considered. However, given the already considerable number of comparative factors, adding another layer of diversity would have made identifying any meaningful patterns difficult. Ultimately, narratives were chosen as the most straightforward and familiar form of literature. Since exploration of interpretative patterns was a priority it was important that groups engaged with several texts and that both biblical Testaments were included. Logistical considerations led to the selection of self-contained episodes, a chapter in length.

As a result of pilot group discussions, gospel narratives were eliminated. The presence of Jesus in the text caused groups to focus their discussion entirely on Christology. Although this is interesting in itself, I decided to avoid narratives that contained the person of Jesus. If his presence within a narrative made him automatically dominant in the minds of participants, then their hermeneutic patterns would probably be different to the ways in which they read other narratives. Clearly further work could be undertaken to explore this phenomenon, but there were a sufficient number of variables without adding this dynamic.

Finally, during the pilot stage groups were convened twice: once to discuss two Old Testament narratives and a second time to repeat the process with New Testament ones. It became evident that the logistics of coordinating the same group twice were not straightforward. Even given the close proximity of pilot group participants I was unable to gather identical groups twice. For both pilot groups only four of seven participants were the same both times. Given the distances involved in running focus groups at participating churches, it appeared unlikely that convening identical groups twice would be feasible. Thus, one, longer session on three self-contained passages was convened for each focus group.[31]

31. E.g., Burgess, "Focussing on Fear," 130–36.

Theological Distinctives

The final consideration was to choose narratives that would provide opportunity for theological discussion on themes that are contentious among British evangelicals. Those chosen were issues of gender, engagement with the supernatural, and violent acts attributed to God.

Women's leadership, the expectation of supernatural experience, and understandings of the nature of God have all generated considerable debate and conflict within British evangelicalism over the past twenty years. I was interested to see how far Generation Y were aware of or concerned about these issues and what their perspectives were. Thus, the following texts were chosen: 1 Samuel 25; the story of interaction between the renegade David, a rich landowner who refuses him hospitality (Nabal) and the landowner's wife (Abigail), who takes initiative to prevent David wreaking vengeance on her household. Ultimately Nabal dies at the hands of God and Abigail marries David. 2 Kings 5 was also chosen; the story of an Aramean general (Naaman) stricken with leprosy who, at the suggestion of an Israelite slave girl, seeks out the prophet Elisha in order to be healed. The episode concludes with his conversion to Yahwism and deception at the hands of Elisha's servant Gehazi, who consequently is struck with leprosy. The final text was Acts 12, which records the martyrdom of the Apostle James at the hands of Herod, the angelic prison break of the Apostle Peter and subsequent death of Herod who is struck by the angel of the Lord. All contain female characters and an act of violent intervention attributed to God, while the latter two both contain miraculous events. All are self-contained and a chapter in length.

I was aware that the Acts 12 text might be more familiar than the others were and that 2 Kings 5 contains a "Sunday School favourite," but both have concluding episodes that proved to be unfamiliar to the groups.

Recruitment of Participants

After churches had been recruited by direct contact with their leaders, material explaining the research was sent to churches and publicized via notice sheets. Volunteers were requested to contact me by email. With the first (Trinity Church) this produced limited results. Only four individuals offered to participate and thus the leader and I concluded that a direct approach from him was likely to be most effective in recruiting appropriate individuals. Therefore, when the other church leaders offered to undertake recruitment I concurred. This was a pragmatic response rather than an issue of gatekeeping, and there was no obvious suggestion that individuals had been recruited to reflect well on the church or articulate official church policy.[32] Leaders did not stipulate control over choice of participants as a qualification for taking part in the project; rather they seemed to be genuinely interested in the ordinary reading of their emerging adults. This willingness to facilitate groups without any suggestion of conditions was one of the advantages of my being an insider researcher; our relationships meant they expressed no suspicion of my agenda, the project or process. Rather, they went to great lengths to facilitate the groups within the requested parameters.[33]

Nine groups were created. I asked the leaders to find British participants with no formal theological education. All of the groups were mixed in terms of gender, although two were not as close to the half male, half female demographic as hoped (one of the younger groups had six male and two female participants and one of the older groups had five females and two males). Seven of the groups contained a non-British participant and, although this was not the original intention, it was representative of the membership of the churches involved. University cities contain considerable numbers of international students and since it would have been offensive and disruptive to ask volunteers to leave, groups were run with those who had volunteered, despite fourteen percent of them not being British.

Inevitably, participants were typically well known to the leaders and thus perhaps of higher than average commitment. Those in the oldest groups tended to have some sort of responsibility within their congregations and had attended the church for some time. Among the mid-aged and younger cohorts, attendance was much shorter, typically one to two years, although the vast majority reported that they had attended evangelical churches for a considerable length of time. They all attended church events at least once, and often twice, a week. Some reported attending additional Christian groups. They were what Guest describes as "Active Affirmers," part of the most consistently frequent churchgoers and those most likely to be "firmly socialized into Christian language and ideas."[34] These individuals are probably the most committed among evangelical emerging adults. They may not therefore be representative of the wider congregation but rather provide information about the most motivated members of evangelical communities.

Participants were required to sign a consent form prior to the session and asked to fill in a short survey about their faith, church attendance and Bible reading practices, which provided valuable background data.

32. Barbour and Kitzinger, *Developing Focus Group Research*, 10.
33. Ibid., 13.
34. Guest, *University Experience*, 41.

Gathering the Data

Observing Church Services

Groups were convened by church leaders over the space of a weekend during which I visited each church and attended services to observe worship and gather some ethnographic data. On one occasion (Central Chapel), I had been asked to preach at the evening service and thus cannot claim to be an objective observer, although it was possible to note the worship, structure and general tone of the service. For each church, I attended two services. This provided only a snapshot of the wider community, but these six occasions provided insight into the congregation and its ethos.

Initial Leader Interview

All three church leaders were interviewed at length prior to the focus groups. These were relaxed and informal conversations. Two took place in their offices at church, the third in the leader's home.[35] These interviews lasted between ninety minutes and three hours. They were semi-structured in order to gather the logistical, theological and structural data for a basic understanding of the history and values of the congregation but flexible enough for improvisation in exploring some of those themes.[36] This allowed the leaders to describe the community to me in their own words and make me aware of any issues they considered pertinent.[37] The conversations were candid, good humoured and provided rich data. All three leaders were extremely generous with their time, and their comments form a significant part of the findings.

A number of factors emerged in conversation which I had not anticipated, forcing me to recognize my own assumptions (and in some cases prejudices) about their values and practices.[38] The interviews also included questions about how leaders anticipated their focus groups would respond to the chosen biblical narratives. They described their expectations, hopes, and, in some cases, fears. These conversations were recorded and subsequently transcribed, coded and analyzed.

---

35. Gillham, *Research Interview*, 9.
36. Wengraf, *Qualitative Research Interviewing*, 5.
37. Gillham, *Research Interview*, 2.
38. Ibid., 3.

Focus Group Meetings

Seven of the nine focus groups were convened in church-related buildings. While I recognize the value of neutral locations, my dependence on church leaders to organise venues meant this was a practical decision.[39] However, since the activity they were undertaking was linked to church practice, I considered that the location would not undermine the findings but might help to illustrate the dominant cultural values of the congregations.[40] Trinity Church offered a classroom space used for weekly Bible studies, and the group was seated round a table in a seminar format. The New Life groups were held in a small office space, with the group seated around a coffee table on a mixture of formal and informal chairs. Two of the Central Chapel groups were held in the leader's home, on sofas, and the third was held in a church lounge. Leaders were not present in any of the groups. Indeed, for the majority of the sessions they were not even in the building. None of them exerted any direct influence over the groups (although there were occasional jokes about what leaders might think of the comments made).

For each session, I introduced myself, describing my background, and explained my interest in understanding how Generation Y read the Bible, including my desire to help leaders understand the consequences of the way they modelled biblical engagement.[41] All members had received and signed copies of documentation around anonymity and confidentiality but this was reiterated and groups were asked for their participation in that beyond the session.[42] To put them at ease, I also emphasized that the discussion was not a test but an exploration of their ideas. Some had completed the background questionnaire in advance of the session, but a majority completed them either before the session while waiting for latecomers, in the comfort breaks, or remained behind afterwards to complete them. Three of the fifty-two participants failed to complete the questionnaire.

Participants were invited to introduce themselves (partly for the tape) and then given a printed copy of the text which they read aloud, taking turns around the room. The rationale for this was to encourage everyone to speak from the outset but also to see whether they would produce their own Bibles to further examine and cross-reference the texts.[43]

39. Powell and Single, "Focus Groups," 201.

40. Kitzinger, "Introducing Focus Groups," 299–302.

41. Common characteristics between researcher and participants are likely to encourage trust and participants are often motivated by the sense that what they are doing may be a forum for change. Race et al., "Rehabilitation Program Evaluation," 36.

42. Powell, "Focus Groups," 502.

43. Kitzinger, "The Methodology of Focus Groups," 105.

The text was used as a discussion starter and, after it had been read, the group were asked about their familiarity with the passage and then asked an open ended question: "What are your thoughts, observations or questions about that passage?" There were no further prescribed questions but rather an open floor for them to discuss whatever had struck them as interesting or significant. As Hennick explains,

> The function of non-directive interviewing is to shift the attention away from the dominance of an interviewer to focus on generating a discussion between participants on certain issues. The discussion element of the method gives participants greater control of the issues raised in the dialogue, as they are essentially discussing the issues between themselves rather than directly with an interviewer.[44]

Focus group methodology suggests five to six structured questions but, since I was interested in the relative importance of themes or interests they displayed, a largely unstructured questioning procedure was appropriate.[45] Initially a number of groups (particularly the younger and mid-aged ones) directed responses and questions towards me, asking for "correct" answers to their questions. Having made it clear that I was aiming to be as non-interventionist as possible and was interested in their ideas, the majority stopped doing this and treated me as a facilitator rather than expert or source of information. Instead, they discussed ideas among themselves and questioned each other.[46] This demonstrated a level of familiarity and comfort with the subject matter and practice of small group discussion.

After instigating the reading and discussion of each text, researcher contributions were primarily prompts: "What does anybody else think?" or "Does anything strike anyone else?" with occasional probing to encourage the contribution of reticent members when they spoke up.[47] I used these prompts when groups appeared reluctant or excessively jocular rather than to steer the content. In some groups, I asked one or two directive questions but, overall, groups were free to direct their own discussion. I presented these questions as hypotheses such as, "Some scholars think that Abigail was manipulating David. What do you think?"[48] The groups appeared to

44. Hennick, *International Focus Group Research*, 5.

45. Powell, "Focus Groups," 201, 108.

46. Barbour and Kitzinger, *Focus Group Research*, 14; Goss and Leinbach, "Focus Groups," 118; Ritchie and Lewis, *Qualitative Research Practice*, 171.

47. Myers, "Enabling Talk," 100.

48. I.e., researcher opinion on such theses was presented as neutral. Krueger, *Focus Groups*, 57.

be comfortable in reflecting on such theories but did not feel compelled to agree. Indeed, only one of the nine groups agreed with the view presented in this particular question. The others were confident to disagree with scholars, despite their frequently expressed desire for expert information.

Discussion of each text lasted about twenty-five minutes before the process was repeated with another. On some occasions, groups appeared to run out of things to say, marking a conclusion. On others, they had to be stopped in order to move on. At this point, a direct question was asked of each group: "Why do you think this passage is in the Bible?" This aimed to crystallize their discussion and meaning-making processes. Overall, including a comfort break with refreshments, the sessions were around two hours in length.[49] In addition to researcher notes, (which included a seating plan and comments on body language and group dynamics) audio recordings were made and subsequently transcribed and coded.

It is worth noting at this point the amount of humour and informality of the discussions (discussed in chapter 8). The positive effects of focus groups on individuals have been well documented, and these groups appeared to follow that pattern. During comfort breaks and at the end of the session, individuals often questioned me about the research project, asked what other groups had discussed and were interested in how far their discussions were typical. Some chose to stay behind after the session to discuss further thoughts and, in a number of groups individuals commented on patterns they saw emerging from the selected texts. For example, several groups commented on the theme of God striking individuals one laughingly commenting, "It's almost like they were deliberately chosen for that!" Where it was appropriate, I answered their questions but was vague about findings in order not to influence subsequent discussion. The older groups appeared to view me as a peer: a number of individuals discussed their own academic or professional research. Participants asked questions about my home church, my relationship with their leader and what I hoped to achieve with the findings, expressing genuine interest in the project. The younger groups were somewhat more hesitant, appearing to view me as an authority figure, but they too relaxed and became animated as time went on. Some even made teasing jokes at my expense, indicating an informality in how they viewed older people or authority figures.[50] Clearly, the tone I attempted to set of being informal, fairly jovial, and relaxed, had an influence and overall the groups appeared to view me as an interested and sympathetic facilitator.

49. Powell and Single, "Focus Groups," 201.

50. Kitzinger, "Introducing Focus Groups," 300.

Coding and Analysis.

Coding was predominantly done by hand although NVIVO software proved helpful in observing conversational priorities. Following Krueger's description of axial coding, the transcripts were initially examined for the three key theological themes under consideration, attempting to identify each time an individual addressed these issues.[51] These were analyzed in turn to explore recurring ideas or unique thought processes. Much of this data was recorded on large spread sheets with grids representing all nine groups and color used to identify patterns across either age or church.

Subsequent coding examined factors related to group dynamics and gender contributions. These included noting silences greater than six seconds, what prompted them and how they were broken. Likewise, episodes of laughter were counted and patterns were measured across age, church, and biblical passage to explore which texts they found most humorous and how humour was used. Episodes of disagreement and conflict were noted, including what provoked them, how the group reacted to them and how (or if) they were resolved. In addition, the total number of lines of conversation contributed by men and women were counted in order to analyze patterns of dominance based on gender and age. Finally, hermeneutic processes were examined, including references to author, context and wider biblical cross referencing.

Beneath individual comments and discussion, I attempted to identify the interpretative strategies groups were using to make sense of the narrative and what their priorities were in engaging with the texts. I remained close to the data, engaging a cyclical process of repeatedly returning both to transcripts and to recordings, reassessing my coding and analysis, ensuring that I had not misunderstood statements, removed them from context or missed tone of voice.[52] A number of conclusions had to be modified, and my analysis has evolved over the course of the project as I realized initial ideas were too simplistic or generalized and that more nuanced examinations of transcripts were required.

Follow-up Leader Interviews

Once factual data had been gathered, an initial summary was sent to the church leaders and a follow up interview was conducted (two by skype for

---

51. Krueger, *Focus Groups*, 128.

52. Hennink, *International Focus Group Research*, 207.

logistical reasons).[53] I did not offer any analysis at this stage but simply reported general trends and asked for their opinions. These discussions lasted between one and two hours and included their observations on the groups' processes, responses, and behaviours. All provided considerable insight into ongoing situations and priorities within the churches, for example, pastoral situations which might have provoked or inhibited discussion of certain topics, or resources their congregations accessed that had possibly influenced their theological reflections.

All three leaders appeared positive about the process, with two asking for advice on how to tackle what they saw as theological deficiencies within the thinking of their groups. One leader suspected that the figures given by his members on personal Bible reading were exaggerated and was certain that they were not typical of the wider congregation. They all appeared to be highly reflexive in examining their church practices and their outcomes, wanting to develop them to be as effective as possible.

Once again, the advantage of my being an insider researcher was evident, and the lack of defensiveness from all three leaders was striking.[54] All of them took the findings seriously and appeared to have spent time reflecting on them prior to the interview. They were encouraged by some findings and curious about others, asking questions about similarities and differences between their own groups and those from other churches. Despite my not presenting analysis or opinion, they all requested it, asking how I understood what I had found, and these interviews became genuine dialogues. It appeared that this had functioned as a consultative process, providing insights into the ordinary reading of their emerging adults and highlighting areas they wished to address or develop within their congregations.[55] However, these episodes of dialogue and asking advice appeared to be directed to me as a peer, a Christian leader and Bible teacher, rather than as a scholar.[56] They clearly viewed me as "one of them" and that trust allowed for more open and frank dialogue than might have occurred with an outsider researcher.

The amount of effort and interest expended by all three churches towards this project is, I believe, related to my being a sympathetic peer, asking questions to which they wished to know the answers. All of them asked for a copy of my final doctoral thesis and hoped that the findings might be useful for the wider evangelical community.

53. Hennink, *International Focus Group Research*, 128.

54. Kitzinger, *Focus Group Research*, 14.

55. Morgan, *Successful Focus Groups*, 15–16.

56. Barbour, *Focus Group Research*, 13.

Methodological Reflections

Inevitably, there are flaws with any project design, and this one is no exception. The creation of artificial groups meant that behaviour varied. In some older groups, participants knew each other well whereas, in younger groups, many had never met, and this seems likely to have influenced the group dynamics and their confidence to discuss texts.

Dependency on church leaders to recruit participants also meant that non-British participants and some who had undertaken informal theological training were included in the sample, thus participants did not all fit the ideal demographic. It also seems likely that those who were particularly interested in the Bible, or highly committed to the church, would have responded to the invitation to participate—thus the groups may be unrepresentative of the wider congregation but reflect the most enthusiastic sections. Likewise, researcher participation was inconsistent since the process of running the focus groups evolved reflexively over the course of the project. As a solo researcher there were inevitably details that I missed that a second researcher might have seen.

While the choice of narratives indirectly raised theological issues, these would have been made more explicit with the use of other forms of biblical literature (such as epistles), thus it was only possible to see a glimpse of opinions on theological diversity without exploring them in any depth. What people find interesting and discuss at length in focus groups is not necessarily what is important to them, and silence does not necessarily imply agreement with majority views, thus any conclusions about priorities or the genuine significance of issues must be appropriately qualified.[57] It is also possible that focus group members with minority views self-censor. Although social similarity helps with this and the groups did have things in common (e.g., age and education level) nor were they complete strangers. They belonged to the same church community, and thus it may be that opinions went undocumented.[58] This would have been helped by follow up interviews to verify intentions and attitudes, but this was beyond the time and financial restrictions of the research and, since the participants belong to a highly mobile demographic, many are likely to have moved on from these churches already.

With regard to questions of faith development through emerging adulthood, longitudinal data is ideal. Comparing a group of nineteen-year-olds with a different group of twenty-nine-year-olds does not provide genuinely

57. Sim, "Qualitative Data," 348.
58. Ibid.,

comparable data. However, longitudinal data was beyond the capacity of this study and thus all patterns observed based on this methodology have to be viewed as tentative and provisional. Similarly, it is dangerous to make generalizations about all evangelical emerging adults based on this sample. They represent nine conversations held by fifty-two individuals at specific times and locations. However, although dialogue in focus groups takes place at specific times and locations, it is historically and culturally situated. Groups do reflect the values and ethos of their habitation. "A single dialogue may be no more than a slice taken out of this historical and cultural habitation," but it does provide information and insight into it.[59]

Some conversations were shaped by circumstances within an individual congregation, others included views of individuals that are unlikely to be representative of a majority of evangelicals. However, the value of case studies is well documented and, within this project, significant patterns have been observed, both across and between churches. Some evidence of developmental and gendered patterns are also clear and, as a process, the project appears to have had an impact both on individual participants (who expressed their enjoyment and learning) and on the churches involved.[60] Thus there have already been positive outcomes prior to the production of this book, and I am optimistic that the findings will be of use to the study of biblicism and the sociology of evangelicalism as well as the British evangelical church. It provides unique data and an adaptable methodology for further academic investigation into theological, hermeneutical and sociological processes within the context of faith-based groups.

59. Markova et al., *Dialogue in Focus Groups,* 24.

60. Goss, "Focus Groups," 119.

3

Interpretative Priorities: What Matters to Young Evangelical Bible Readers?

Introduction

A CENTRAL RATIONALE BEHIND this project was the observation of exactly how young evangelicals engage biblical narrative. Two key research questions underpin this. One was around their interpretative priorities; what they paid attention to in the text as illustrated by the types of question they asked of it. The second was how far young adult readings were typical of wider evangelical hermeneutical practices, whether they varied across the tradition and whether they altered throughout this developmental period?

The following chapters explore these two questions. Although they are interrelated and thus discussion overlaps, this chapter examines their interpretative priorities before chapter 4 discusses more broadly, how far their reading parallels other evangelical practices. They have been placed in this sequence in order to provide the reader with a sense of the actual discussion of the focus groups and provide nuance prior to the broader observations of chapter 4.

Asking Questions of the Text: Ordinary Interpretative Priorities

A wide range of questions can be asked of any biblical text and, in a field as under-researched as ordinary hermeneutics, discovering those that young evangelical readers chose to focus on is important in illustrating what they expect of and hope for from the Bible. In order to identify and create helpful categories to situate these priorities, comparison with a range of scholarly biblical interpretations have been undertaken. Other comparisons—with older evangelicals, other Christians, or even non-believers would be interesting. However, there is a dearth data on these. Biblical scholarship provides a good sample of issues that could be addressed in each text. The purpose of this chapter then is not to critique the available academic literature but to use it to identify the interpretative priorities and categories that help analyze the interpretative moves that ordinary readers made.

Each narrative will be examined in turn and, although space precludes discussing every aspect of all three texts, key issues that raised significant interpretative priorities are explored.

1 Samuel 25

The story of the encounter between David, Abigail, and Nabal in 1 Samuel 25 was unfamiliar to the focus groups. However, scholars have shown considerable interest in this episode. Much of this has been literary, focussing on allusions, patterns and types within the text, comparing it to other biblical episodes.[1] Some have paid attention to the historical character of David and the wider political and theological issues of monarchy in ancient Israel.[2] There has also been interest in the significance of marriage within the Davidic narrative.[3]

However, the issues of interest discussed both by scholars and by ordinary readers do not fit into neat categories; rather they overlap. In order to provide some structure for comparison, they have been divided into five areas: 1. David's reputation; 2. Issues around a divinely appointed monarchy; 3. The acquisition of wives; 4. The development of David's character; and 5. Themes of wisdom and folly embodied by Abigail and Nabal. Some additional areas of concern for ordinary readers conclude the section.

---

1. E.g., Levenson, "First Samuel 25," 11–28; Green, "1 Samuel 25," 1–23; Berger, "Ruth and Inner-Biblical Allusion," 253–72; Murphy, 1 Samuel.

2. E.g., Gordon, "David's Rise and Saul's Demise," 37–64; Gunn, The Fate of King Saul; Jobling, 1 Samuel; McKenzie, King David; Campbell, 1 Samuel; Firth, 1 & 2 Samuel.

3. E.g., Levenson and Halpern, "David's Marriages," 507–18; Berlin, "David's Wives," 69–85; Miscal, 1 Samuel; Bach, The Pleasure of Her Text; Nicol, "David, Abigail and Bathsheba".

David's Reputation

Scholarly works typically have a political orientation, focussing on the impact of David's reputation on the subsequent royal line. Several note this chapter as situated within a trilogy of narratives which seek to establish David's rise to power as free of blood guilt.[4] Others identify his journey to understand the exercise or restraint of power.[5] Alternatively, Berger suggests that the Ruth-Boaz narrative is designed to illustrate a more wholesome bloodline, rehabilitating the Davidic line from the moral ambiguity both he and Abigail demonstrate.[6]

David's reputation was of some interest to the ordinary readers; however, no wider parallels were drawn, and it was not a political but rather a moral reading. Instead of understanding this as pro-Davidic propaganda their concern was that David should be protected from sin which might damage his relationship with God. Two groups did note the situating of the text within the trilogy of episodes but did not explore the significance of that. Indeed, a key interpretative factor was that none of the groups attended to an authorial horizon in their readings. They engaged with the world within the text, particularly the relationship between David and God, rather than any wider agenda, and there was no reflection on the legitimacy of the Davidic line.

Divinely Appointed Monarchy

An overlapping theme was of David as divinely appointed; the text as an endorsement of his destiny to reign as God's choice. Scholarly suggestions are that responses to David are shown as synonymous with attitudes to God.[7] That this is a narrative about the ethics and legitimacy of kingship and is thus a post-exilic comment on the appropriate way for Israelite monarchs to ascend the throne.[8] Several understand it as an allegory for the wider Saulide-Davidic conflict. Nabal represents Saul, suffering the same fate: doomed because he stands in the way of God's favourite, with this chapter as a redressing of Saulide factions.[9]

---

4. Campbell, *First Samuel*, 221; Klein, *1 Samuel*, 246; Gordon, "David's Rise," 185.

5. Miscal, *1 Samuel*, 150.

6. Berger, "Ruth and Inner-Biblical Allusion," 253.

7. Campbell, *1 Samuel*, 257; Gunn, *The Fate of King Saul*, 102.

8. Berlin, "David's Wives," 77; Green, "1 Samuel 25," 3–7.

9. Jobling, *1 Samuel*, 152; Gunn, *The Fate of King Saul*, 102; Gordon, "David's Rise," 40.

For the ordinary readers, the divine nature of David's kingship was a significant theme in their discussions, but again they had a different emphasis. Seven of the nine groups were aware of the historical setting of the passage and discussed the Saulide-Davidic conflict. Several noted significance around Samuel's death, Israel having lost his stabilizing force. However, only one group identified Nabal directly with Saul, suggesting his rejection of David was an act of loyalty towards the existing monarch.

There was a universal acceptance of David as God's chosen king and that all faithful Israelites should therefore have acquiesced to his request. Their primary concern was theological; to reject David was understood to be a rejection of God. Nabal then was siding against God, while Abigail, in supporting David, sided with him. This mirrors scholarship at a basic level; however, all three of the Trinity Church groups extrapolated this theme further. They emphasized Jesus as a Davidic descendant and thus understood a rejection of David as a rejection of Christ which left Nabal, like all unrepentant sinners, under God's judgement. As before, there was no reflection on authorial political agendas. Their interest was in contemporary theological and pastoral implications, particularly that of conversionism and the acceptance or rejection of God.

Acquisition of Wives

Scholars have explored the political and ethical issues around David's acquisition of wives in this text. Some argue its significance is in demonstrating that Abigail was claimed without bloodguilt, showing a pure triangle of relationship in contrast to the later, lascivious one involving Bathsheba and Uriah.[10] Others draw contrasts between David's "types" of wives.[11] Some suggest that the author is presenting David's marriage to Abigail as legitimate *and* strategic establishing David's power base in Hebron.[12] Many observe the significance of taking multiple wives as a sign of kingship, identifying Abigail, Michal, and even Ahinoam as pawns in the power struggle.[13]

Among ordinary readers, David's marriage was of interest to eight of the groups. However, their primary focus was a moral one; a resounding rejection of polygamy. All were certain that God disapproved and speculated about David engaging in such activity. One group concluded he was following the example of pagan kings and two others reflected on women

10. Gordon, 1 & 2 Samuel, 185; Nicol, "David, Abigail and Bathsheba," 140.

11. Berlin, "David's Wives," 70–74; Bach, The Pleasure of her, 33.

12. Miscal, 1 Samuel, 156; Levenson, "1 Samuel 25," 26.

13. Miscal, 1 Samuel, 156; Levenson and Halpern, "David's Marriages," 514–15.

as a sign of power or prestige, one individual identifying Saul withholding Michal as a political game. Thus, there was some awareness of marriage as a political activity. However, it was noticeable that they did not critique their own understanding of heterosexual, monogamous, contemporary marriage. There was an assumption that it was preferable to ancient forms, with no reflection on context. One undergraduate woman speculated that David must have held modern attitudes towards women since he was "a man after God's own heart." This was one of the areas where participants criticized David's behaviour even though the narrator did not overtly do so. Rather than functioning as straightforward, compliant readers, they were prepared to critique events from an ethical position when they felt strongly enough about it.

David's Character and Development

A number of scholars describe this narrative as a significant marker in David's psychological development.[14] Some suggest it shows an unrevealed dark side, a foretaste of the bloodshed involved in the Bathsheba episode and a future echo of David's fall from grace.[15] Alternatively it is seen as a tilting between good-David and bad-David, Miscal noting that David's triple greeting of peace is replaced with a parallel triple reference to violence.[16] Similarly, Klein observes the furious vulgarity of David's vow to kill all those "who piss against a wall."[17]

There is also considerable discussion about David's request to Nabal: an innocent, culturally appropriate request based on benevolent actions, or a protection racket?[18] Some are critical of David accusing him of arrogance and deliberate provocation, identifying a pattern for all who stand in David's way. However, others argue for this as a decisive point in David's psychological development, in which he learns that if he restrains himself from using violence to claim the throne YHWH will defend him.[19]

Eight of the nine focus groups explored this theme. The majority were critical of David's violence, although they saw it in terms of an overreaction

---

14. Campbell, *1 Samuel*, 258; Berlin, "David's Wives," 79.

15. Klein, *1 Samuel*, 250; Levenson, "1 Samuel 25," 24.

16. Miscal, *1 Samuel*, 150–1.

17. Klein, *1 Samuel*, 250.

18. Bosworth, *The Story Within*, 99; Steussy, *David*, 75; Gunn, *The Fate of King Saul*, 96; Shields, "A Feast Fit for a King," 39; Halpern, *David's Secret Demons*, 22; Cartledge, *1 & 2 Samuel*, 293.

19. Gordon, "David's Rise," 39; Firth, *1 & 2 Samuel*, 237.

rather than a murderous dark side and were convinced that the refusal of hospitality was a serious crime. They demonstrated a response to David that was primarily sympathetic, but repeatedly referred to him as a flawed individual, one group citing the Bathsheba episode and another briefly speculating as to whether David's request was menacing. The majority considered that the text described David's intention as benevolent and none demonstrated the levels of criticism scholars raised. Their emphasis was on David being "like us," learning in the way they learnt from their mistakes. It was an exemplar reading, demonstrating considerable wider knowledge of David as a biblical figure. He was understood as a hero of the Judeo-Christian faith and thus they were prepared to criticize his actions without perceiving him as an oppressive figure. Repeatedly, groups talked about him being restrained by God working through Abigail, learning to control his temper and not to take justice into his own hands. One group related this to "learning how to be a leader," but most understood it as a lesson in personal morality: part of David's spiritual journey. Once again, the primarily concern was that David's relationship with God should not be sullied by sin.

Wisdom and Folly

The final widely discussed theme among scholars is that of Abigail and Nabal as representatives of wisdom and folly. Abigail is compared with the personification of wisdom in Proverbs and the embodiment of Proverbs 31 the ideal wife.[20] She is identified as having the longest prose speech of any woman in the Old Testament, being respected by her servants and stepping outside social convention to protect both men.[21] She is described as a prophetess, gifted with the Holy Spirit, David's redeemer, saviour, defender, and the intentional protector of his reputation.[22] Some see her becoming David's queen as a reward for loyalty, and their relationship as pure and romantic.[23] Bach describes a "good sense mother provider who controls David's temper like a parent," soothing David's passions rather than enflaming them as Bathsheba does.[24] However, others are more suspicious of her motives,

20. Shields, "A Feast Fit for a King," 44.

21. Bach, *The Pleasure of Her Text*, 26–30.

22. Klein, 1 *Samuel*, 251; Levinson and Halpern, "David's Marriages," 23–27; Bach, *The Pleasure of Her Text*, 28; Campbell, 1 *Samuel*, 261; Firth, 1 *& 2 Samuel*, 273; Jobling, 1 *Samuel*, 152.

23. Berlin, "Characterization," 79; Nicol, "David, Abigail and Bathsheba," 136; Levenson, "1 Samuel 25," 18.

24. Bach, *The Pleasure of Her Text*, 30–31.

describing her as obsequious, employing "loquacious flattery" to ingratiate herself.[25] Others see her as protecting her own interests and being vicious and self-seeking, her actions calculated to hurt, even kill, her husband.[26] McKenzie believes she was "ruthless or at least desperate" and "willing to conspire with David to murder her husband in order to forward his career and secure her own future."[27] Shields takes the middle ground, perceiving her as trying to avert bloodshed while having ambition for herself too.[28]

Academic opinion, then, is divided on Abigail and, likewise, the interpretation of Nabal as the representation of folly. Levenson sees him as rejecting any authority but his own and therefore fitting the description of the "fool who says there is no God."[29] Much debate centres on Nabal's name, and whether anyone would name a child "Folly," but rather its possible meaning being "flame," "sent," "noble," or "skilled."[30] The absence of family names is also noted, Gordon suggesting that Keleb (Dog) is close to Caleb (Nabal's tribe) and a statement on his character rather than illustrating ties to a national hero and powerful clan.[31] Also noted are Nabal's extreme wealth; his gluttonous (possibly orgiastic) feasting is contrasted with his refusal to feed David's men.[32] Likewise, his leadership is unfavourably contrasted with David's.[33] Boyle argues Nabal's death from "hardness of heart" was not a medical condition (since ancient Israel had no knowledge of the circulatory system) but rather stubbornness, a refusal to repent, which consequently led to God striking him dead.[34] What most agree on, however, is that Nabal is a supporter, representation or surrogate for Saul; he rejects David and allies with Saul, launching a scathing attack.[35] Essentially they are parallel; "David serves both and suffers harm in return."[36]

Ordinary readers made a widespread exploration of the characters of Abigail and Nabal, and the language of wisdom and folly was regularly used.

---

25. Campbell, *1 Samuel*, 257; Miscal, *1 Samuel*, 152; Steussy, *David*, 75.

26. Gunn, *The Fate of King Saul*, 101; Jobling, *1 Samuel*, 155–56.

27. McKenzie, *King David*, 101.

28. Shields, "A Feast Fit for a King," 54.

29. Levenson, "1 Samuel 25," 15, 22.

30. Klein, *1 Samuel*, 248.

31. Gordon, *1 & 2 Samuel*, 182.

32. Klein, *1 Samuel*, 251.

33. Nicol, "David, Abigail and Bathsheba," 133.

34. Boyle, "The Law of the Heart," 402–5.

35. Firth, *1 & 2 Samuel*, 268; Gordon, "David's Rise," 181; Jobling, *1 Samuel*, 152; Gunn, *The Fate of King Saul*, 97.

36. Bosworth, *The Story Within*, 71.

However, none of the groups drew on wider allusions to embodiment of these qualities. It may be that, since they read events as historically factual, it did not occur to them to draw allegorical parallels. Alternatively, it is possible that a lack of familiarity with biblical wisdom literature meant they did not identify such patterns. Three of the groups did use the language of them as hero/villain or types but this was largely with regard to how far they functioned as role models rather than wider biblical patterns. Essentially, they were useful for the spiritual development of readers in the same way that David's learning process provided a model.

Groups expressed almost universal approval of Abigail, viewing her in messianic terms: a "sort of Jesus" mediating and protecting David. She was described as a replacement for Samuel and used by God. However, one group was critical of her, accepting the scholarly thesis that she was self-seeking. Although eight of the groups strongly rejected that idea, the two older groups from the egalitarian church (New Life) allowed her mixed motives, seeing her as a real woman caught in a difficult situation. Groups identified her as a leader, faithful to God and a peacemaker. Some made comments that her support for David was motivated by a rejection of the Saulide line and acceptance of David as divinely appointed. The type she embodied was faithful believer rather than a personification of wisdom. With regard to her marriage to David, some groups viewed it as a reward while, in two of the elder groups, women presented a romantic reading of David saving Abigail from widowhood. On both occasions men had a more cynical opinion seeing a pragmatic decision based on her wealth, beauty and skill set.

Nabal was frequently referred to as a fool, selfish, exploitative and arrogant. Like some scholars, a number of the groups felt that he was out of touch with his servants and saw his feasting while David's men went hungry as tyrannical and abusive (although this was tempered by their uncertainty about ancient hospitality customs). One of the groups noted his "unfortunate naming," but no one questioned this as a historical fact or read it as any form of metaphor. Eight of the groups were highly critical of him, and several described him as a stereotype of "the bad guy." The Trinity Church groups were the most critical of his actions, reading his rejection of David theologically as a rejection of Christ and pronouncing him "deserving of death." He was a type of unrepentant unbeliever. His death raised considerable discussion, and speculation over literal and figurative understandings of the described cause. However, they were more concerned with theological and ethical questions of God's actions.

There were overlaps with scholarly interests, but the ordinary assumption that this was an accurate historical account meant that they did not tend to draw wider literary parallels or demonstrate literary critical concerns. Certainly, there was no sense of an allegorical reading, although some parallels were drawn, such as Abigail with Christ (demonstrating a Christocentric hermeneutic). Parallels between Saul and Nabal were essentially simplistic. Nabal was taking Saul's side, rather than functioning as a representative. Again, this appears to be rooted in a belief in the historical facticity of the events described by a trustworthy (if unidentified) narrator and concern for what they, as readers, might learn from the behaviour of the characters.

Other Ordinary Concerns and Some Conclusions

It is clear that there were both overlaps and differences between scholarly and ordinary readings of this narrative. One of the most significant variations is that the dominant theme for seven of groups was Nabal's death at the hands of God. This theological question was extremely pressing and is further discussed in chapter 6. None of the scholarly works focussed on this verse, but to many of the ordinary readers it was highly significant and challenged their understanding of the character of God, illustrating theological priorities in their reading.

The second significant difference is that all nine groups referred to applying the text or what they could learn from it. This typifies the devotional nature of evangelical and ordinary Bible reading. Some viewed the three characters as role models or warnings, others drew lessons of revenge being in God's hands alone, and some found encouragement in David's character flaws. All of the Trinity groups drew parallels to Christian conversion. An interesting point of note is that these were individualistic readings, focussing on David, and his relationship with God. Similarly, the applications they drew were personal: not to be selfish but rather hospitable and generous; not to take revenge into one's own hands but to trust it to God; how to learn patience or to control one's temper. There was no discussion of the nation or politics of Israel, the reputation of the Davidic line, or corporate responses to the text. It was a story about individuals, their relationships and God's behaviour within those.

Overall, ordinary readers presented theological and devotional priorities. They did not appear to recognize an authorial horizon but demonstrated a partially naïve reading; they believed the text's version of events and trusted that the authorial voice was reliable. There was no awareness that this might represent post-exilic, pro-Davidic propaganda or parallel other scriptural texts. Nor did they engage in any literary critical analysis of the text. It was, however, not a fundamentalist reading; they were aware of the need for cultural information and scholarship in order to understand events. Indeed, a number of the groups expressed frustration at not knowing the cultural norms on issues like hospitality, obeisance, and gender roles. It was not then an entirely naïve reading, but neither did they engage with the same critical frameworks as scholars or demonstrate resistant reading; rather they trusted the text and explored theological and devotional consequences of the events described.

2 Kings 5

The second narrative discussed was more familiar, although groups differentiated between "The Naaman bit" and the unfamiliar "Gehazi bit" (verses 20–27). Several mentioned sermons or Bible studies they had attended, particularly as children in Sunday school. However, scholarly attention tends to focus on issues such as form criticism, the story as part of an Elisha saga,[37] literary emphases,[38] historical,[39] feminist,[40] and theological readings,[41] as well as Christological focuses.[42] On this occasion there was considerable overlap of interest between ordinary readers and scholars, although once again priorities and reading strategies varied. Findings are structured into three sections: 1. Issues of structure; 2. Literary style and purpose; 3. Engagement with characters; and 4. Other theological themes.

Structure, Literary Style, and Purpose

Scholars spend considerable time considering the sophisticated narrative structure of 2 Kings 5, dividing it into multiple sections.[43] A number identify its complexity and uniqueness as an Elisha story, and some propose Gehazi as a later addition.[44] Literary reflections also raise the idea of stereotypes:

37. Bergen, "Elisha".

38. Hobbs, *2 Kings*; Brodie, *The Crucial Bridge*; Cohn, *2 Kings*.

39. Gray, *I & II Kings*; Fritz, *1 & 2 Kings*.

40. Kim, "Retelling Naaman's Story," 49–61.

41. Brueggemann, *1 & 2 Kings*; Hens-Piazza, *1–2 Kings*; Briggs, *The Virtuous Reader*.

42. Ellul, *The Politics of God*; Provan, *1 and 2 Kings*; Leithart, *1 & 2 Kings*.

43. Nelson, *First and Second Kings*, 176; Cohn, *2 Kings*, 35–36; Hens-Piazza, *1–2 Kings*, 257; Hobbs, *2 Kings*, 58–59; Kim, "Retelling Naaman's Story," 51.

44. Cohn, "Form and Perspective," 171; Hens-Piazza, *Kings*, 257; Hobbs, *2 Kings*, 62; Wiseman, *1 and 2 Kings*, 206; Gray, *I & II Kings*, 50; Hobbs, *2 Kings*, 58.

"The good-hearted maiden, the foreign ruler who learns his lesson and the greedy assistant."[45]

In terms of purpose, Kim argues that the theme of master-servant power dynamics is at its heart, but more typically scholars focus on national, political, and cultic purpose, including suggestions of an exilic or post-exilic dating: an exhortation to Israelites to follow the slave girl's example in engaging their oppressors.[46] It is also considered a comment on temple worship or critique of the ongoing ineffectualness of the monarchy.[47] As an Elisha saga it is viewed as a power demonstration narrative which establishes him as a prophet with significance beyond Israel.[48]

Theological readings typically understand it as demonstrating God's inclusivity, sovereignty and impartiality in judging both Gentiles and Israelites.[49] The engagement of this narrative with New Testament themes is also noted, including Jesus's use of this story in Luke 4.[50] Some with a Christian theological perspective argue that it anticipates Christian baptism with Elisha being a Christ figure.[51]

Ordinary readers demonstrated some similarities with scholarly readings, but typically had different priorities. With regard to the literary structure, a number referred to it as having two halves. Only one group addressed the structure of the text, with some insight, speculating about how many sermons it might be divided into. Otherwise, there was no structural or literary criticism of the narrative and no discussion of sources or it being post-exilic literature. However, the ordinary understanding of the purpose of the narrative did overlap with scholarly themes. Frequently raised was the theme of power dynamics between servants and masters. Rather than an overarching purpose as Kim suggests, they viewed it more as Brueggemann does: a demonstration of God's inclusivity in using the weak to influence the strong.[52] This was particularly important to the Central Chapel and New Life groups suggesting a democratic emphasis typical of their church ethos and generational focus on both justice and individualism.

---

45. Nelson, *Kings*, 177.

46. Kim, "Retelling Naaman's Story," 51; Leithart, *1 & 2 Kings*, 196; Bergen, *Elisha*, 119.

47. Moore, *God Saves*, 83; Brueggemann, *Testimony to Otherwise*, 48; Cohn, "Form and Perspective," 176.

48. Hobbs, *2 Kings*, 68; Hens-Piazza, *Kings*, 257.

49. Brueggemann, *Testimony*, 59; Cohn, *2 Kings*, 42; Ellul, *The Politics of God*, 13.

50. Brueggemann, *Testimony*, 59; Wiseman, *Kings*, 209.

51. Leithart, *Kings*, 192–93; Nelson, *Kings*, 181; Ellul, *The Politics of God*, 9.

52. Brueggemann, *Testimony*, 60.

The most common understanding of the narrative's purpose was missional: namely God's concern for the salvation of Gentiles, Israel's role in that, and the idea of Naaman as a missionary to Aram. A second, almost universal theological understanding was that this was a story about grace, a "sort of New Testament story in the Old Testament." Gehazi's crime was undermining God's freely given grace and it provided a cautionary tale. Three groups paralleled Naaman's healing with Christian baptism, one describing it as the "archetype Christian conversion story." Two groups compared it with healings performed by Jesus, although no direct parallels between Elisha and Jesus were drawn. Another recurring theme among five of the Trinity Church/Central Chapel groups was the sovereignty of God. This went beyond scholarly readings to include divine orchestration of a range of events to bring about Naaman's "salvation."

Their reading then was theological, focused on conversionism and having an emphasis on the revelation of God's character and purposes. It also demonstrated a canonical and salvific understanding; a reading of the narrative in the light of New Testament themes and concepts. These were primarily grace and participation by humans in God's purposes. There was evidence of devotional reading, but on this occasion the text was understood more as being about God and his nature and plans. No attention was paid to an authorial horizon or questions of literary criticism.

Characters in the Narrative

In this sophisticated narrative, scholars have reflected on the characters in considerable detail. Naaman, his slave girl and servants, the King of Israel, Elisha and Gehazi have been widely discussed. What is significant is the considerable similarity between scholarly and ordinary interests on the first four of these. Rather than explore all four, one (Naaman) has been chosen as a case study to illustrate the parallels. However, since scholarly and ordinary readings around Elisha and Gehazi differ, they will be discussed individually.

Case Study: Naaman

Almost all scholars note the contrast between the greatness of Naaman's reputation and the issue of his health. The extensive description of his virtues is widely perceived as a "lavish and positive appraisal."[53] Brueggemann

---

53. Bergen, *Elisha*, 112; Ellul, *The Politics of God*, 25; Brueggemann, *Testimony*, 46;

calls him an anonymous Israelite, while Hobbs cites Josephus's attributing the slaying of the apostate King Ahab to him.[54] Whether he led raiding parties or traded for captives seized by tribesmen, Naaman is a wealthy, successful military figure.[55] The substance of his leprosy include suggestions that Aramean attitudes did not include ostracism.[56] It is variously identified as eczema, psoriasis or an embarrassing skin disease but not the sort that debarred one from society.[57] Hens Piazza notes however that he was desperate enough to travel to enemy lands to seek a cure.[58]

The process of his "conversion" or humbling before the God of Israel has also been widely discussed. The vast amount of wealth he took is noted as far beyond any normal tribute payments, thus a representation of his dignity: a vast gift to prove that "he is no charity case."[59] Elisha's rebuffing of his expectation of deference was part of this humbling process, and his refusal to do something as simple, but public, as dip in the Jordan reflects Naaman's anger at this treatment.[60] His expectation that spectacular magic would be performed upon him is noted but that ultimately, talked around by his servants, he submits and goes down into the Jordan.[61]

A number of scholars comment on God's requirement of perfect obedience (hence seven dippings), symbolic submission and of Naaman's need to act on his own behalf.[62] His internal transformation is noted. "Arrogance has become reverent humility before the prophet and his God. The "Lord" of an Israelite servant has become the "servant" of the Israelite prophet."[63] This conversion is confirmed by Naaman's desire to worship the God of Israel exclusively, his humility (in descending from his chariot) and his generosity towards the duplicitous Gehazi.[64] Most agree, Naaman's humbling himself

---

Cohn, "2 Kings V," 172; Gray, *Kings*, 504; Moore, *God Saves*, 71; Cohn, 2 *Kings*, 36; Hens-Piazza, *Kings*, 258.

54. Brueggemann, *Testimony*, 47; Hobbs, 2 *Kings*, 63.

55. Bergen, *Elisha*, 112; Gray, *Kings*, 504.

56. Bergen, *Elisha*, 112;

57. Gray, *Kings*, 504; Nelson, *Kings*, 177; Wiseman, *Kings*, 207; Hobbs, 2 *Kings*, 63.

58. Hens-Piazza, *Kings*, 258.

59. Wiseman, *Kings*, 207; Brueggemann, *Testimony*, 46.

60. Hens-Pizza, *Kings*, 260; Leithart, *Kings*, 193; Fritz, *Kings*, 258.

61. Brueggemann, 1 & 2 *Kings*, 261; Cohn, 2 *Kings*, 37; Hens-Piazza, *Kings*, 261; Cohn, 2 *Kings*, 177; Kim, "Retelling Naaman's Story," 55.

62. Wiseman, *Kings*, 208; Brueggemann, *Testimony*, 49; Cohn, 2 *Kings*, 38; Hens-Piazza, *Kings*, 261.

63. Cohn, 2 *Kings*, 38.

64. Hens-Piazza, *Kings*, 264.

has brought about physical and spiritual transformation, Leithart calling it "Naaman's baptism."[65]

Similar to scholarly work, the ordinary focus groups showed considerable interest in Naaman. They noted the description of his power, his God-given victories, and briefly discussed the substance of his leprosy. The majority concluded that he had contracted it only recently, although some speculated that perhaps it was another skin disease rather than modern leprosy. All nine groups explored his "conversion" and transformation in some detail. The majority noted his displeasure at Elisha's apparent neglect and instruction to dip in a "dirty Israeli river." They also discussed the process of humbling he underwent, the role played by powerless characters in that, and God's desire for his obedience in contrast to his intention to "buy his healing." The majority noted that the healing was much less dramatic than he expected, and described his transformation of character. "God changing his heart" was manifest in his generosity towards Gehazi and his desire to continue to worship God (although only two groups noted his request for soil).

There are therefore considerable overlaps with historical scholarly readings. The main differences were based on a lack of contextual or historical knowledge, such as normal tribute payments or status of military personnel in ancient cultures. Similar interests are observable with Naaman's slave girl and other servants and with the King of Israel. However, ordinary readers reflected on them as real people, speculating about their emotional responses and actions. Like scholars, they reflected on the political situation between Israel and Aram although, as with 1 Samuel 25, they did not consider any politically motivated authorial agenda, such as a wider criticism of the Judean monarchy.[66] Nor did they consider the slave girl as an exemplar for exiled Israelites which, again, was related to their lack of reflection on the authorial horizon or dating of the text. Ordinary readers drew fewer parallels between characters within the narrative than scholars do but were more prone to comparisons with other biblical narratives, for example, comparing the slave girl with Daniel or Esther.[67] Thus they paid less attention to literary themes within the text but did cite it within the wider biblical canon. This drawing of parallels and cross referencing exhibited both exemplar and canonical hermeneutics. However, when engaging

---

65. Leithart, *Kings*, 193.

66. Brueggemann, *Testimony*, 48; Cohn, "2 Kings V," 176.

67. Moore, *God Saves*, 71–72; Brueggemann, *Testimony*, 57; Cohn, 2 *Kings*, 40; Hens-Piazza, *Kings*, 263; Moore, *God Saves*, 80; Nelson, *Kings*, 180; Kim, "Retelling Naaman's Story," 57.

the characters of Elisha and Gehazi the readings of scholars and ordinary participants diverged.

Elisha and the Role of YHWH

Although this is an Elisha narrative, the prophet appears in person only once, and twice sends terse messages. His authority, however, is undoubted. Bergen notes that YHWH is absent in the story, suggesting that Elisha stands in the place of God.[68] However, the majority of scholars agree that his refusal to accept Naaman's payment illustrates his desire to ensure the Aramean understands that YHWH has done the healing and to take no personal credit.[69] A number comment that this miracle confirms Elisha's place as the prophet of God, his refusal to perform the sign Naaman hoped for illustrating his desire for Naaman to understand that the prophets do not control the gods but rather YHWH requires submission and humility.[70] "Naaman stands in humility before Elisha, but Elisha stands in humility before God refusing the gifts and giving him the credit."[71] Ellul argues for Elisha as a Christ figure, while a number note both his awareness and exaggeration of Gehazi's deceitful actions suggesting that his role as a religious official make his deed particularly reprehensible.[72]

A significant difference in readings is highlighted at this point. All nine focus groups considered God not only to be present, but a central figure within the narrative. They understood his presence as demonstrated through the slave girl's testimony, Naaman's healing and Elisha's knowledge of Gehazi's actions. However, the Central Chapel and Trinity Church groups also discussed God orchestrating events. Some considered his Spirit had already been at work "softening Naaman's heart," others believed that he had intentionally placed the Hebrew slave girl in Naaman's house for this purpose. Some were unwilling to go that far but agreed God could "make the best of bad circumstances" to bring about Naaman's conversion. Either way God was central to events; this was a narrative that demonstrated his character and his desire to show grace, even to violent pagans such as Naaman. However, submission to his will and his plans were an absolute

---

68. Bergen, *Elisha*, 115.

69. Cohn, *2 Kings*, 39; Hens-Piazza, *Kings*, 262; Moore, *God Saves*, 77; Provan, *Kings*, 192.

70. Provan, *Kings*, 191; Moore, *God Saves*, 77.

71. Nelson, *Kings*, 179.

72. Ellul, *The Politics of God*, 9; Hobbs, *2 Kings*, 66; Hens-Piazza, *Kings*, 263; Cohn, *2 Kings*, 42.

prerequisite for receiving such blessing; essentially this was a story about God's sovereignty.

Elisha, proportional to the attention given him in the narrative, received limited attention. Eight of the groups mentioned his refusal to perform in the way Naaman expected. All were clear that Elisha's intention was for glory to go to God. One group did speculate about his wider function in Israel's history, but the majority focussed on this narrative and one or two surrounding episodes rather than considering his reputation or theological function. Little was made of Elisha as a type; no parallels were drawn to Christ, and there was no reflection on the wider function of his ministry, or indeed the role of prophets. Despite their tendency for cross-referencing and canonical reading, the participants almost took this story as a standalone episode. It seems likely that unfamiliarity with this portion of the Old Testament and prophetic literature meant they had limited information to use in their analysis. Thus, in contrast to their conversations about David (of whom they had considerable knowledge), their wider exploration of the character of Elisha was minimal. He was perceived as a faithful servant of God, but their attention was primarily on God himself.

Gehazi

Gehazi is widely denounced among scholars as a liar and critic of his master, who cites his lies in Elisha's mouth and inflates himself, as Naaman has humbled himself.[73] Likewise, he is described as an extortionist, greedy and sordid, exploitative of Naaman's innocence and new faith.[74] He is described as racist and disrespectful, expressing no thanks or the traditional salutation of peace on his departure from Naaman.[75] Some argue that he should have understood known his master would not derive material gain from the use of his gifts.[76] However, a slight tone of sympathy comes from Hobbs who notes that, presented with such vast affluence in a time of famine, resisting the opportunity to accrue wealth was simply too much for Gehazi.[77]

Finally, Gehazi is frequently seen as symbolic by scholars. "Gehazi represents an Israel rejected in favor of the Gentiles," his greed on a par with the worst excesses of Israelite Kings.[78] He is contrasted with the generosity

73. Bergen, *Elisha*, 120; Brueggemann, *Kings*, 336; Moore, *God Saves*, 82.

74. Brueggemann, *Testimony*, 58; Nelson, *Kings*, 179; Gray, *Kings*, 508.

75. Cohn, *2 Kings*, 40–41.

76. Nelson, *Kings*, 180; Fritz, *Kings*, 261.

77. Hobbs, *2 Kings*, 68.

78. Leithart, *Kings*, 196.

of Elisha, who healed for free; Naaman, who offers twice what he requests; and the slave girl, who used her position to bless rather than exploit.[79] Cohn calls him a "foil to the God-fearing foreigner," an ironic contrast, since the non-Israelite behaves in a more honorable way than the servant of God's prophet.[80] His curse is understood as the sequel to Naaman's healing, the inheriting of Naaman's leprosy as a demonstration of impartial prophetic justice.[81] Moore contrasts the journeys of Gehazi and Naaman as illustrating a fitting quid pro quo outcome.[82] "For having stolen Naaman's possession, Gehazi now inherits his disease as well."[83] The ending is described as satisfying given the heinousness of his crime.[84]

Ordinary readers reflected extensively on Gehazi. All nine groups were critical of him, variously describing him as devious, greedy, a liar, exploitative, and "really horrible." Their main concern was that he had undermined Elisha and the concept of grace through obedience modelled to Naaman. Four groups reflected on him exploiting a "new believer" and five considered that as the servant of a prophet he should know better than to seek material gain.

However, in contrast to scholars there was also some sympathy towards him. Two groups speculated that perhaps it was difficult to know when it was appropriate to accept a gift. Only one group unequivocally thought his judgement as fitting, others considered it harsh. That punishment would continue to his descendants was of particular concern, with many commenting that it was unfair, highlighting their individualism. One significant pattern was that all of the New Life groups felt the punishment was unfair. They spent considerable time discussing whether God had actually inflicted this punishment, one group speculating whether Elisha had abused his power. This discussion makes up a considerable part of chapter 6 but was noticeable in its divergence from both scholarly work and the more conservative groups who tended to view his judgement as harsh but appropriate. Concerns then were primarily theological and about the nature of divine judgement.

Once again, none of the ordinary readers saw Gehazi as a literary type or symbolic criticism of the nation of Israel. They drew occasional

79. Brueggemann, *Testimony*, 57; Cohn, 2 *Kings*, 40; Hens-Piazza, *Kings*, 263; Moore, *God Saves*, 80; Nelson, *Kings*, 180; Kim, "Retelling Naaman's Story," 57.

80. Cohn, "2 Kings V," 180.

81. Brueggemann, *Kings*, 337; Cohn, "2 Kings V," 182.

82. Moore, *God Saves*, 81.

83. Cohn, "2 Kings V," 182.

84. Provan, *Kings*, 192.

comparisons between his faithlessness and the faith of Elisha or Naaman but otherwise, rather than engaging with literary patterns or an authorial agenda, they saw Gehazi as a real, historic character. He provided another exemplar, although on this occasion one to avoid emulating. He was not a literary vehicle, foil or allegory but a real man, who made bad choices and paid a severe price for them—a lesson they should learn from.

Other Theological Themes

Theologically, the question of monotheism is among the most interesting in this narrative. As Briggs comments, many scholars do not engage with Naaman's concerns about the necessity of his bowing to Rimmon despite his conversion to Yahwism.[85] Some note Elisha's enigmatic response to "go in peace" and comment on the soil noting the irony that, "he who previously disdained the waters of Israel's river now asks for two mule loads of soil with which to return to Aram."[86]

With regard to forgiveness for bowing to Rimmon, scholars varyingly suggest that Elisha's response as an act of charity, allowing him to gradually explore and adapt his practices in the light of his new-found faith or an illustration of God's gentleness towards this tricky moral dilemma.[87] "Go in peace" is seen as an ambivalent response, relying on some leniency from YHWH, or as non-committal but giving tacit approval; the act of glorification having been enough.[88] Alternatively, a number regard Naaman's actions as naïve: the sign of a weak, juvenile faith.[89] Bergen suggests that the whole episode was intended to reinforce the need for temple worship in the minds of readers and remind them of the structure of normal worship which this violated.[90]

This question of monotheism was discussed by five groups of ordinary readers. They explored it in varying detail, but the elder cohort were particularly concerned. One group queried why Naaman was not expected to act like Daniel: faithful in the face of pagan practices? In another, two women explored parallels within their own conversion narratives. Some concluded that God would continue to teach Naaman and that he had gone home "as

---

85. Briggs, *The Virtuous Reader*, 155.

86. Hens-Piazza, *Kings*, 262.

87. Briggs, *Virtuous Reader*, 58–160; Leithart, *Kings*, 195.

88. Fritz, *Kings*, 260; Nelson, *Kings*, 180, 183; Brueggemann, *Testimony*, 57; Cohn, "2 Kings V," 179.

89. Gray, *Kings*, 507; Wiseman, *Kings*, 208.

90. Bergen, *Elisha*, 119.

a witness that the God of Israel was the true God." There was overlap with scholarly discussion about the ethics of Naaman's request, but no reflection on its wider symbolism or cultic significance. As with David in the previous text, this was the moral dilemma of an individual attempting to avoid sin and damaging their relationship with God rather than an authorial statement on wider issues. Essentially their theological concerns were devotional and focussed on how the faithful should act to maintain relationship with God.

Some Conclusions

Overall then, there was much resonance between academic and ordinary readings of 2 Kings 5. However, as before, the authorial horizon and wider political context were not of significance to the ordinary readers, and nor was there any serious literary critique. On this occasion, cultural context seemed of less concern, or at least the groups appeared more confident that they understood the setting and culture within which events occurred. It seems that increased familiarity with the narrative was responsible for this confidence. However, the lack of comparison with other prophetic stories suggests a lack of wider knowledge of this period or appropriate Old Testament literature.

Although they paid varying amounts of attention to different characters within the narrative, attitudes were similar across all nine groups. They read *with* the text, accepting the narrative voice as trustworthy and referring to textual details to confirm or discredit ideas. As with 1 Samuel 25, the New Life and some Central Chapel groups were concerned about theological questions that the narrative was not fully accurate in its portrayal of God inflicting judgement. This did not constitute a resistant reading *per se* but rather a wrestling with their understanding of his character.

There was evidence of exemplar hermeneutics: the slave girl, Naaman and Elisha as examples to follow while Gehazi and the King of Israel were negative ones to avoid. This illustrated a devotional reading although it was less pronounced than the salvific or theological themes in which they were particularly interested. It is interesting to note that although they did not use the language of grammatico-historical hermeneutics (i.e. the meaning intended by the author) groups all focussed on a central theme which they understood to be the purpose of the story. This was salvation of the nations and access to God's grace through obedience. Thus conversionism and explorations of the character and nature of God were their primary concerns. It was clear that they had a canonical understanding of how to read the Old Testament—"reading back" into an Old Testament narrative to draw parallels with Christian themes, rather than engaging with it as ancient Hebrew literature.

Acts 12

Introduction

The final narrative under consideration was Acts 12. It is described as one of several self-contained literary units within the book of Acts, presenting a rounded narrative in which God's people are vindicated and his enemies brought to justice.[91] It is also the last significant episode in the story of Peter and marks a change of focus from the spread of the gospel centred on Jerusalem to Paul's Gentile mission. Witherington describes the Luke-Acts narratives as a "scholarly battlefield."[92] In order to decipher the conflicts, an outline of the major interpretative fields is helpful. Scholarship falls into two categories: historical-critical and literary-critical. Historical-critical readings aim to establish the accuracy of the text and range from theologically conservative works[93] to more critical/liberal readings.[94] Two categories of literary-critical readings exist, one comparing Acts with other ancient literature[95] the other providing modern literary readings.[96] Finally, some scholars draw on a literary background to inform historical questions.[97]

These distinctions provide a helpful framework for assessing the questions ordinary readers asked of the text. Findings are grouped into two sections, firstly the areas where scholarship and ordinary readings overlapped (The purpose of the narrative and the death of James), and secondly five themes in which priorities differed.

91. Gasque, *Acts*, 205.

92. Witherington, *Acts of the Apostles*, 1.

93. E.g., Marshall, *Acts of the Apostles*; Bruce, *Acts*; Stott, *The Message of Acts*.

94. E.g., Hanson, *Acts*; Ludemann, *Early Christianity*.

95. E.g., Gasque, *Acts*; Harrill, "Dramatic Function," 150–57; Clark, *Parallel Lives*; Pervo, *Acts*.

96. E.g., Spencer, *Acts*; Chambers, "Knock, Knock," 89–97.

97. E.g., Conzelmann, *Acts*; Dunn, *Acts*; Witherington, *The Acts of the Apostles*.

Similar Scholarly and Ordinary Readings

The Purpose of the Narrative

Scholars argue that Acts 12 performs a variety of functions within the wider narrative. Some consider the transition of leadership from Peter to James within the early Christian community to be central.[98] However, many agree that the central theological theme is of a power struggle between God and persecutors of the believers, concluding with an editorial exhortation that God will ultimately triumph.[99] Ordinary readers held a universal understanding of the purpose of the narrative. All nine groups perceived this text as an encouragement to persecuted believers, an exhortation that the power of God was superior to any human force. All of them understood it in terms of a power struggle between Herod and God and were clear that Luke's purpose was to show divine sovereignty and authority. None of the groups reflected on transfer of authority away from Peter. Their view was that Peter had been rescued since he had not yet completed his part in God's plans. They were certain he was still the rock on which Jesus was building his church, and a vital part of its mission.

Death of the Apostle James

Historical critics engage with the death of James on two levels: clarifying the details of the event but primarily engaging the theological questions it raises. A number believe the execution to be politically motivated.[100] Barrett suggests it resurrects the theme of persecution in the minds of readers and acts as a foil to Peter's eventual escape (illustrating that readers should not automatically expect divine rescue).[101] Others agree that Luke was highlighting ongoing persecution, painting a picture of the deteriorating situation for the church in Jerusalem and heightening the desperation of Peter's situation.[102] In terms of the theological issues, it is identified as the fulfilment of Jesus's prophecy in Mark 10:39; his martyrdom as part of God's sovereign plan.[103] Others argue for it as evidence of the mystery of

---

98. Barrett, *Acts*, 479, 570–72; Larkin, *Acts*, 186; Marshall, *Acts*, 206; Witherington, *Acts*, 383.

99. Barrett, *Acts*, 570; Stott, *Acts*, 213; Larkin, *Acts*, 183.

100. Bruce, *Acts*, 233; Larkin, *Acts*, 182; Longnecker, *Acts*, 204.

101. Barrett, *Acts*, 479.

102. Pelikan, *Acts*, 144; Peterson, *Acts*, 360.

103. Bruce, *Acts*, 233; Stott, *Acts*, 209.

divine providence, or that divine protection is extended to those who are necessary servants to the ongoing gospel mission, implying James's part is complete.[104] Stott Summarizes, "The chapter opens with James dead, Peter suffering and Herod triumphing; it closes with Herod dead, Peter free and the word of God triumphing."[105] Larkin also suggests that the power of the state is contrasted with the power of the church for whom "prayer is the only weapon it has, but it is more than enough."[106] The author, however, simply reports events and does not answer questions about James's death or the efficacy of prayer despite Peterson's suggestion that he has a special interest in encouraging prayer among his readers.[107]

Responses to the death of James were mixed among the ordinary readers but there are considerable overlaps with scholarly readings. Many of them explored the idea of martyrdom and James having completed his purposes. The New Life groups particularly focussed on an eschatological perspective. Almost all of them saw the contrast between Peter and James, and several groups explored the emotional impact of James's death on the early church and their need for reassurance. Two of the Trinity Church groups identified a political agenda behind Herod's actions, while one group described beheading as a merciful form of execution, noting that the majority of the apostles were martyred eventually.

However, the theme of prayer was one of the most widely discussed and significant amongst the ordinary readers. This is further explored in chapter 5 but, in short, was central to six of the discussions, many readers drawing parallels with their own prayer lives or understanding of the power and significance of prayer.

Divergences between Scholarly and Ordinary Readings

Dating the Text

By contrast to the previous two narratives, a key issue raised amongst historical-critical scholars is the dating of events reported in Acts 12. Josephus's corroborating account creates general agreement for Herod's death in AD 44. However, lack of clarity on other historical events means it is only possible to speculate on the date of Peter's imprisonment.[108] Ordinary

104. Bruce, *Acts*, 237; Peterson, *Acts*, 362; Larkin, *Acts*, 184–85.

105. Stott, *Acts*, 213.

106. Larkin, *Acts*, 183.

107. Peterson, *Acts*, 363.

108. Ibid., 368.

readers, by contrast, raised few introductory questions around the date of the text. Although some wondered how long these events took place after the execution of Jesus, or where they fit in relation to the conversion of the Apostle Paul, they did not appear to feel the need for an exact dating.

Historical and Mythical Readings

A second significant difference is in attitudes towards the supernatural aspects of the chapter. These are the rescue of Peter from prison by an *angelos* and the death of Herod.

The rescue of Peter is one of three divine jail breaks in Acts and although there are some differences between types of scholarship, historical scholars tend to ask literary questions rather than engage with the historicity of this aspect of the narrative. Some, coming from evangelical traditions do ask theological questions with regard to the existence of divine beings, but a majority focus their attention on ancient escape narratives. Discussion about the *angelos* (which can be understood as a human messenger) has largely focussed on the likelihood of the escape being an "inside job."[109] For example: "Without taking the angel *au pied de la lettre* we can reasonably see here an imprisonment of Peter from which he managed to escape because of bribery, negligence, or simply a change of mind on the part of the authorities, all of which are well evidenced in the ancient world."[110]

Some note Luke's propensity for describing supernatural activity in his works, and Stott, Dunn, and Marshall all consider that *he* clearly believed this to have been a divine *angelos*.[111] However, rather than wrangle with the existence of the angelic and historicity of events, scholars of various persuasions note that Peter's dramatic escape follows in a long tradition of epic or heroic escapes.[112] Conzelmann argues that it closely fits the pattern of Greco-Roman escape narratives and is thus an "old Peter legend."[113] Pervo concludes that this marks a "thrilling and memorable exit" to Peter's ministry.[114]

---

109. Bruce, *Acts*, 236; Ludemann, *Acts*, 145.

110. Hanson, *Acts*, 133–34.

111. Bruce, *Acts*, 236; Pervo, *Profit*, 7; Stott, *Acts*, 209; Dunn, *Acts*, 161, 163; Marshall, *Acts*, 209.

112. Barrett, *Acts*, 571; Bruce, *Acts*, 236; Conzelmann, *Acts*; 93; Ludemann, *Early Christianity*, 143; Pervo, *Acts*; 304.

113. Conzelmann, *Acts*, 93–94, 54.

114. Pervo, *Acts*, 301–10.

Literary theological discussions understanding the *angelos* in a variety of ways such as, "A Jewish way of describing miraculous deliverance or intervention."[115] Alternatively part of the Old Testament tradition of rescue by the angel of the Lord and the "ongoing rescue-exodus narrative."[116] Theological parallels include Acts 5, Acts 16, and the passion of Christ (this being Peter's resurrection).[117] Pelikan alternatively suggests that Luke's inclusion of angelic activity is a rebuttal of rationalist Sadducee arguments and part of a strategy to affirm the doctrine of resurrection.[118] Clearly, applying rational methodologies to supernatural events is a difficult process but it is noticeable how many scholars do not even discuss the question of the *angelos* in their work, most engage with literary questions of rescue narratives or Luke's wider theological agenda.

However, the *angelos* was a source of considerable discussion for the ordinary readers. All nine groups unequivocally believed that Peter was rescued from prison by a divine, angelic being. Their translations all stated "angel," but even so no mention of human intervention was made. They believed that the account was historically factual: Peter had met an angelic being, God caused the chains to fall from his wrists, divinely blinded (or in some other way incapacitated) the guards, and opened the gates. The majority of them noted Peter's confusion, but there was no question of anything other than a reading of these events as a "proper miracle," and some made references to contemporary examples of what they believed to be angelic activity or compared this with other biblical rescue narratives. These episodes were cited as similar events: proof that God had acted in this way more than once. In essence, they did not engage with an authorial agenda beyond Luke's desire to report historical events that would encourage Christian believers and, once again, had theological and devotional and experiential priorities.

The second angelic episode describes the death of Herod in Acts 12:22–23. "The people kept shouting, 'The voice of a god, and not of a mortal!' And immediately because he had not given glory to God, an angel of the Lord struck him down, and he was eaten by worms and died."

Historical-critical scholars typically compare this account with that of Josephus which, although lengthier, follows a similar pattern and conclusion. Although he attributes the death to fate and Luke to an angel of the

---

115. Kaye, *The Supernatural*, 67.

116. Peterson, *Acts*, 363.

117. Clark, *Parallel Lives*, 216, 323; Pervo, *Acts*, 309; Marshal, *Acts*, 206.

118. Pelikan, *Acts*, 145.

Lord, both agree that Agrippa's demise was self-inflicted.[119] A number of scholars note it as divine retribution but, again, few comment on the *angelos* to whom it was attributed.[120] Indeed, even evangelical scholars prioritize rationalist discussion as to what kind of medical condition killed Herod.[121]

Literary scholars tend to take a different approach. Pervo argues for Herod as a type. Since Agrippa never used this title, Luke uses "Herod" to refer to a tyrant in the mind of his readers. One Herod slaughtered the infants; another beheaded John the Baptist, thus the type includes any oppressor of God's people.[122] A number note that death by worms was an established ancient description for the death of an oppressive tyrant who defied or despised God.[123] Indeed, 2 Maccabees describes the death of Antiochus in similar terms.[124]

The main discussion around Herod's death for the ordinary readers was one of confusion. Several of the groups were initially unclear about the episode's function in the story (and noted that their strong familiarity with the text did not include this short episode) but resolved the tension by reflecting on the literary structure of the text. It was evident that, when pushed, some groups *did* look for literary patterns and structure, showing awareness of the text as constructed literature.

Five of the groups focussed on the worms, with great hilarity. Although no one made medical suggestions per se, one group did reorder the text, deciding that after he was dead Herod's decomposing body was eaten by worms. The majority did not appear to feel the need to justify or defend such events rationally; understanding what disease had killed Herod was not a concern. Three groups noted the angelic involvement in this death, however, they were more concerned with ethical questions around whether God had indeed killed Herod or not. One individual did suggest it might be a type of death, a humiliation for a corrupt ruler; however, this went unexplored. Seven of the groups noted Herod's demise as the result of his self-glorification and four articulated that he deserved it, showing none of the concern they had demonstrated towards Gehazi; they were certain judgement was in order. There was no sense of Herod as a literary type or of his death fitting that pattern. Instead, the majority, once again, saw it as a

---

119. Josephus, *Antiquities,* 19.8.2.

120. Peterson, *Acts,* 368–69; Stott, *Acts,* 213; Larkin, *Acts,* 188.

121. Bruce, *Acts,* 242; Stott, *Acts,* 213; Larkin, *Acts,* 187–88.

122. Pervo, *Acts,* 303; Witherington, *Acts,* 382; Dunn, *Acts,* 162.

123. Dunn, *Acts,* 167; Conzelmann, *Acts,* 96–97; Ludemann, *Early Christianity,* 144; Bruce, *Acts,* 242; Peterson, *Acts,* 320.

124. 2 Maccabees 9:9.

record of historical events even if, on this occasion, some recognized them as shaped by Luke to make a theological statement.

The Death of Peter's Guards

Verses 19–20 report, "When morning came, there was no small commotion among the soldiers over what had become of Peter. When Herod had searched for him and could not find him, he examined the guards and ordered them put to death."

A surprisingly small number of scholars mention these verses in passing, presuming them to be the fulfilment of the Code of Justinian 9.4.4.[125] This, however, states that "low hirelings" such as the jailor (and presumably individual soldiers) should not be executed in place of a missing prisoner.[126] In the light of this, the execution of the bewildered soldiers can be seen not an act of Roman justice, but of personal fury.

Six of the nine ordinary groups commented on the death of the guards. Some of the younger and mid-aged groups were extremely concerned at what they perceived as an injustice which raised theological questions. However, the older groups from Central Chapel and Trinity Church simply considered them unlucky: in the wrong place at the wrong time. No one referred to the code of Justinian though a number paralleled this text with Acts 16, assuming execution as a norm in such a situation. Several drew canonical parallels, comparing the experiences of Paul's jailor and the guards at Jesus's tomb. Others stated that they expected such brutality from Herod, but no one saw this as part of a deliberate agenda to present him as a tyrant, the execution of James had already convinced them of that. They viewed the guards as unfortunate or the victims of a human, or possibly divine, injustice.

Use of Humor and Irony

Another significant point of diversity is the literary mechanism of humor used in Acts 12. Historical scholars tend to note the use of irony or gentle humor to add realism.[127] However, literary scholars widely emphasize the

---

125. Conzelmann, *Acts,* 5; Peterson, *Acts,* 367; Witherington, *Acts,* 385; Bruce, *Acts,* 240.

126. Blume, "Justinian".

127. Peterson, *Acts,* 363; Stott, *Acts,* 211; Bruce, *Acts,* 238; Larkin, *Acts,* 185.

function of humor.[128] Dunn finds amusement in the fact that "Peter who has just walked through gates manned by soldiers is left at the door by a maid servant."[129] Spencer adds to the theme of gate related irony noting that an iron gate cannot contain Peter but he cannot get through a wicker one.[130] While Pervo acknowledges "nail biting suspense, savoured with amusement. . . . Getting chains off is no problem, getting Peter dressed is!"[131]

Pervo understands Luke's jailbreak stories as a "series of escapades" by the book's heroes, designed to entertain and inspire.[132] This is part of a significant literary discussion as to whether Luke was writing primarily to entertain or educate his readers. Pervo sees Luke holding pleasure and instruction together for ordinary, uneducated hearers, but Witherington considers inspiring Theophilus in his Christian faith or comforting readers was Luke's priority rather than entertaining or amusing them.[133] Chambers however argues that Luke uses the methodology of a raconteur to challenge power structures within the early church.[134] She does note, however, that "[t]he humour is juxtaposed with very real and serious issues; the death of James, threat of death to the apostles and believers. Despite the humour, the spreading of the gospel can be, literally, deadly serious."[135]

There has also been considerable scholarly work around the comic function of the slave girl Rhoda. Some consider her as proof of Acts as lowbrow literature, since they understand her as an ancient comedic device—a *Servus currens* (running slave).[136] Harrill argues that she is intentionally ridiculed by the author, although others consider that it is Peter and the early church, who refuse to believe the testimony of a woman, that are being mocked.[137] Walaskay summarizes: "Luke brings down the curtain on this section of Acts with a note of great irony: a great and godlike king, intent on destroying this young movement, cannot even defeat the likes of Peter, a somewhat bumbling and very fallible Christian leader. Instead God put an

---

128. Pelikan, *Acts*, 148; Walaskay, *Acts*, 118; Witherington, *Acts,* 387.

129. Dunn, *Acts,* 164.

130. Spencer, *Acts*, 126.

131. Pervo, *Acts*, 304.

132. Pervo, *Profit*, 18.

133. Pervo, *Profit*, 13; Witherington, *Acts*, 379, 338.

134. Chambers, "Knock, Knock," 89.

135. Ibid., 94–96.

136. Pervo, *Profit*, 13; Harrill, "Dramatic Function," 151.

137. Harrill, "Dramatic Function," 151; Walaskay, *Acts*, 118; Witherington, *Women in the Earliest Churches*, 147; Spencer, *Acts*, 127–28.

end to the King."[138] The final joke is not on Peter, Rhoda or the believers; it is on the authorities who oppress the early church. Thus, scholars note that Luke skillfully weaves many emotions through this chapter, ending with his optimistic editorial comment.[139]

Much of the ordinary response to humour is discussed in chapter 8, but, in summary, none of the groups overtly engaged with literary reflections on the use of irony or humour. Many commented, "It's hilarious" or "I love it that . . ." and there was plenty of laughter, particularly around Herod's death. Four of the older groups did comment on editorial inclusions and the use of understatement or deliberate building of tension; they were aware of it as a crafted piece of literature. However, this was a background factor; it was more the case that they found the story funny rather than noticing literary comedic devices. They were entertained, educated, inspired, and comforted, much as original readers might have been, but there was no discussion about Luke's intentions to do so nor of this being low-brow literature. Put simply, they functioned as partially naïve readers. However, all nine groups noticed the final editorial comment as such and were encouraged by its assertion of the sovereignty and power of God both for themselves and the wider church, particularly contemporary persecuted believers.

Engaging the Early Church

A final theme is the response of the gathered church to the rescue of Peter. Beyond James, the two members mentioned by name are women. Although theological discussion rages over Luke's attitude towards women, these female protagonists appear only briefly.[140] Mary and (in particular) Rhoda have received considerable scholarly attention. Much of the interest amongst historical scholars towards Mary is focussed on her home, rather than her matriarchal role. It is noted that she is identified via her son, implying that she was a widow or married to a non-believer and that John Mark was probably well known amongst Luke's second-generation readers.[141] Many recognize her wealth: owning a house big enough to hold such a meeting, and having a "cosmopolitan household" with at least one slave.[142] However, much of the discussion speculates on the function of Mary's home as the site

---

138. Walaskay, *Acts*, 121.

139. Acts 24.

140. E.g., Seim, *The Double Message*, 3.

141. Barrett, *Acts*, 583; Bruce, *Acts*, 238.

142. Pervo, *Acts*, 306; Bruce, *Acts*, 238., Barrett, *Acts*, 584; Glancey argues modest households might own a slave. *Slavery in Early Christianity*, 40.

of a house church and possibly the last supper or Pentecost.[143] Little comment is made on Mary as a "mother of the church," although Witherington notes her courage and generosity and Richter Remier's feminist reading assumes Mary was involved in the organization and preaching of the early church, commending her for creating a community where the equality of Galatians 3:28 was embodied.[144] Chambers however sees an implied criticism suggesting, "Luke exalts a slave woman over a wealthy woman."[145]

By comparison, the ordinary readers paid no attention to Mary. Beyond a clarifying question—"Which Mary is this?"—she was entirely ignored, even by those women readers who tended to focus on female characters. They were not interested in the historical details of her home, which was somewhat surprising given the creative attention they had paid to the household of Abigail. Given their propensity to focus on "little people" in other narratives this is surprising but it may be the case that so little information combined with the more dramatic events of the text to distract their attention from this. Alternatively, their familiarity with the text did reduce their examination of cultural context and attention to Mary may have suffered as a result of this.

Aspects of scholarly work on the character of Rhoda have already been addressed, but historical scholars who do not focus on her as a comedic type typically identify her as a believer whose over-excitement creates tension by leaving Peter outside the door.[146] That her words are dismissed causes debate around the faith of the praying believers and their suggestion that Peter's angel is knocking at the door.[147] Little is made of her gender, other than the likelihood of her testimony being dismissed based on prejudices of the time, although some identify intentional Lukan parallels with the women at the tomb of Jesus.[148] Feminist scholars identify her courage and determination to succeed in delivering her message to the incredulous community.[149] Spencer describes her as the embodiment of the Pentecost promise that slave girls will prophesy, noting that hers is only the second female voice heard in Acts and suggesting Luke's intention may have been to

143. Peterson, *Acts*, 365; Barrett, *Acts*, 184; Bruce, *Acts*, 238; Marshal, *Acts*, 210; Stott, *Acts*, 210.

144. Witherington, *Women*, 155; Richter Reimer, *Women in the Acts*, 242.

145. Chambers, "Knock, Knock," 196.

146. A sympathetic reading suggests it appropriate for a slave to seek the homeowner's approval before admitting a visitor. Glancey, *Slavery*, 39.

147. Peterson, *Acts*, 366; Pelikan, *Acts*, 146; Larkin, *Acts*, 185; Dunn, *Acts*, 164.

148. Chambers, "Knock, Knock," 95; Seim, *Double Message*, 24; Walaskay, *Acts*, 119–20.

149. Richter Reimer, *Women*, 242.

rebuke those who were not willing to accept the testimony of women within the church.[150]

Rhoda received more attention from ordinary readers than Mary had. All nine groups commented on her actions with more than half commending her for having faith despite the doubts of others. Some (of both genders) articulated a sense of identification with her, having been mocked for their own faith in some way. As with other figures, there was no consideration of her as a type, although two groups did identify a parallel between her and the women at Jesus's tomb, with another suggesting that Luke had a pro-women agenda.

The final grouping ordinary readers paid considerable attention to was the gathered church, desperately praying. Where scholars paid little attention to them beyond the location of their meeting several ordinary readers stated that they identified with this group and could imagine their experience, appearing to collapse 2,000 years. Their prayer was seen as inspirational and their doubts as understandable (if frustrating). On some occasions, readers overtly expressed a sense of continuity between this prayer meeting and their own faith, referring to them as "we." Thus, a sense of solidarity and continuity between the early church, themselves, and contemporary persecuted believers was significant and distinctly different from scholarly interests.

Some Conclusions

This text was by far the most well-known. All the New Life groups were highly familiar with it, as were the older groups from both other churches. Even those who were less familiar had still heard it and had more confidence in discussing it, although the death of Herod was unknown. The most noticeable pattern in comparing academic and ordinary readings was that ordinary readers did not engage in literary-critical methodology. They appeared to be aware of an author and some commented on his literary craftsmanship and editorial comments. They considered the structure of the passage in order to make sense of the unfamiliar final episode, but that was as far as their engagement with the text as literature went. There was no comparison with extra-biblical literature, although there were inter canonical parallels drawn. Occasional references to "types" did occur but they were fleeting and unexplored. The implication was that the groups did not regard the narrative as an ancient text; rather they seemed to view it as an accurate account of church history and something with which they

150. Witherington, *Women*, 147; Spencer, *Acts*, 127–28.

could identify. At one level, they functioned as original readers becoming caught up in the narrative, engaging with the emotions it provoked and reflecting on its theological messages rather than analyzing it in any significantly critical way.

With regard to historical-critical scholarship, there was more overlap. Unsurprisingly, their readings resonated more with theologically conservative scholars. They were less concerned, however, with validating the historicity of the text or rationalizing miraculous events; instead, they embraced a factual reading. The other significant difference was that they read the text with high levels of empathy. James, Peter, Rhoda and the early church were all embraced within a sense of Christian unity. They were inspiring, frustrating, amusing, and "like us." Their priorities were typically theologically driven, with the sense of God being faithful to his people, the power of prayer and the ongoing spread of the gospel as most important. They read the narrative in a devotional manner, as personally encouraging and inspiring for contemporary as well as ancient believers. Overall then, there were theological overlaps but literary and historical distinctions in reading priorities. The historical-critical ideas and methods they adopted were used to serve a devotional reading and inspire their faith.

Overall Conclusions

Having explored the reading priorities of a large number of scholars and fifty-two ordinary readers, a number of patterns have become evident. These ordinary readers demonstrated some resonance with historical-critical scholars, particularly those from similar traditions. However, they were not concerned with introductory questions, such as accurately dating the passages or finding rational answers to supernatural or medical questions. The historical information they used, or wanted, was cultural information in order to make sense of the world within the text. However, the more familiar a text the less they focussed on this information. It seemed to be the case that with an unfamiliar passage they read the text more closely and cultural detail helped them make sense of the narrative. With episodes they knew better, there was greater inclination to read more swiftly and move straight to theological issues.

Ordinary readers also demonstrated a universal understanding of the narratives as historically factual. On no occasion was this view challenged. The narrative voice was considered trustworthy and, although they might have questions about issues raised, they rarely challenged the content itself. They were compliant readers, demonstrating elements of naïve and devotional reading in their practices rather than intentionally critical ones. They did raise ethical concerns both with the behaviour of humans and of God; however, it was rare for them to demonstrate awareness of or critically reflect on their own cultural background, expectations, or attitudes. Despite recognizing an historical gap between the text and their own world, as their leaders had expected, they were not obviously self-aware readers.

Although they engaged some historical methodology, the ordinary readers did not engage in literary-critical practices in any meaningful way. They demonstrated minimal inclination to understand characters as types or representatives. Instead, they understood them as real people having actual experiences. There was a tendency to notice "little people" and to adopt an exemplar hermeneutic using identification and empathy. God was also understood as a character in the narrative: often silent but never passive. He was perceived as actively involved in events, and they understood that his character could be deduced from the narratives, although some found this challenging at times.

In line with rarely recognizing the text as literature, participants did not engage with the authorial agenda of Old Testament narratives at all and showed no awareness of texts making political or cultic statements. Original readers were not something they considered. However, some of the older groups did engage with the author of Acts. On this occasion, they considered the episode to be a cleverly crafted piece of literature with a theological agenda which they accepted as accurate. However, in the same way that they used historical information to understand unfamiliar texts, they also noted literary structure to bring clarity. Thus, although it was not a priority, some groups did reflect on the shape and themes within a text when they deemed it necessary.

Finally, the groups demonstrated a canonical reading, frequently drawing parallels across the breadth of the Bible, citing a wide variety of biblical literature. It was evident, however, that there were sections of the Bible where their knowledge was stronger. Acts 12 was clearly the most familiar passage and many cited sermons and teaching they had heard on the majority of it. Despite not knowing 1 Samuel 25, they demonstrated wide knowledge of the Davidic story. By contrast, 2 Kings 5 was familiar but there was little evidence of knowledge of wider prophetic literature or the surrounding historical background. It was clear that evangelical biblical engagement is patchy and that certain sections of narratives are more widely examined while others, even among long standing evangelicals are left relatively unexplored. In terms of the canonical parallels they drew these were rarely explored but rather cited as occasions when something similar had happened. This did not tie into any reflection on authorial intention, but did demonstrate an understanding of the canon as an interrelated whole that helped to interpret itself. It was evident that they read Old Testament texts in the light of Christian themes which functioned in a devotional capacity to inspire their faith and actions as believers.

Overall, ordinary readings among these young evangelicals prioritized theological questions and personal spiritual reflection. They showed individualistic and altruistic concerns, but relationships demonstrated between individuals in the text and God were of greatest interest and functioned as exemplars for Christian discipleship. As Malley noted they were reading for relevance, and as De Wit suggests they had an existential rather than analytical priority.[151] None the less, they used a variety of analytical tools to service these concerns. Particularly with unfamiliar passages reading became slower and more focussed on cultural details and literary structure. Therefore, it is clear that although ordinary evangelical emerging adults at one level function as naïve readers, trusting the biblical text, their reading is not entirely pre-critical and they are more than willing to ask difficult questions of the themes it raises.

151. Malley, *How the Bible Works*, 119; De Wit, *Eyes of Another*, 8–9.

4

Ordinary Hermeneutics: How Do Young Evangelicals Read Scripture?

Evangelical Hermeneutics

Introduction and Historical context

As ESTABLISHED IN CHAPTER 1, generalising about British evangelicalism is difficult. Interpretations of biblical texts and Christian doctrines are extremely varied and despite the centrality of Scripture to evangelical faith there is no prescribed hermeneutic. However, there are some general trends, rooted in historical developments of the late twentieth century.

Hermeneutics became a focus for British evangelical churches in the 1970s, most notably at the National Evangelical Anglican Conference in 1977. Here Anthony Thiselton introduced Gadamer's theories of interpretative horizons to evangelical vocabulary.[1] A proliferation of popular Bible translations had created awareness of interpretative variety and, combined with concern over ethical teaching on contemporary social concerns, this created uncertainty about establishing biblical meaning. What had once seemed obvious was no longer straightforward, and hermeneutics became a divisive issue.[2] Conservatives were concerned that it would lead to an increase in liberal thinking, further undermining biblical authority, while more creative evangelical scholars propounded it.[3] Simultaneously, James

1. Thiselton, "Understanding God's Word," 90–122; Capon, *Evangelicals Tomorrow.*
2. Bebbington, *Evangelicalism,* 269.
3. Ibid., 269.

Barr reignited historic accusations of fundamentalism among British con-servative evangelicals.[4] While a number of scholars attempted to refute his accusations, questions of how the Bible should be read and the meaning of "inerrancy" were firmly placed on the agenda of evangelical scholars and church leaders.[5]

Subsequently, aspects of Thiselton's work were popularized by John Stott.[6] Challenging readers and preachers to recognize their cultural preju-dices, he propounded the need for "bridge building" to allow hearers to cross the "broad divide of 2000 years" and explored the idea of interpreta-tive horizons.[7] He described a dialogue between Scripture and reader that should demonstrate a "dynamic interplay between text and interpreters," ex-horting his readers to have a little patience in learning such skills, insisting that the new hermeneutic had not "put biblical interpretation beyond the reach of all but the professionals."[8] This increasing openness to scholarship led to writers from different ends of the evangelical spectrum encouraging popular audiences to engage with dual interpretative horizons and pro-nounced that the aim of Bible reading was to "discover what the text meant when it was originally written."[9] Such information might then be applied to the faith and life of the believer; the fusion of horizons taking place at the point of application. Ultimately this double listening, attending to both authorial and reader horizons, became established as something of a nor-mative evangelical practice for exegesis and preaching in the second half of the twentieth century, although, in the light of post-modern hermeneutics, debate still continues.[10]

In order to examine how far these attitudes have trickled down into ordinary readings, five categories of typical evangelical practice will be ex-plored in further detail.

---

4. Barr, *Fundamentalism*; Harris, *Fundamentalism*, 53–56; Warner, *Reinventing English Evangelicalism*, 190–91.

5. E.g., Stott, "Are Evangelicals Fundamentalists?" 44–46; Goldingay, "James Barr on Fundamentalism," 295–308; Henry, "British Fundamentalists," 22–26; Packer, "Un-derstanding the Bible," 50.

6. Thiselton, *Two Horizons*; Stott, *I Believe in Preaching*.

7. Stott, *I Believe in Preaching*, 137–38.

8. Ibid., 185–87.

9. Packer, "Infallible Scripture," 339–40 ; Fee, "Hermeneutics and Common Sense," 182.

10. E.g., Meadors, *Four Views*.

Literalism, "Common Sense" Reading, and Rationalism

Evangelicals believe that the Bible is "the word of God": divinely inspired and faithfully written by human authors.[11] The text is presumed to be reliable and comprehensible to any believer. It is often assumed then that evangelicals are literalists, taking the text at face value, since they understand it as an exact account of historical events.[12] However, Barr convincingly argued that conservative evangelicals were less concerned with literal readings than with the doctrine of inerrancy, which informed their reading attitudes and practices. "The Bible must be so interpreted as to avoid any admission that it contains any kind of error. In order to avoid imputing error the Bible fundamentalists will twist and turn back and forward between literal and non-literal interpretations . . . in particular by abandoning the literal sense as soon as it would be an embarrassment to the view of inerrancy held."[13] Barton states, "Conservatives do avoid literal reading at times and opt for more remote readings," including allegorical ones, particularly to avoid conflict with scientific evidence.[14] This oscillation results in the harmonization of conflicting passages, vagueness over textual difficulties and inconsistency of attention—skating over certain passages while emphasizing others.[15]

The evangelical-fundamentalist relationship is complex and a number of schemas to differentiate between them exist.[16] Suggestions include the observation that evangelicals are less anti-intellectual, demonstrate an "ethic of civility" (which prevents them from being overly dogmatic), and have less authoritarian leadership with regards to doctrinal "soundness."[17] However, Harris understands evangelical reading strategies to be informed by the overriding principle of inerrancy and Rogers identifies both fundamentalist and evangelical characteristics among English conservatives.[18] This is not the place for a detailed exploration of the doctrine of inerrancy, but it is

11. E.g., Evangelical Alliance statement of faith, We believe in "The divine inspiration and supreme authority of the Old and New Testament Scriptures, which are the written Word of God—fully trustworthy for faith and conduct." www.eauk.org/about/basis-of-faith. Accessed October 5, 2014.

12. Barton, *Biblical Criticism*, 23.

13. Barr, *Fundamentalism*, 40–46.

14. Barton, *Biblical Criticism*, 95–96.

15. Barr, *Fundamentalism*, 54–58; Perrin, *Inspiring Women*, 7–8.

16. E.g., Ammerman, "Operationalizing Evangelicalism," 170–71; Bebbington, *Evangelicalism*, 275–76; Marsden, *Understanding Fundamentalism*; McGrath, *Evangelicalism*; Stott, *Evangelical Truth*.

17. Boone, *The Bible Tells Them So*, 6, 84–87, 103; Crapanzano, *Serving the Word*, 7.

18. Harris, *Fundamentalism*, 311; Rogers, "Ordinary Hermeneutics," 251.

fair to say that whether evangelicals use this language or not (and many prefer the terms infallible, authoritative, or reliable) a sense of defending the authority of the Bible has been central in shaping their reading practices.[19]

It is also true that, except on occasions when the straightforward readings of the text cause irrevocable problems (such as the creation narrative in Genesis), evangelicals usually practise a common-sense reading.[20] Typically, they understand that a text means what it appears to say and that the narrative voice presents a trustworthy report of actual events. They often ignore (or are unaware) of literary theories on interpretation, thus, unless texts cross certain lines, resistant reading is unlikely. Rather, evangelicals typically behave as "compliant readers" operating a "hermeneutic of trust."[21] Following the Reformers, they do not typically look for allegorical, figurative, or mythical meanings in biblical texts.[22] It is true that they recognize the significance of genre (for example, parables are considered stories),[23] but books containing narratives are typically regarded as historical accounts of actual events rather than redacted community or oral traditions. Village notes that Anglican evangelicals report belief in miracle accounts as historical events. This he considers to be a form of resistant reading, acknowledging problems of rational credibility but deliberately proving their faith by believing the scriptural account.[24] Charismatic evangelicals are particularly inclined to do this, believing miraculous events such as healings still occur today, but Village contrasts them with Pentecostal pre-critical readings, suggesting that their evangelical roots made charismatics more inclined to engage with historical and literary background.[25]

By contrast, Barr notes that despite their complaint that historical-criticism dismisses the supernatural, conservative evangelical commentaries often ignore or rationally explain miraculous episodes, typically describing them as natural phenomena orchestrated by God: a form of deist rationalism.[26] Thus, although evangelicals usually believe biblical events to

19. Holmes argues that inerrantism is an American priority, British evangelicals typically preferring "authoritative." "Evangelical Theology and Identity," 26, 31.

20. Harris, *Fundamentalism*, 303.

21. Powell, *What Do They Hear?* 67; Rogers, "Ordinary Hermeneutics," 46.

22. Harris, *Fundamentalism*, 281; Barton, *Biblical Criticism*, 89; Malley, *How the Bible Works*, 100; Barr, *Fundamentalism*, 50; Crapanzano, *Serving the Word*, 2.

23. Barr, *Fundamentalism*, 48; Village, *The Bible and Lay People*, 65; Bielo, "On the Failure of Meaning," 16; Malley, *How the Bible Works*, 92.

24. Village, *The Bible and Lay People*, 67.

25. Ibid., 146.

26. Barr, *Fundamentalism*, 247.

be factually accurate, they engage different perspectives on how such events occurred and whether they might still occur today.

Christ-centred Readings

A second pattern embraced by a majority of evangelicals is a canonical reading, which emphasizes a salvific hermeneutic: the centrality of Christ's atoning sacrifice for humanity. Some argue that a Christological hermeneutic dates back to the Apostles and that understanding both Testaments in the light of New Testament themes focussed on Christ is what makes a reading Christian.[27] Birch claims that Baptist hermeneutics particularly focus on Christ: his presence within both Testaments; his existence before Scripture; his authority over Scripture; and his ability to communicate through Scripture.[28] Whether or not this is peculiarly Baptist is debatable since Christocentrism is an evangelical priority, and crucicentrism is a core belief. Indeed, a common criticism is that evangelicalism's focus on Christ's divinity and death distorts the gospel message.[29]

Engagement with Scholarship

One frequently cited distinctive between evangelicals and fundamentalists is their relative willingness to engage with biblical scholarship. The past forty years have seen significant shifts within British evangelicalism, and changes in hermeneutic practices have influenced the educative processes of clergy, encouraging engagement with scholars from both outside and within the tradition. Similarly, the Pentecostal movement and charismatic renewal have had dramatic effects in many areas of evangelical life including engagement both with pre-critical and post-modern readings.[30]

---

27. Rogers, "Ordinary Hermeneutics," 39–40.

28. Birch, "Baptists and Biblical Interpretation," 159–68.

29. Barr, *Fundamentalism*, 28.

30. Moore argues that evangelical traditions are moving towards Pentecostal interpretative strategies focussing on narrative and experience, while Pentecostals are adopting traditionally evangelical practices. "A Pentecostal Approach to Scripture," 13

Attitudes towards Scholarship

Historically, evangelicals were sceptical of modern historical-critical methodology and nervous of hermeneutical changes.[31] Fears that practices such as source criticism would undermine biblical authority and confuse ordinary believers meant that many dismissed such scholarship as anti-Christian.[32] Much of this fear was rooted in the core value of the Bible being accessible to all believers rather than only to a scholarly or religious elite.[33] However, over recent decades an integration of scholarly theology and traditional handling of the Bible has taken place among evangelicals in the UK.[34] A number of evangelical scholars on both sides of the Atlantic have adopted historical-critical practices within a faith framework sometimes named "believing criticism" and, in an effort to resource the church, some have also produced popular work.[35] Whether such practices have widely filtered into congregations is a legitimate question. Traditional evangelical habits such as focussing on the meaning of individual words,[36] verse by verse exegesis,[37] and extensive cross referencing[38] have diminished. Often influenced by literary theory from writers such as Fee, who argues that "Words only have meaning in sentences, and biblical sentences for the most part only have clear meaning in relation to preceding and succeeding sentences."[39] Thus, many evangelicals are more open to using modernist critical tools although many still demonstrate a reluctance to engage with fields like form criticism.[40]

Textual Transmission

Alongside this mixed engagement with biblical scholarship, there is also evidence of naiveté in understanding the process of textual transmission and translation among ordinary evangelicals. There is often an assumption

31. Harris, *Fundamentalism*, 293.

32. Marshall, *Beyond the Bible*, 17.

33. Harris, *Fundamentalism*, 293

34. Sparks, *God's Word*, 20.

35. Marshall, *Beyond the Bible*, 20; Sparks, *God's Word*, 19; Briggs, "The Bible before Us," 14–28.

36. Crapanzano, *Serving the Word*, 2; Bielo notes the prioritization of individual words over lengthier discourse segments among American fundamentalists. "On the Failure of Meaning," 15.

37. Marshall, *Beyond the Bible*, 17.

38. Boone, *The Bible Tells Them So*, 13; Crapanzano, *Serving the Word*, 7.

39. Fee and Stuart, *How to Read the Bible*, 2.

40. Marshall, *Beyond the Bible*, 22.

of inerrancy in the "original sources" and that translations are substantially accurate.[41] Malley notes the importance evangelicals place on their English translation being faithful representations of what they understand as "ancient revelation-events."[42] He and Bielo observed belief that ambiguity in the English translation might be resolved by the original language or an alternative translation.[43] This suggests a misunderstanding about the origins of the biblical text and the processes of its documentation, and Barr suggests that many have a socialized rather than logical doctrine of Scripture.[44] It seems likely then that rather than confuse congregations with complex issues of transmission and translation, preachers may well avoid engaging such questions for fear of undermining their congregations' confidence in the Bible.

Grammatico-historical Reading

In terms of the scholarship that ordinary evangelicals *have* engaged with, many use a quasi-critical, "grammatico-historical" reading, which is rooted in a resistance to historical-critical methods (although it can be understood as a subset of historical criticism).[45] It emphasizes a search for authorial intention and concentrates on introductory or opening questions such as the date and place of writing, historical, geographical, and cultural context.[46] While it is possible to argue that this demonstrates engagement with scholarship, pre-critical readers have always asked such questions; thus, much ordinary evangelical reading has pre-critical elements even if scholars and clergy engage with critical practices.[47] Indeed, Powell notes a significant difference in the engagement with scripture by clergy and laity. "Clergy prefer a two-stage process: first identify what the author meant to communicate, and then extrapolate meaning for the present that is compatible with the author's intent. The laity, in this study, tended to skip the first step."[48] He concluded that training alters hermeneutic process. Clergy practise exegesis with some concern for scholarly issues, while laity perform eisegesis,

---

41. Barr, *Fundamentalism*, 84; Boone, *The Bible Tells Them So*, 29.

42. Malley, *How the Bible Works*, 49.

43. Ibid.; Bielo, "On the Failure of Meaning," 13.

44. Brogan, "Can I Have Your Autograph?" 107; Barr, *Fundamentalism*, 81.

45. Porter, "Hermeneutics," 102.

46. Barton, *Biblical Criticism*, 24; Crapanzano, *Serving the Word*, 2.

47. Barton, *Biblical Criticism*, 26.

48. Powell, *What Do They Hear?* 93.

their concern being the personal implications of the text.[49] However, use of grammatico-historical practices has provided a moderating alternative to a dogmatic approach (reducing Scripture to theological proof texts) or an impressionistic one (the Bible as a source of blessed thoughts).[50]

A number of the popular books have been written to help ordinary evangelicals engage with this two-step reading strategy. In *How to Read the Bible for All It's Worth*,[51] Fee and Stuart, repeatedly emphasize: "Exegesis is the careful systematic study of the Scripture to discover the original intended meaning. This is basically a historical task. It is an attempt to hear the word as the original recipients were to have heard it."[52]

Reader response hermeneutics are not appropriate in this schema, and the prevention of relativistic readings is paramount. Interestingly, they contrast this with devotional reading in which, it appears, the Holy Spirit can use the text in a wider variety of ways within "careful controls." However, reading "to learn and understand" the text needs to undertake recovery of authorial intention before any principle can be applied to life.[53] This practise is emphasized across the evangelical spectrum. Packer positions himself in opposition to "naïve reading or preaching." Instead he argues for "what the text objectively means, what it meant at, and from, the time of writing must be the reader's priority."[54] It is to be expected then that ordinary evangelical readers might consider there to be an objective meaning to any text, understood as what the author intended, and that, consequently, they would adopt this semi-critical practice, although engagement with literary scholarship, redaction and source criticism seem unlikely.

Interpretative Horizons

The subject of hermeneutics itself is a popular contemporary issue among some British evangelicals.[55] Some have awareness of the unintentional interpretative bias they bring to the text, but many more have an understanding of a gap between the world of the text and that of the reader.[56] Although they

49. Ibid., 92.

50. Marshall, *Beyond the Bible*, 16.

51. Fee, *How to Read the Bible* .

52. Ibid., 23.

53. Ibid, 29–31.

54. Packer, "Infallible Scripture," 339–40.

55. The Bible Society course, *H+ Making Good Sense of the Bible* ,is aimed at ordinary readers.

56. Stott, *Preaching*, 294; Warner, *Reinventing English Evangelicalism*, 190.

may not describe this in terms of interpretative horizons, or be consciously intentional in their reading, Village notes a preference for a reader-orientated horizon amongst laity, but observes that higher education increases focus on authorial or textual horizons.[57] Rogers found a focus on text horizon both in his charismatic and his conservative churches, although he considered that "fusion processes were often rapid."[58] Harris and Warner both comment that, rather than consistently applying this two-step process, if plain reading can make sense of a text, evangelicals typically see no need for hermeneutics and undertake it only to resolve textual difficulties.[59]

However, different texts are difficult for different groups, and evangelical readings are often dependent on other doctrinal values. For example, some conservatives take a "plain sense" reading on women's leadership but undertake hermeneutical processes to deny contemporary charismatic gifts. Alternatively, egalitarian charismatics take a "plain sense" reading of 1 Corinthians 12–14 on gifts but undertake interpretative processes in understanding the role of women. Bartkowski similarly identifies underlying worldviews as informing divergent (and contradictory) readings among conservative evangelicals.[60] Briggs argues that such screening "will ultimately simply get the Bible to echo back to us what we already believed anyway."[61] Nevertheless, scholarly work (particularly by fellow evangelicals) can alter understanding on doctrinal issues and thus it is possible for evangelicals to move theological position while maintaining a framework of biblical authority, even inerrancy, the error being understood to be with the interpretation not the text itself.[62] Similarly, post-modern and liberationist readings have had influence on many younger evangelicals who are embracing readings that promote social justice and transformation, an activism reminiscent of earlier evangelical traditions.[63]

Motivation for Reading

A fourth significant factor in evangelical hermeneutics centres on the motivation for reading: the belief that the Bible is relevant to the life of believers.

57. Village, *The Bible and Lay People*, 83.

58. Rogers, "Ordinary Hermeneutics," 134.

59. Harris, *Fundamentalism*, 284; Warner, *Reinventing English Evangelicalism*, 191.

60. Bartkowski, "Beyond Biblical Literalism," 259–72.

61. Briggs, *Reading the Bible Wisely*, 96.

62. Marshall, *Beyond the Bible*, 28.

63. E.g., Myers, *Binding the Strong Man*; Hays, *Moral Vision*; Bebbington, *Evangelicalism*, 69–72.

Malley argues that the primary function of evangelical exegesis is to affirm the relevance of the Bible to ordinary readers with an assumption that there will always be a personal application (although their search is not always successful).[64] De Wit, likewise, argues that all ordinary reading, evangelical or not, "is intent on appropriation."[65]

Traditionally, some forms of evangelicalism have emphasized their rationalist roots, prioritizing reading the Bible to "inform the mind and acquire correct doctrine."[66] However Grenz argues that this is becoming an outdated epistemology. He suggests that there is a revival in a Pietist-Puritan process of reading to sustain the soul.[67] Malley found evidence for both: a desire to establish and justify doctrines but also an "Expectation that God will speak to them, either corporately, as part of the universal church, or individually, in the particular circumstance of their lives. And they expect God to say things that are important."[68]

An interest in establishing doctrinal truth as well as devotional reading is often held alongside some measure of engagement with scholarship by evangelicals. Many use study Bibles, which contain scholarly comment, or read popular scholarly work. Specific mixed-mode reading strategies have been developed, such as that devised by Wink, who encouraged the use of scholarly findings alongside readers' intuition and imagination.[69] Powell has developed a model of expected and unexpected readings which considers reader empathy with characters in the text.[70] However, Briggs criticizes what he sees as the contemporary evangelical concern to deduce principles from the biblical text for application.[71] He argues that rather than going beyond the text in order to apply it, good reading goes deeper into the text allowing it to set the agenda.[72] The search for a second-stage application diminishes Scripture, and he prefers readers to immerse themselves into the Bible and emerge transformed by the experience rather than reduce it to a book of moral lessons.[73] Whether this model can influence the deeply held evangelical expectation that the Bible will be highly relevant for their

---

64. Malley, *How the Bible Works*, 112.
65. De Wit, *The Eyes of Another*, 10.
66. Grenz, "Introduction," 11.
67. Ibid.
68. Malley, *How the Bible Works*, 79–81, 105.
69. Wink, *Transforming Bible Study*.
70. Powell, *What Do They Hear?*
71. Briggs, *Reading the Bible Wisely*, 96.
72. Briggs, "These are the Days of Elijah," 158.
73. Briggs, *Reading the Bible Wisely*, 101.

daily lives is unclear. Both devotional engagement and reading beyond the text are driven by a search for immediate relevance that may not create the patience and ability to hold uncertainties in tension, which Briggs's model necessitates.

In terms of the process of application, Birch describes a sense of continuity with the biblical narrative among Baptists which he calls, "then is now": a desire to "actualize the apostolic faith in each new age."[74] Pentecostals also echo a sense of continuity with the early church, "collapsing the distance between the original context of Scripture and the context of the reader."[75] Both they and charismatics tend to follow in the primitivist footsteps of the Montanists and Anabaptists in anticipating similar experiences to those of biblical characters who should be followed as role models, an "exemplar hermeneutic."[76]

Pinnock adds that, like Pentecostals, charismatics operate a "Spirit-hermeneutic" that causes them to be very open to diverse readings, creating "endless reflection" and "treasure old and new" from the text.[77] Indeed, some charismatics have adopted a "this-is-that" hermeneutic. Stibbe argues that, led by the Holy Spirit, he used an analogical or Pesher reading to understand the Toronto blessing phenomena of the 1990s as comparable to Ezekiel 47. This was removed from its original historical context, but, he argues, was an acceptable reading following in the tradition of New Testament writers appropriating and reinterpreting parts of the Old Testament.[78] Despite criticism, it has considerable overlap with pre-modern practices and was observed by Rogers amongst British charismatics who used text-linking, Pesher, and allegorical hermeneutics, along with what he called "spring-board" preaching.[79] Such sermons were almost entirely focussed on the reader horizon, simply using a Bible passage to "jump off" from.[80] It may well be the case that other types of ordinary evangelical readers draw similar inspired parallels in their devotional reading, appropriating texts apart from their historical context. But whether they do this when engaging with small group reading of the text is another matter.

74. Birch, "Baptists," 157.

75. Martin, *Pentecostal Hermeneutics*, 3.

76. Ibid., 8.

77. Pinnock, "The Work of the Spirit," 238–41.

78. Stibbe, "This Is That," 184.

79. E.g., Smith, "This Is That Hermeneutics," 33–62.

80. Rogers, "Ordinary Hermeneutics," 192–96.

Interpretative Limitations

A final point is that typically evangelicals do not believe that the Bible can mean just anything one wishes. They follow in the footsteps of the Reformers whose emphasis on *Sensus literalis* functioned as boundaries on meanings.[81] However, despite instructions to find the objective meaning of a text, it is rare for evangelicals to consider there to be an exclusive, definitive meaning for a passage. Malley notes a tendency for preachers to offer *a* rather than *the* meaning of a passage.[82] Evangelicals are typically untroubled that people may take different things away from a text—God is actively speaking to individuals after all.[83] But overall authority lies with God's communication through the inspired writer, not the reader. "Evangelicals believe that human beings are judged by the Bible and called to change in the light of it, rather than standing in judgement over the Bible and rejecting those parts that are not in line with their own sensibilities."[84]

Thus there are interpretative limits to what may be concluded from the text. However, groups define these boundaries differently. Stott describes the Bible as the senior partner in the spiral of interpretation, something readers should "sit under."[85] Pinnock, arguing for a Spirit-hermeneutic, states, "[t]exts of the Bible do have definite meanings in the historical situation and that meaning is the anchor of our interpretation. But the total meaning cannot be restricted to that. Texts carry implied meanings too, but they cannot mean just anything we want. Some interpretations are more plausible than others." [86]

Barton, however, describes evangelical practices as a straightjacket for the text[87] and Briggs complains that, "[t]he problem lies with the habit, deeply ingrained across the theological spectrum, of reading off an agenda from the surface of the text what happens to fit very neatly into a system of values already held."[88]

Certainly interpretative boundaries vary and they may be doctrinally constituted. People do demonstrate confirmation bias, finding evidence

---

81. Barton, *The Nature of Biblical Criticism*, 99.

82. Malley, *How the Bible Works*, 125.

83. Ibid., 125–26.

84. Larsen, "Defining and Locating Evangelicalism," 8.

85. Stott, *Between Two Worlds*.

86. Pinnock, *The Work of the Spirit*, 241.

87. Barton, *Biblical Criticism*, 107.

88. Briggs, *Reading the Bible Wisely*, 130.

to support their existing values and ignoring what is contrary to them.[89] However, theological and societal shifts have influenced these boundaries. Some insist that New Testament imperatives are absolute and that established readings from trusted commentators should not be challenged.[90] However, an emphasis on the overarching narrative of Scripture, empathetic readings, and a recognition of the polyvalence of legitimate interpretations is growing.[91] Nonetheless, Rogers found that even those who encourage polyvalence of reading do so within an expectation of meaningfulness and canonical coherence.[92] Furthermore, referring to his imaginative model, Wink states, "This does not mean anything goes, but simply that the truth is like a multifaceted diamond."[93] Thus evangelicals are increasingly open to consider alternative readings, but for most there are interpretative limits—however these might be determined.

Summary

It is clear that there is both homogeneity and diversity within evangelical interpretative practices. Although evangelical scholars may be more nuanced, amongst ordinary readers, maintaining the authority of the Bible is a central principle. The Bible is the Word of God, trustworthy and useful in its final form. That it should be accessible to all and inform lived practices is also crucial and for the most part a common sense or plain reading is adequate. The narrator of any text is a trustworthy voice and the described event is an accurate, factual account of an historical episode. Among many, there is a suspicion of wider historical or literary criticism. Scholarship is typically engaged when it helps to resolve difficulties within the text, but equally the pre-critical practices of harmonization, text-linking, and in some cases Pesher readings occur alongside the avoidance of complex passages.

For ordinary readers there is typically recognition of a gap between the original author/readers and contemporary society and some use of hermeneutical techniques to bridge it. However, this fusion of horizons is typically a one-way process and often ordinary evangelicals are not aware of the cultural or theological agenda they bring to the text. There is also a perception that the overarching meaning of the text is what the author intended, although it is unusual for preachers or readers to be insistent that theirs is

89. Malley, *How the Bible Works*, 120.

90. Boone, *the Bible Tells Them So*, 78; Rogers, "Ordinary Hermeneutics," 146–47.

91. E.g., Wright, *Scripture and the Authority of God*.

92. Rogers, "Ordinary Hermeneutics," 210.

93. Wink, *Transforming Bible Study*, 37–38.

the only understanding of this. However, there are interpretative limits: a text cannot contradict the canonical metanarrative, in particular the salvific actions of God through Christ. Thus, there is resistance to relativism in the meaning but tolerance of multiple applications.

Since they understand Hebrews 4:12 to describe the biblical text as "living and active," it is natural to evangelicals that God might use it in a variety of situations, although its overarching meaning will be consistent. However, it should also be noted that despite their core value of biblical authority, evangelicals can be guilty of selective reading.[94] Of being "devoted Bible admirers but not daily Bible readers."[95] Concerns over biblical literacy are widespread.[96] "Despite claims about the centrality and authority of Scripture, the amount of engagement with the Bible for normal evangelical Christians, is in fact, minimal."[97]

Finally, individual evangelicals approach the biblical text with different agendas and reading practices. These might be: *devotional*—for personal faith or drawing close to God; *therapeutic*—reading for comfort or consolation and to make sense of experience;[98] *analytical* or *educational*—for exploring and testing new ideas or for preaching; *practical*—for addressing particular contemporary or ethical issues; and *confessional*—in defending doctrines and church structures.[99] They may read alone or in groups, and individuals within the same congregation may hold various priorities simultaneously.[100] Despite claims to hold the Bible as authoritative, to read it plainly and to allow it to shape their faith and lives, evangelical Bible reading is not a simple matter.

Participating Churches and Practices of Bible Engagement

Before exploring the hermeneutic processes undertaken by ordinary readers it is helpful to consider what their churches publically articulate about the Bible. This information is derived from leader interviews, attendance

94. Hollenweger, "Crucial Issues for Pentecostals," 164.

95. Whitney, "Teaching Scripture Intake," 164.

96. 76 percent of regular church-goers failed to place ten biblical stories in order of appearance. Although evangelicals reported the highest rates of personal Bible reading (82 percent several times a week and 52 percent daily), the majority of these were ten minutes or less. Field, "Is the Bible Becoming a Closed Book?" 503–28.

97. Peppiatt, "Response to Stephen Holmes," 38.

98. Roland, "More Than Alone with the Bible," 331.

99. Dare, "In the Fray," 233–35.

100. Ibid., 235.

at services and information on their websites. This is not an ethnographic survey, but does provide some context and allow for reflection on how far groups typify the official values of their churches.

Central Chapel

Central Chapel models many typical evangelical practices. Ken described the Bible as "God breathed and useful" and himself as "an inerrantist." Although other leaders preferred to describe the Bible as infallible, all agreed Scripture was "utterly reliable, authoritative and without error." He explained that there was a broad range of views within the congregation, including "literalists" (by which he meant seven-day creationists). The Bible was expected to inform and transform faith and behaviour. He stated, "We want to hear God's word in our lives and obey it, to grow in Christlikeness and fruitfulness for the kingdom." Ken also articulated some engagement with scholarship and grammatico-historical priorities. The church prides itself on "responsible Bible teaching" and trains preachers in "basic principles of handling the text." This includes respecting genre and context. Ken did not emphasize authorial intention or refer to the text as having a single objective meaning. Rather, he emphasized canonical priorities, holding both Testaments together as a continuous revelation and having a Christocentric emphasis. "Every passage should, in some way, be pointing us to Christ and the gospel." He qualified this adding, "At the same time doing respect to genre and proper context." Although they aimed to preach through the whole canon every decade, Ken acknowledged some parts received less attention than others.

Central Chapel demonstrates typical evangelical pragmatism and desire for relevance. They alternate between systematic and topical teaching, aimed at theological and discipleship issues. The decision to alter the church's position on women's leadership is a good example of the principles of scriptural authority and an interpretative community in action. Ken explained that personal conviction, "staying abreast of contemporary thinking and publications" and pressure from egalitarians within the community had led to the conclusion that, "The current understanding of the Scriptures was not the best understanding of the Scriptures—therefore our theology and our practice needed to be reconsidered." Scripture had not changed, it was still authoritative and without error, but rather their interpretation and thus application had radically altered.

Ken anticipated that groups would use an instinctive rather than self-conscious hermeneutic, and he expected them to draw both theological principles and discipleship applications from the texts.[101] He anticipated that they would be unfamiliar with the 1 Samuel 25 narrative but hoped that they would identify cross-canonical themes, in particular a christocentric pattern, identifying references to Jesus throughout all three texts.

New Life

Sarah, expressed a variety of evangelical interpretative patterns despite her reluctance to use the label. She described the church as having a "high view of Scripture" and repeatedly expressed concerns about biblical illiteracy amongst young adults.[102] They intentionally focussed on increasing biblical knowledge, running Bible overview courses and teaching from both Testaments. She also described training preachers to use a "two-step" interpretative process. The emphasis was on exploring the cultural context of passages before applying them to lived faith, and she was confident that members would recognize a cultural gap between the world of the text and their own lives. However, she was concerned that this first exegetical step might be neglected. "They probably won't spend enough time in terms of the original—what it meant for there and then as well as what it means for here and now."

New Life demonstrates a double reading hermeneutic and elements of a Grammatico-historical approach. This is significant given their charismatic ecclesiology. Sarah did not describe a "Spirit-hermeneutic" but typical evangelical practices. She encouraged devotional reading through other interpretative processes, but with regard to the public teaching of Scripture, New Life demonstrated attention to original meaning and cultural context rather than a naïve or experience-driven hermeneutic process. Sarah also distinguished between "straightforward passages" where "what it says is what it means" and more difficult texts where understanding "culture and context is really needed," confirming the selective use of hermeneutics when plain sense reading appears unhelpful.

New Life has particular concern for relevance in its Bible teaching. Describing it as "informal, multi-layered and creative," Sarah explained her passion for good communication and diversity of style. Half of their preaching was systematic biblical exposition, the other half focussed on topical issues although it was still "rooted in Scripture." Preaching was adapted to

101. Rogers notes that hermeneutical processes are largely unconscious and instinctive among ordinary church members. "Ordinary Hermeneutics," 139.

102. Similar concerns are noted in Cocksworth, "Holding Together," 142; Rogers, "Ordinary Hermeneutics," 180.

suit their two congregations, and it was evident from the services I attended that pragmatism and relevance were priorities. Both sermons were topical, one with limited biblical references while the other included an exegetical exploration of 1 Samuel 18:1–11. Interestingly, the preacher dismissed the verse, "An evil spirit from the Lord rushed upon Saul," stating, "I don't agree with that, it's not how God does things." This was not explored or explained; she did not engage an interpretative process to defend the authority of the text but demonstrated an undeveloped resistant reading. Whether this is typical or an anomaly is unclear. Sarah emphasized New Life's presentation of the Bible as authoritative, although she also explained that the church "actively resists being seen to be narrow or judgemental." In turn, this influenced the way in which they explained the biblical text.

Finally, Sarah did not anticipate a dominant Christocentric priority among the New Life groups. She explained that they joked about "the Sunday School answer always being Jesus." Although she was keen to emphasize the centrality of Christ, she did not expect the groups to "crow-bar" Jesus into any given text. Like Ken, she anticipated instinctive rather than self-aware hermeneutic processes, although she too feared that they would focus primarily on personal application.

Trinity Church

Biblical engagement at Trinity Church was unique in a number of ways. True to its Reformed background, correct thinking was important. Will described deliberate attention to doctrine and apologetics, including teaching on sovereignty, grace, and the Nicene Creed, which used cross referencing to demonstrate "how to put your systematics together." However, he emphasized that their Sunday morning sermons were different from those of most conservative evangelicals. Inspired by Timothy Keller and others he had, "changed [his] mind about what preaching was meant to be."[103] Sermons at Trinity now tended "not to show [their] working out." But rather, "[the] aim is for people to be transformed after the likeness of Christ, by hearing His word. I don't want people to leave on Sunday mornings so much saying "I learnt something new today" as saying "I have learnt to love Christ more today."

Will expected preachers to handle the text with careful reading, understanding of context and "working out the main idea of the passage." These grammatico-historic practices express an established evangelical

103. Timothy Keller is the founding pastor of Redeemer Presbyterian Church, New York. He is a prolific writer and his podcasts are hugely popular.

understanding in a way that the other two churches did not. However, like the others, he hoped for a transformative effect from Bible engagement. He explained this move away from doctrinally oriented practices:

> Most of us come from an academic, analyze everything to death kind of background . . . quite a lot of us [are] fed up with the only application of the Bible teaching being "Read your Bible, pray more and do more evangelism." Our expectation [is] that when the Scripture is preached (in the context of a group of people who love the Lord and who are spiritually searching) [that] the normal effect of that is that some people will be converted and most people will grow.

Certainly this demonstrates evangelical attitudes: the transformational power of the Bible; an expectation of relevance in the lives of readers; the need for thoughtfulness, and some scholarly engagement in understanding the text. But Trinity Church is intentionally moving away from dogmatic or authoritative forms of conservative evangelicalism while still being concerned for sound thinking among its members.

Will anticipated that ordinary readers might "exemplify characters." His main hope was that they would observe theological ideas in the texts, particularly grace, and that they would prioritize a Christocentric hermeneutic.

Summary

All three leaders were clear that they engaged in double reading hermeneutics and aspects of grammatico-historical practices, modelling this to their congregations. All were concerned about biblical literacy and expected the Old Testament narratives to be least familiar. They also emphasized biblical education amongst their congregations, which, particularly for preachers, involved Bible-handling tools. They considered that these were skills necessary for faithful Bible reading rather than a naïve or common-sense approach. No one mentioned literal readings as normative, although Sarah did distinguish between complex passages and straightforward ones, and it seems fair to assume that the others may hold this view.

Only Ken, at Central Chapel, overtly explored ideas of inerrancy in the light of the diversity of opinion among their very mixed congregation. New Life informally expressed biblical authority, their website declaring, "We believe the Bible is inspired by God and tells the story of his love for and relationship with humanity. God calls us to immerse ourselves in his story, to meditate on and interpret it, and ultimately to live out that story today."

This unique narrative emphasis (reflecting N. T Wright's narrative model) reflects their highly relational ethos and desire for contemporary relevance.[104] By contrast, the Trinity Church website describes the Bible as follows: "As originally given it is true in its entirety, and it is the supreme authority by which all human conduct, creeds, opinions and beliefs should be tested." This common evangelical approach avoids using the language of inerrancy.

Ken and Sarah expressed concern that their groups would largely focus on personal application. Ken and Will both anticipated a Christocentric focus to their groups' readings. Even so, in all three cases there was a hope that groups would identify a gap and engage in reflection on cultural context as different from their own situation. There was also an expectation that reading the Bible was transformative and taught some sort of lesson, be it a revelation of God, a personal application or a doctrinal truth. Thus, these churches illustrate both diversity and similarity across the breadth of British evangelicalism.

Observed Ordinary Hermeneutics

With regard to the ordinary hermeneutic practices of these ordinary readers, the most striking finding was that regardless of their denominational background or age, highly similar strategies were used by all nine groups. Clearly generalities about all British evangelicals cannot be made from this sample, but given the diversity of background they came from this is a striking finding. In the following section core similarities are explored followed by some of the contrasts and comparisons that were noticeable based on age and denomination.

Similarities in Ordinary Hermeneutic Practices and Interpretative Priorities

Historical Facticity

As discussed in the previous chapter a central observation was that no one suggested that the texts were anything other than accurate representations of historical events. Angelic rescue, healing from and striking with leprosy

104. Wright, *Scripture and the Authority of God.*

were all accepted as factually accurate. No attempt to rationalize these events was made. However, Village is correct in noting that "Evangelical belief is not blind literalism—but a principled position."[105] Participants were aware that those outside their faith did not believe in such events. Nonetheless, they were adamant that God could do anything and that it was part of their faith to believe supernatural accounts described in the text. This is further explored in chapter 5, but one technique used to justify extraordinary events was that individuals would cite similar episodes from within Scripture. No one saw these as allusions or intentional literary parallels but rather proof that God had done something like this before, or subsequently and thus it was believable on this occasion too.

This hermeneutic of trust and belief in the reliability of the narrative voice meant that just as events were accurate, so characters were read as real people. Unlike scholars who recognize characters as types or allusions (for example: Abigail and Nabal as the embodiment of wisdom and folly, or Gehazi as the embodiment of faithless Israel), ordinary readers did none of this. Abigail was a wise woman who was faithful to God's will. Nabal a selfish and rebellious individual who opposed God's anointed. Gehazi was a man who made a bad decision and suffered the results of that. Characters were only "types" in as far as they were like other persecuted believers (James), like other followers of God who made errors (David), or like a new convert (Naaman). They were real people not literary figures or illustrations. Similarly, wider literary questions and devices were not commented upon. It was clear that participants were not inclined to engage with the Bible as constructed literature, redacted oral traditions, or use literary techniques to decipher them. Rather they understood narratives as factually accurate and reliable narrative.

The only exception to this facticity was some debate as to whether violent acts attributed to God were correctly described. The younger Trinity Church and Central Chapel groups ultimately conceded that, although they were unhappy about them, such things must be true. New Life groups used various interpretative strategies (discussed in chapters 5 and 8) to explain statements that did not agree with their understanding of God's character. These included the possibility of mistranslation (the original was presumed to be accurate) and rationalist readings: interpreting accounts as biological and geological events explained as divine activity by primitive people. The interpretative dilemma was that the text clearly stated something they did not want to believe. Only one individual from New Life was prepared to state overtly that he did not believe the text's version of events.

105. Village, *The Bible and Lay People*, 67.

Similarly, when presented with an alternative and partially resistant reading by the researcher (that of Abigail as manipulative and self-seeking), the only group which embraced the idea was the youngest New Life group. While this group accepted and expanded it, eight groups rejected the idea as "not what the text says." This bears some resemblance to Rogers's findings of greater willingness to question and read texts in a more unorthodox manner among charismatics, although it did not amount to intentional resistant reading.[106]

Essentially, it was accepted by the vast majority that the narratives gave an authoritative account. It was common practice for participants to state, "but the text says . . ." to prove their point or challenge someone else's view. Interestingly, it was rare for this tactic to be countered with an alternative comparable text. The plain reading of the narrative triumphed on almost every occasion, and it was evident that the groups largely trusted the narrative voice, demonstrating a compliant, although not passive, reading. Participants were prepared to wrestle with difficulties and to question the text, although ultimately they typically submitted to it as authoritative and their own understanding, or possibly the translation, being where confusion lay. One could interpret these ordinary readings as pre-modern or fundamentalist, but this is not the case. Engagement with other strategies demonstrated a more nuanced hermeneutic process.

Situating the Text

As a key interpretative step scholars of varying persuasions spend much time and energy attempting to date biblical texts. Either their date of composition, or the dating of events they report. Among these ordinary readers, however, there was no concern for dating the episodes. Instead there was interest in situating them within wider biblical chronology. They asked questions about time frames, but not specific dates. For example: Where did Naaman's healing fit in the history of Israel? Which King was 2 Kings 5 describing? Where in the rise of David did this episode take place? Likewise, where did Acts 12 fit within the wider narrative of the early church? How long after the death of Christ was it? Had Paul been converted yet? The readers identified key events and wanted to situate the texts in relation to them. Most demonstrated awareness of the wider canon and wanted to situate the narratives within that larger biblical framework.

In some (predominantly older) groups there was sufficient biblical knowledge to accomplish this task. In others individuals pulled out their

106. Rogers, "Ordinary Hermeneutics," 208.

own Bibles and flicked through to try and locate the episode chronologically. Some were unable to do this and clearly frustrated by that expressing a desire for expert advice.

Indeed, situating the narratives within that wider framework was something most groups intentionally did as a first step in their reading. This suggests that it is something they have seen modelled as an appropriate way to read the Bible rather than simply taking any given text in isolation. However, as with other interpretative tools this action was most pronounced with unfamiliar passages and was less important with the Acts 12 narrative (with which all groups were most familiar).

Interpretative Horizons

Related to this question of dating is the question of which interpretative horizon the ordinary readers paid most attention to. Interpretative horizons are key theoretical constructs in biblical interpretation.[107] Village, adapting Ricouer's language, suggests three "worlds" which readers of narratives might inhabit: The world *behind* the text; the world *in* the text; and the world *in front* of the text. Thus attention might be paid to "understanding the intention of the author *or* recreating imaginatively the events described in the text *or* applying the text in some way to one's life."[108] This is somewhat different to a two-step or double reading hermeneutic which prioritizes authorial intention as the "original meaning." Despite Powell's observation of horizon preferences and Rogers's findings of rapid fusion of horizons the groups in this study did something slightly different.[109]

It is possible that a different form of literature found within Scripture (such as epistles or gospels, with allegedly clear authorship) might have brought to light the author-reader horizon dichotomy more clearly. However, given the use of narratives, focussing on the *textual* horizon was a clear priority. For the Old Testament narratives, there was no acknowledgement that an author even existed thus the readers asked no meaningful questions about authorial intention. There was no sense of political or historical agenda behind the texts or of them as crafted literature. 1 Samuel 25 was not considered as pro-Davidic propaganda. No-one reflected that 2 Kings 5 might have post-exilic origins influencing its reporting of the events around Naaman's healing. The authorial horizon and subsequent questions it raises were not engaged at all.

107. Village, "Biblical Interpretative Horizons," 158.

108. Ibid., 159.

109. Powell, *What Do They Hear?* 93; Rogers, "Ordinary Hermeneutics," 134.

Interestingly, New Testament engagement was somewhat different. Whereas Old Testament authorship had been ignored, a number of the groups did identify an author, "Luke" for Acts 12, and there were occasional comments about his agenda or skills as a writer. There were also vague references among the older groups to an original Gentile or Jewish audience. Thus, the world *behind* the text was something of which they were vaguely aware, but it was not a significant interpretative factor. This mirrors Bialecki's observations of authorship as presumed but only rarely referred to among evangelicals.[110]

Differentiation between Old and New Testament authorial awareness was raised with the church leaders in follow up interviews. Will and Ken reflected that since the authorship of Old Testament texts was often contested amongst scholars, it was not something they tended to communicate to their congregations, whereas New Testament books with named authors were presented as such. This appears to have created an understanding of Old Testament narratives as anonymous but reliable historical records rather than identifying an author with an agenda, as they did with Acts. Nevertheless, finding an objective meaning, the author's meaning, which evangelical literature encourages as a first interpretative step, was not the priority of the ordinary readers. Instead, understanding the world *within* the text, the events described and their context were more important.

Contextual Priorities

The most significant interpretative process undertaken in all nine groups was consideration of cultural context of the world within the narrative. Regardless of age or church, the primary concern was to understand the cultural background, showing clear awareness of a cultural gap between the world of the text and their own. This was particularly pronounced with 1 Samuel 25, with which they were least familiar, 82 percent claiming to be entirely unfamiliar with it. Groups put a lot of time and energy into discussing cultural norms, including speculation about hospitality codes and marriage practices in ancient Israel. With 2 Kings 5, ancient warfare, politics and slavery played a key part in the discussions alongside geographic and historic details. It was interesting to note that discussion of such information decreased as familiarity with the narrative increased, so it was limited with Acts 12. It appeared that difficult or unfamiliar passages caused participants to engage most clearly in intentional hermeneutic processes such as this.

110. Bialecki, "The Bones Restored to Life," 142.

Groups pooled cultural and historical knowledge and cross-referenced to other parts of the Bible, demonstrating greater general knowledge the older they became. Interestingly, even though they were unfamiliar with 1 Samuel 25 most had good knowledge of the wider Davidic narrative. By contrast although they knew the Naaman episode it was evident that they had limited wider knowledge of Elisha narratives, or prophetic literature. This suggests an unequal or selective engagement with Old Testament literature among the wider evangelical tradition from which most came.

The majority were aware of and repeatedly expressed a desire for scholarship or expertise to resolve their uncertainties (although asking Google appeared to be equivalent!). The oldest New Life group had access to a study Bible and frequently deferred to its owner, who read its comments aloud. At no point was the interpretation questioned. There appeared to be an assumption that not only the text but also the explanations were reliable. In other groups, individuals took on the role of expert, explaining cultural points (some of which were accurate). By contrast, others expressed a sense of inadequacy at their ability to understand cultural situations. This was most noticeable among the younger cohort and newer converts. One individual in the New Life youngest group stated,

> I think that, if this is the kind of passage that I read on my own, I'd read it, go "I've got no idea what that means" and Google it. I'd get a lot more out of it if it were a sermon. This is something that I don't feel I would get anything useful out of until it's explained in context.

Clearly there is an openness to some sorts of scholarly expertise among these emerging adults; indeed, this seemed more prevalent than the idea of plain reading. They assumed a need for assistance to read and at times felt disabled without it.

Consistent patterns such as these do confirm that interpretative processes are learnt. Will explained that in mid-week Bible studies, contextual understanding was encouraged. Sarah stated that New Life worked hard to explain the cultural context of New Testament passages in order to promote their position on women's leadership. Thus, she was not surprised that their groups followed that model. Understanding the world described within the text was the of primary concern among all the groups, although Ken did speculate that perhaps in a less artificial setting, such as a home group or personal reading situation, readers might be more inclined to premature fusions of horizons and immediately jump to personal application.

Empathy as a Hermeneutic Tool.

Despite their largely compliant reading, groups frequently used a form of creative engagement with the events described, prioritizing empathy. Several groups "imagined" their way into the text, creating additional dialogue for characters, speculating about their feelings and motivations and expressing a sense of identification with them. David's short temper, Naaman's irritation, Rhoda's excited confusion all produced comments of "I'm like that" in some form or another.[111] Characters in the texts were viewed as inspiration role models, or salutary warnings. Where scholars are often highly critical of David in 2 Kings 5, identifying a dark side or a foreshadowing of future violence, the ordinary readers saw his actions as an over-reaction.[112] Certainly unacceptable, but something both he and they could learn from—part of his learning how to lead and to trust God. Abigail's courage was viewed as inspirational, Naaman's slave as generous—characteristics for them to imitate. Similarly Rhoda being mocked for her faith or Naaman's need to submit to God's will were experiences individuals expressed identification with. This exemplar hermeneutic was frequent and occurred across all ages and churches.

There were also some gender-related trends, with women frequently identifying and empathizing with female characters (further explored in chapter 4).[113] Identification was particularly pronounced with Acts 12. A number of individuals expressed their ability to imagine the early church's prayer meeting and the believers' anxiety. This parallels the documented practice of closely relating biblical figures with contemporary converts and understanding them as linked through time and space.[114] Participants appeared to collapse the intervening 2,000 years, using "we" and "us" to describe the early believers, seeing themselves as part of a continuous trajectory from the early church.

This empathetic hermeneutic and focus on the world within the text included creative expansion of the narrative in a form of midrashic activity. For example, Abigail was described exhorting the women of her household to help gather food, and the experiences of Naaman's slave girl were explored. It was primarily older groups who did this, suggesting a greater confidence to expand and explore beyond exact textual wording. Powell

111. Friend-Harding noted typological interpretations, the linking between biblical, historical and personal stories and readers situating themselves within the biblical narrative. *The Book of Jerry Falwell*, 55–56.

112. Klein, 1 *Samuel*, 250; Levenson, "1 Samuel 25," 24.

113. Perrin, "Searching for Sisters," 114–15.

114. Murphy, "The Trouble with Good News," 21.

notes the use of empathy in Bible reading, commenting that readers may not empathise in a predictable manner. Changes in social conscience influence the empathy choices people make, which the original author could not have anticipated.[115] That appears to be true. While older groups empathized with the dominant character, such as Peter, others (particularly New Life and younger groups) expressed sympathy for his executed guards. Equally, while some identified with Naaman, others were concerned for Gehazi and his descendants. Overall, younger and mid-aged groups expressed these concerns most frequently while older groups focussed on the hero or dominant characters. One could argue that this focus on less obvious characters falls within Powell's category of unexpected reading, but it seems to demonstrate a strong sense of humanitarianism, an ethical concern for injustice against the "little people" rather than a simple compliant reading. This might also demonstrate post-modern sympathies, the altruistic individualism attributed to Generation Y, and the deep-seated concern about fairness they tend to hold.[116]

An alternative interpretation is that the older readers were demonstrating conformity with normative conventions; they have learnt to read "with" the text and to pay less attention to minor questions. Younger readers were more prone to distraction and inclined to pick up on smaller details. It could be argued that this is a closer reading, paying more attention to the text, but alternatively the older groups' readings could be regarded as more canonical, engaging the major themes and characters of the passage within the wider sweep of Scripture.

Appropriation of the Text

Related to this exemplar reading is the process of appropriation of the text. All three leaders expressed concern that their emerging adults would be primarily interested in applying the text to themselves. While they were not averse to this in principle (believing Bible teaching should be transformative), they were concerned that the groups would demonstrate a self-centred engagement with Scripture and appropriate the text without sufficient analytical process. However, these concerns were unfounded: groups *did* express concern to deduce or apply principles from the texts to their own situations, but it was not their primary consideration. On at least two occasions when individuals expressed concern to "find the main point" (by which they meant a timeless truth for personal application, not the author's

115. Powell, *What Do They Hear?* 31.
116. Arnett, *The Dangers of Myth Making*, 17–20.

intention) groups censured this concern. On one occasion, there was a somewhat irritated explanation that the conversation had just begun, implying that application would be found, but after a process of examination and discussion; the individual was premature in expecting an application. On the other occasion, a new believer asked for advice on what to "take away" from the narrative. The group did not censure her but gave a variety of possible applications and quickly moved back to analysis. Again, it was apparently too soon in the process for application to be appropriate. It is noteworthy that both of these episodes of "hermeneutical apprenticeship" took place in Trinity Church groups and involved new believers, echoing Rogers's findings of conservative evangelical "apprenticing ordinary readers in text horizon engagement."[117]

Despite intermittent minor comments of identification and appropriation, it was clear that the norm, across all three churches, was to examine and interpret the text *before* making any application. However, they evidently considered that there would be something of relevance in any given biblical passage, a lesson or principle to learn. When asked, at the end of each text, "Why is this passage in the Bible?" almost all responses focussed on the learning of theological truths or a personal lesson: "to teach us . . ." or "to show us . . ." were frequently used statements. All groups had a strongly devotional priority in their reading. It appeared that they understood the Bible as primarily written for the benefit of believers but that there was a necessary interpretative process to undertake first. It was a two-step hermeneutic, but modified from the established evangelical ideal of authorial meaning.

Theological and Theocentric Priorities

In addition to a devotional priority in their reading, ordinary readers across all groups and churches expressed a tendency to focus on theological questions once their cultural questions had been explored. They all explored the nature of God, and were cross canonical, drawing Old and New Testament themes together. Salvation, grace, mission, monotheism, and sovereignty were all discussed in varying degrees. Very often the groups focussed on the same theological themes as scholars even though they used different techniques to examine the text.

Similarly they all identified God as a central figure in all three passages. Even in those where he was barely mentioned, God was identified as a driving force behind or resolving events. Much of the discussion of the

117. Rogers, "Ordinary Hermeneutics," 134.

younger groups in particular was around the nature of God as they wrestled with his reported actions, but their reading drew God into all aspects of the narratives. Personal relationship with God was at the heart of these episodes for the ordinary readers. Abigail was faithful to God, Nabal was not. Their concern over David's behaviour was that sin would damage his relationship with God. Herod deserved his comeuppance for his defiance of God and persecution of the believers. There was a strongly individualistic aspect to this reading and again, priority for their personal encouragement from the narratives, but these narratives first and foremost were stories about God and his engagement with humanity.

Polyvalence of Interpretation

Despite holding the Bible as authoritative, and in some cases inerrant, evangelicals tend to be polyvalent in their Bible reading.[118] "Polyvalence refers to the capacity—or perhaps inevitable tendency for texts to mean different things to different people."[119] This study provides further evidence of this. Groups explored theological questions and proposed alternative understandings without a need to bring about a definitive answer. Mirroring Bielo's findings, topics were often left unresolved while the groups moved on to another subject.[120] There did not seem to be a pressing need for doctrinal closure or indeed establishing definitive answers, implying that relationships and inclusiveness are often a higher priority than resolving theological dilemmas.[121]

When it came to appropriation of the text, some participants agreed with each other's suggestions, but often they framed alternatives with phrases such as, "For me . . ." or "Personally, I'd take from this . . . ." None of these were contested. Although there were interpretative limits (see chapter 7), the text being applied six different ways to six people appeared normal. It was simply a case of what from the discussion had struck them the most.[122] There was a sense of searching for insight together rather than needing correct answers. Some groups articulated a self-awareness that their reading was probably different to those of other cultures or generations, but this went unexplored, with no critiquing of their own cultures or the agendas

118. E.g., Bielo, "On the Failure of Meaning," 102.

119. Powell, *What Do They Hear?* 3.

120. Bielo, "On the Failure of Meaning," 2; Todd, "The Interactions of Talk and Text," 70.

121. Ibid., 81.

122. Searl, "The Women's Bible Study," 102.

they brought to the text. Rather, contemporary attitudes were considered preferable to ancient ones. While there was a clear awareness of a cultural chasm between the events described in the text and their interpretations, this was not a self-conscious or intentional reader-oriented hermeneutic. The groups read, as their leaders had anticipated, in a largely unreflective manner. The function of the text was to encourage faith, discipleship and provide a mechanism for God to speak directly into their lives. Thus polyvalent applications according to the needs of individuals were acceptable, but there were appropriate interpretative processes to engage with before applications could be drawn and limits on acceptable interpretations.

Other Evangelical Hermeneutic Practices

In addition to the practices previously describe, there were some others, often associated with evangelicalism, articulated by a small minority. This suggests that they remain within evangelical interpretative frameworks but may no longer be dominant. They included focussing on individual words.[123] One participant stated, "I'm convinced that everything and every word that is written had been guided by God and so every word in the Bible has its own importance." On a second occasion, there was discussion around the significance of the word "but" in Acts 12:24 which ultimately led nowhere constructive. This focus on exact wording implies an understanding of the English version as a word-for-word translation of the text, and may be something some have seen modelled although it was far from dominant.

There were also sporadic references to translation issues, with a vague sense that the original language was more reliable. On one occasion, participants checked various translations to clarify a theological point, being frustrated that there was no significant result from the process. However, translation issues appeared to be a background factor rather than a priority.

There was also evidence that the groups regarded the Bible as a continuous and integrated literary form: a "collection of texts that tells a cohesive story about the nature and purpose of God, humanity and the unfolding of time."[124] Situating the texts within wider biblical chronology was an initial activity for many groups. Likewise, all nine groups made cross-references to other biblical texts, some extensively so, citing narratives, Jewish law, epistles, and Gospel parables.[125] These references were not always accurate,

123. Bielo notes this as "a very Protestant thing to do," citing Crapanzano, Coleman, and Keane. "On the Failure of Meaning," 15.

124. Bielo, "On the Failure of Meaning," 10.

125. Rogers, "Ordinary Hermeneutics," 139, 195.

but it was typical for groups to regard the texts under consideration as part of a wider authoritative canon, frequently referring to theological themes across Scripture. It seemed normal for groups to draw threads from one passage of Scripture to another, suggesting that they view the text as an integrated whole. Distinctions, nonetheless, were regularly drawn between Old and New Testaments. These were most common among the younger and charismatic groups. Differentiation between the behaviour and character of God was the main point of discussion although, in all cases, it was articulated that they also understood that God had not changed. There appeared to be an understanding that they *should* see the text as continuous but were unsure how to reconcile what they saw as conflicts between the two Testaments. Older groups appeared less perplexed by this issue, presumably having resolved such dilemmas at some level.

It is clear then, that these emerging adults read using established evangelical hermeneutical patterns. They demonstrated a clear hermeneutic of trust and considered the narrative voice reliable while being prepared to ask difficult questions of the text. They focussed on the textual and reader horizons, but in a clear two-step process. Theological and devotional priorities were uppermost in their thinking but they used aspects of scholarship—particularly cultural contextual information of the world within the text to do so. That all the groups did so suggests greater homogeneity across sections of evangelicalism than one might have expected.

Contrasts and Comparisons

Contrasts between Churches

The significant similarities across the groups having been described, it should be noted that there were interpretative variations. It might have been expected, given its charismatic ethos, that groups from New Life would adopt some form of "Spirit-led" hermeneutic, collapsing intervening history to transpose biblical events onto contemporary ones. In the event, there was no evidence of this at all. The New Life groups engaged in a typical evangelical, grammatico-historical influenced practice.[126] Although there was theological variation in their readings compared to the other churches, their methodology was not significantly different. This was the only church where dissenting voices challenged the narratives. The dissent was not widespread, and it would be an exaggeration to say it represented a fully

126. Village also noted this among charismatic Anglicans, *The Bible and Lay People*, 146–47.

engaged resistant reading, but they did appear to show greater freedom to ask critical questions of the text.

The Central Chapel groups were inclined to read the texts with a mission-oriented focus. It was common for them to identify biblical parallels around conversionism, and there were significant conversations about contemporary evangelism and personal faith sharing. This matched the priorities of the Sunday service I attended and it is possible that this theme, current at the time in the church's teaching, influenced the discussions.[127] Conversionism appeared to be a central interpretative key, even though imaginative and empathetic readings were also pronounced in the older groups. The younger group tended to focus on uncertainties over doctrinal issues.

The most distinctive interpretative pattern was demonstrated by Trinity Church groups. In addition to hermeneutical apprenticing, all groups worked hard to situate Jesus in the narratives. Although mentioned in none of the passages, groups intentionally and repeatedly identified references or parallels to Christ plus themes of grace, forgiveness, repentance, and conversion. This highly Christological hermeneutic was pronounced and at times laboured. There was some measure of this in the Central Chapel discussions but it was nowhere near as prolific as amongst the Trinity groups. The Christological hermeneutic, with an emphasis on penal substitution, is typical of Reformed practices. A majority of participants had significant experience of other Reformed churches and organizations which, it is fair to assume, follow this hermeneutic pattern. This conservative theological norm was endorsed by the Trinity leader.

> If there is a tendency I would rather that it be to go "this is a book about Christ, where is he?" and perhaps be slightly implausible in your readings—in a slightly church-fathers-esque kind of way, than "principally this is a book about me, how do I find what the book has to tell me?" Not because that's necessarily evil but because the cultural dominant thing is to read all texts as essentially being about me and about my life. And so just trying to overturn that and say this book is focussed on somebody else I think is a good thing.

127. Recent teaching had significant influence on a number of findings. E.g., a number of New Life participants cited Proverbs as their favourite biblical book. This, it emerged, had been the subject of a recent teaching series.

Age-related Patterns

One final set of comparisons are age related and consider evidence for hermeneutic development among evangelical emerging adults. Significantly, only a few patterns were noticeable.

Firstly, confidence to engage with unfamiliar texts increased with age, as did cultural knowledge. This should be no surprise, given that older members had typically been believers and attended their churches for longer and had therefore experienced more sermons and undertaken the most Bible study. Faced with an unfamiliar text, they quickly appropriated hermeneutic tools, whereas younger groups verbalized their uncertainty. A number of the elder cohort held positions of responsibility within the communities and had attended informal theological training. Indeed, the new believers in older groups were particularly conspicuous by their lack of knowledge and less nuanced reading practices. Older groups were also most inclined to adopt midrashic practices, reading behind the text, suggesting a confidence in using their imaginations as reading tools. Although they were not prepared to contradict the text, they were prepared to expand a back story to fill in the narrative gaps. Older groups were also least likely to become involved in serious discussions over minor points. There was frequent humour about minor themes—an indication that they were playfully engaging with what they understood to be a red herring.

This appears to show a developed discernment over what they considered significant major (typically canonical) themes, whereas younger groups often focussed attention on minor details in the text. It may indicate an inclination to see minor textual points as less important, demonstrating a developmental ability to identify wider themes through Scripture, rather than focus on the details of an individual text. They were also inclined to be somewhat facetious about "correct" answers, although the majority still expressed views that were orthodox for their tradition. This indicated an awareness of stereotypical responses and some ability to critique their own tradition.

Older groups also appeared to express views most in keeping with the doctrinal positions of their churches and had fewer theological uncertainties. It would appear that on certain issues that confused younger readers they had worked out what they thought and either felt no need to engage those questions or resolved them quickly.

Beyond these trends, there were few clear developmental patterns. One might have expected a greater emphasis on doctrinal rather than devotional application among older groups, since developmental models suggest that relevance is particularly pertinent to younger adults. However, this was not the case. It may be that among contemporary emerging adults this priority is extended into one's later twenties or simply indicative of evangelicalism as a whole. Given the emphasis all three leaders placed on relevance in their Bible engagement, this seems likely. There was some evidence of the older groups understanding the function of narratives as being to describe the nature and character of God rather than to prescribe behaviour, and greater awareness of authorial intention, but neither of these functions were consistently demonstrated.

In terms of reading practices, there were few differences that could not be ascribed to familiarity with the text and greater experience of reading it. It is possible that these similarities can be explained by the fact that the majority of participants had been members of evangelical churches and organizations for a long time. Participants were asked at what age they considered themselves to have converted or developed an active Christian faith. Their answers were highly similar.[128] For men, the average was 15.42 years old (Trinity), 16.3 (Central), and 15 (New Life). For women slightly younger: 14.42, 15.85, and 12.6 years accordingly. Only four of the fifty-two participants described their conversion to evangelical Christian faith in the past three years. It seems plausible that evangelical converts adopt an interpretative practice over the first few years of their faith. They are taught how to read the Bible by the community, often through the modelling of exegesis in sermons, and this creates enduring habits throughout their young-adult faith—the observed changes being indicative of greater gathered knowledge and confidence and establishing of a world view.[129] Whether these practices alter as they pass into later adulthood is impossible to conclude from these findings, but the consistency of findings here suggests that the majority have common, unspoken rules of how to engage the texts which, it can be surmised, were learned as part of an earlier socialization in church.

Conclusions

Overall, it is possible to observe a number of patterns, which are summarized in four categories.

---

128. Evangelicals emphasize conversion as a significant point in a believer's faith. 92 percent of participants identified a specific point when this had occurred, although it might have been the result of a gradual process. The rest made comments such as "all my life."

129. Village notes the significance of interpretative communities in creating learning patterns and the residual effects of these as members cross churches. *The Bible and Lay People*, 137.

Firstly, participants followed typical evangelical patterns in viewing the Bible as authoritative and relevant to their lives. They were primarily compliant readers, trusting the narrative voice, but were by no means passive and were prepared to discuss things that were problematic for them. They appeared to operate under typical evangelical assumptions around translations and the authority of original languages and cross-referencing was widespread.

Secondly, all participants appeared to view the Bible as a continuous narrative and understood their faith as a continuation of that demonstrated by followers of God in both Testaments. This included exemplar hermeneutics and the use of identification and empathy with major figures and minor characters. Situating the narrative within a biblical framework was important for some groups, particularly those from Central Chapel and Trinity Church.

Thirdly, their hermeneutic processes involved a recognition of the gap between the world of the text and their own. This they endeavoured to cross by focussing on understanding the cultural context described *within* the text before exploring theological themes and appropriating principles for their own lives. These principles were sometimes doctrinal but often focussed on individual behaviour and a polyvalence of such readings appeared to be perfectly acceptable, within interpretative limits.

Finally, despite evangelical instruction to find the objective meaning, defined as the author's intention, few of the groups demonstrated this. The world *in* the text and how it related to the reader's horizon were their priorities rather than the authorial horizon. For the New Testament text, some of the older groups made vague reference to authorship, but none did so with the Old Testament texts; the authors appeared to be invisible. Groups expressed interest, indeed desire, for external expertise to understand the textual context and were clearly not opposed to scholarship. However, this need was focussed on historical and cultural detail; there was no real sign of engagement with scholarly interpretative practices beyond a few comments about literary structure and authorial intention in the Acts 12 text.

Overall, there was surprisingly little hermeneutic diversity across the churches. The charismatics operated as evangelicals in their reading, and the conservatives were as interested in appropriation of the text as they were in doctrinal correctness. This may of course be the influence of transdenominationalism across the three churches.[130] One difference was that the groups from Trinity Church and the older Central Chapel readers were

130. Diversity was most pronounced among the Central Chapel groups. Other participants tended to have belonged organizations situated within their "tribe."

more inclined towards a christocentric hermeneutic in all the texts, and the charismatic groups were slightly more inclined to question events as reported by the text. However, while they may have had different theological interests and questions, essentially the groups appeared to read in the same manner.

Likewise, there were some developmental similarities: older groups demonstrated greater confidence, historical knowledge and compliance with the reading practices of their traditions. They tended to focus on major themes within the texts, were least likely to debate doctrinal questions and most likely to engage in imaginative or midrashic readings. They were also most likely to be aware of an authorial horizon but still demonstrated a preference for textual and reader ones.

Engagement with a different sort of biblical literature might have highlighted other interpretative strategies but, in terms of reading biblical narrative, these emerging adults viewed the text as the reliable story of their forebears, and they were willing to engage and learn from it even if, at times, they were uncertain about its meaning or uncomfortable with its content. There was evidence of pre-critical reading patterns and some post-modern influences but, as Todd suggests, "The interpretative approach of the groups is not driven primarily by the philosophical concerns of a particular interpretative strategy."[131] However, it would be accurate to say that participants operated an intentional hermeneutic of belief. They knew that non-believers would read these texts differently and that there were complexities in understanding ancient narratives, but for them as practising evangelicals these texts were important, informative, to be read thoughtfully and with extra biblical resources if necessary in order to inform their own faith and life.

131. Todd, "The Interactions of Talk and Text," 81.

5

Evangelical Theological Distinctives: Engaging with the Supernatural

Introduction

THE PREVIOUS CHAPTERS IDENTIFIED significant similarities in the hermeneutical processes undertaken by evangelical emerging adults; the following three explore some of the key theological issues raised in their discussions. These themes have been chosen based on the diversity of opinion they create across the spectrum of British evangelicalism. They are referred to as "theological markers" since they represent some of the fault lines within evangelical belief.

This chapter addresses reader engagement with the supernatural. Chapter 6 considers their responses to the violence of God; and chapter 7 reflects on attitudes around issues of gender. For each theme theological and cultural context are introduced before ordinary readings are discussed and compared.

Engaging the Supernatural: Some Definitions

Clearly, there are theological concerns when using the word "supernatural" and thus it needs defining. Until the seventeenth century it was an adjective or adverb to describe the enabling of someone or something to behave "above their ordinary station" and thus inappropriate to describe the actions of God.[1] However, it, "Began to connote a realm of being, a territory of existence 'outside' the world we know. With 'nature' now deemed single, homogenous and self-contained we labelled 'supernatural' the 'other' world

---

1. Lash, *The Beginning and the End*, 168

inhabited (some said) by ghosts, poltergeists, by demons, angels and such-like extra-terrestrials—and by God."[2]

God became an entity one did or did not believe in rather than a relational being intimately engaged in his creation. Since the seventeenth century there has been an increasing sense that God is somehow not involved in the natural (or scientifically observable), but only in that which is non-natural or spiritual.[3] While western culture has developed a predominantly materialist paradigm, traditional cultures continue to understand both seen and unseen forces as part of nature.[4] The Enlightenment "essentially drove apart God and the created order. Laws replaced the ongoing actions of God. The realm of nature no longer required divine agency."[5] Berger cites elimination of the transcendent in monotheistic Judaism, arguing that Protestantism subsequently divested Christian, and western thinking of the numinous.[6] The danger then with using "supernatural" is that it sets up a dichotomous view of the universe: the natural or material parts of existence (which science can interpret and often manipulate) are identified as real and the super, spiritual or non-measurable parts are not. The latter are often considered less significant or dismissed as irrational within an Enlightenment framework.[7] Many western Christians with secular, materialistic educations struggle to hold together natural law and divine activity. This risks reducing the divine to the "God of the gaps," a God who interacts with creation only under special circumstances, contradicting orthodox Christian understanding of his ongoing involvement in the universe.[8] Similarly, contemporary non-theists often describe any type of non-rational experience as supernatural, detaching the term entirely from religious usage.[9] Thus, to describe an event as "supernatural" is not straightforward.

The biblical texts explored in this project all describe some measure of overt divine activity, and many of the groups discussed non-rationalistic themes including prayer, the angelic, divine healings, curses, and miracles. "Spiritual activity" might be an appropriate description for these, however it could encompass any manner of religious (and non-religious) entities, practices and beliefs. Keener suggests "para-normal" as appropriate, but its

---

2. Lash, *The Beginning and the End*, 168.

3. Keener, *Miracles*, 7.

4. Twelftree, "Introduction," 7.

5. Del Colle, "Miracles in Christianity," 248.

6. Berger, *The Sacred Canopy*, 111–20.

7. Keener, *Miracles*, 173–74.

8. Thiselton, *The Holy Spirit*, 105.

9. James, *Religious Experience*, 50–61.

popular associations with ghosts, psychic activity and the like make it unhelpful.[10] Alternatively, he suggests "supra-human" to describe the activity of non-human beings, but since much of the discussion involved human activity (like prayer), this is not appropriate either.[11]

Extra-ordinary or extra-normal might be used to describe events beyond the normal experience of the majority.[12] However, extra-ordinary is widely used to describe anything remarkable and both ordinary and normal are relative terms. For many, prayer may be extra-normal, but for practising Christians it is entirely normal. Likewise, charismatics may consider praying in tongues ordinary, but it is extra-ordinary to many Christians. Certainly a dramatic healing or angelic visitation might be more widely viewed as extra-normal but, since Pilch suggests 90 percent of the world today accept both ordinary reality and non-ordinary reality, the question must be raised: what *is* "ordinary" or "normal," and for whom?[13]

In the light of these complications, and because a wide range of spiritual activities and experiences are under consideration, I shall follow Keener's example and use the phrase "supernatural" in its popular rather than technical form.[14] Despite the potentially dualistic implications, it is a helpful generic term to describe the non-rational spiritual activities and experiences of human beings. It is also the language used by the participants and thus is methodologically appropriate since ordinary theology specifically values the language of research subjects.

A second linguistic consideration is of the term "miracle." Much debate has taken place within Protestant and Catholic traditions on the nature of the miraculous. Aquinas saw miracles as acts of God perfecting, rather than violating, nature.[15] In the medieval period, they were considered signs of God's continuing presence in his creation, events above or beyond, rather than counter, to nature's laws. "*Miracula exterior* and *miracula interior* [were] both expected with authentic works of power, whether exterior or interior, intended to increase sanctity."[16] Bede allowed for miracles, but considered them more frequent and spectacular at the start of the church and tended to stress inner conversion over outer transformation.[17] The re-

---

10. Keener, *Miracles*, 3.

11. Ibid., 7.

12. Ibid., 3.

13. Pilch, *Flights of the Soul*, 17.

14. Keener, *Miracles*, 8.

15. Twelftree, *Miracles*, 9.

16. Del Colle, *Miracles*, 239–40.

17. Thiselton, *The Holy Spirit*, 226.

formers were cautious and, partly rooted in a rejection of Catholic excesses, expressed cessationist views; the days of marvel or miracles were over and God's work was largely internal.[18] They argued that miraculous events had functioned to accredit the ministry of Jesus and message of the apostles but were limited to that epoch.[19] Influenced by Enlightenment rationalism and Humean arguments against the reality of the miraculous, theologians such as Bultmann, "Reduced miracles in Scripture to novelistic flourishes of legendary accreditations which required them to be read differently from the rest of the work."[20] Schleiermacher defined miracle as, "The religious name for event" but predominantly describing religious feeling and conversion.[21] Tillich argued for "sign-events" pointing to divine mystery but only understood *as* miracles by those with faith.[22] Finally, Warfield, the "father of contemporary cessationism" revived traditional Reformation views of "miracles as limited to epochs of special divine revelation" thus almost certainly non-occurring today.[23]

However, some contemporary academics are re-embracing the idea of the miraculous event. Keener's extensive two-volume project considers contemporary global accounts of miraculous healings and argues for academic re-consideration of anti-supernaturalism.[24] Larmer defines them as events that would not have taken place except through the intentional actions of the divine, furthering God's purposes because they are sufficiently extraordinary to be recognized as such.[25] Basinger defines miracles as public, direct acts of God which are benevolent and have a desirable outcome (although acknowledging that this is relative).[26] He suggests that, regardless of how theists understand the mechanics of the miraculous, "a miracle is an awe-producing event that points to the divine."[27] Larmer summarizes, "The conclusion to be drawn is that on scientific, philosophical, and theological grounds belief in miracles is entirely rational. Far from being an

---

18. Del Colle, *Miracles*, 241.

19. Ruthven, *Cessation of the Charismata*, 189.

20. Brown, "Debates on Miracles," 282; Keener, *Miracles*, 15.

21. Del Colle, *Miracles*, 248.

22. Ward, *Divine Action*, 177.

23. Ruthven, *Cessation*, 189.

24. Keener, *Miracles*, 2.

25. Larmer, "The Meaning of Miracles," 36.

26. Basinger, "What is a Miracle?" 20–24.

27. Basinger, "Miracle," 31

embarrassment to religious faith they are signs of God's love for, and continuing involvement in, creation."[28]

Moberly notes that there is no world for miracle in Hebrew, suggesting that the most accurate way to understand such events in the Hebrew Bible is as "an enhancement or temporary elevation of power beyond the natural, rather than the breaking of natural law."[29] None of the texts used include the word miracle, but participants frequently used that language to describe unusual or dramatic events. Again, in line with methodological considerations, participant language will be used. However, distinguishing between *miracula exterior* and *miracula interior* is helpful to describe publically observable events and the inner working of the Spirit experienced by an individual.[30]

British Evangelicalism and the Supernatural

Despite commitment to Scripture as authoritative, and in some cases inerrant, British evangelicals present an interesting combination of attitudes towards supernatural events. A spectrum of opinion exists: at one end are those who accept miracles in Scripture, but are functional rationalists, with little expectation of contemporary events. Some extend this to cessationism, rejecting the possibility of a contemporary *miracula exterior* (including charismatic gifts).[31] At the other end, Pentecostals and charismatics often read biblical accounts of divine activity as a model for ministry, anticipating contemporary interventions and embracing a theology of "spiritual warfare."[32]

In his seminal work on congregations, Hopewell noted attitudes towards the supernatural as a key distinguishing factor. Using literary terms to describe four Christian worldviews, he argued that each emphasized

28. Larmer, *Miracles*, 50.

29. Moberly, "Miracles in the Hebrew Bible," 58–60.

30. Del Colle, *Miracles*, 240.

31. Warner, *English Evangelicalism*, 229; Bebbington cites the development of the Anglican "Reform" movement as a reaction to the influence of the Charismatic renewal in this and other theological areas. "Evangelical Trends," 104.

32. Pentecostals and charismatic beliefs are not identical. Charismatics typically do not follow the classic Pentecostal requirement of tongues as evidence of Spirit baptism. Robbins, "Globalization," 120. "Spiritual warfare" is a term rooted in 1990s missiology, which emphasizes the reality of battles between demonic and angelic powers in which Christians are called to participate. Two influential writers were Wagner, *Confronting the Powers*, and Prince, *They Shall Expel Demons*. Scotland cites this as a core charismatic value, *Charismatic Movement*, 282.

different aspects of Christian tradition—including engagement with the supernatural. Most applicable to the churches under observation are his canonic/tragic and charismatic/romantic categories. The canonic category anticipates gradual decline as the norm of human existence, with resolution or salvation only available through suffering and perseverance. It demonstrates a high reliance on and exclusive submission to the Bible. The charismatic/romantic category describes a more optimistic worldview, the solution to life's dilemmas being through spiritual adventure in which one can be a hero. This emphasizes triumph through adversity and encountering the transcendent spirit to empower and equip one for this adventure.[33]

The churches participating in this study hold differing official positions along the spectrum of attitudes towards the supernatural and within Hopewell's model. New Life is charismatic, encouraging the use of tongues and prophecy, engaged in prayer for healing with at least one member who reports regular experiences of the angelic. Sarah anticipated that discussion of the supernatural events in the texts would be straightforward, assuming that the groups would be open, comfortable and expectant of supernatural experiences today. It might be expected that their groups would demonstrate a romantic reading of the texts. Central Chapel has historic Brethren links but uses a contemporary worship band and some charismatic songs. However, it is not charismatic in its theology or praxis. Songs were not used as a sacrament—focussing on the divine and using repetition as a form of meditation—typical of charismatics.[34] Instead, they were used as hymns, declarations of faith or exhortations to the community, typical of traditional evangelical worship.[35] Ken did not expect significant discussion of the supernatural.

> I have very low expectations, if I'm honest, of supernatural manifestations taking place today. I do believe that healings happen, but with nothing like the frequency of intensity that they did in the first century. I'm not cessationist, I do believe that there are signs, wonders and miracles around today . . . we just don't teach that you should expect them very often. The greatest miracle, and the greatest healing is that of the conversion [so] let's be working really hard for that. We have low expectation of the miraculous in our congregation and if they are strongly shaped by the way we teach; I suspect that will come across.

33. Hopewell, *Congregations*, 58–69.

34. Steven, *Worship in the Spirit*, 127–29; Bonnington, "Charismatic Spirituality," 31.

35. Montgomery, *Sing A New Song*, 36.

This emphasis on *miracula interior* over *miracula exterior* has a long tradition.[36] Ken's low expectation of "spiritual manifestations" reflects a form of cessationism that stretches back to Chrysostom and Augustine.[37] It anticipates little by way of signs and wonders but is reluctant to rule them out entirely. Rather, it emphasizes the interior work of the Spirit in a believer's life. Cessationism has always been a minority Protestant view; however, significant numbers appear to have adopted this form of "mild" cessationism.[38] Keener states, "Many modern cessationists do not exclude God's supernatural activity in the present but simply argue that it does not occur to the same degree or in the same form as in the New Testament."[39] Cessationism may not be the best description for this; indeed, Ken actively resisted this label, wishing to distance the church from hard-line cessationism and remain open to the (in his view unlikely) possibility of contemporary miracles. In Hopewell's terms, this suggests a "canonic" worldview with little expectation of believers experiencing the dramatic power of the transcendent spirit in the form of *miracula exterior*.

Will, at Trinity Church, gave a more mixed response. Since they are a Reformed community, I had anticipated a cessationist position; however, he explained that they considered themselves them to be charismatic or "continuist" in their theology.[40] Describing cessationism as "A doctrine that is a peculiarity of some branches of protestant Christianity," he criticized it as a poor interpretation of Scripture and church history, explaining that by charismatic he meant, "We don't object to gifts although they're not regularly demonstrated in our meetings." He explained that the church leadership wanted to encourage prophetic contributions but that the congregation were reluctant. In response to questions about their use of charismatic worship songs without the typical emotive worship practices he explained, "I don't think that what you described as the charismatic spirituality of the contemporary Pentecostal and charismatic movements is the only or definitive way of expressing charismatic convictions in your doctrine." In other words, one can be charismatic without demonstrating the charismata or their frequently associated worship practices. Will was concerned about what he perceived as excesses of the charismatic movement but happy to embrace some aspects of the tradition, using the label in an aspirational and

36. Del Colle, *Miracles*, 239.

37. Ibid., 237.

38. Keener, *Miracles*, 260.

39. Ibid., 260.

40. The New Frontiers network is both Reformed and charismatic. Kay, *Apostolic Networks*, 64–80.

theoretical manner. With regard to supernatural activity, he anticipated that the groups would not have problems with the texts as historical records but would have no real expectation of such experiences today.

> I think there will be some people who feel disappointed by that, so I'm sure there will be some people who wish that there was more obviously divine, supernatural intervention. I think within the church we would have a number of people who would be much more sort of "If we believed in this more it would happen more"—a lack of faith sort of thing. The majority will be "It could happen but it probably won't," and that may stem from either a healthy and realistic understanding of the nature of the miraculous, which is by definition miraculous, or from a somewhat sceptical modernist worldview. And it's often hard to distinguish.

This identifies the tension many modern British evangelicals experience: a rationalist education has taught them to prioritize scientific understanding, and their experience of *miracula exterior* is limited. However, their understanding of Scripture as historically accurate, combined with the influence of the charismatic/Pentecostal movement, has perhaps raised expectations of the type of dramatic action God might perform. Although this is comparable to Central Chapel (their worship service used a similar format), Will presented Trinity Church as more intentional about its desire to engage with charismata such as prophecy, which marks it as unusual for an FIEC affiliated church. Returning to Hopewell's model, Trinity appears to be "canonical" in its worldview while its leaders aspire towards the "romantic." All three leaders anticipated that their groups would understand accounts in the text to be describing a literal historical event. No one anticipated the rationalization or understanding of biblical events as metaphorical or figurative. Thus the three churches are officially situated at various points along the evangelical spectrum and might be described as follows:

- *New Life:* "Actively charismatic" evangelicals: fully open to the supernatural and miraculous in both Scripture and contemporary experience, seeing one as a continuation of the other and demonstrating Hopewell's "romantic" worldview.

- *Trinity Church:* "Open but cautious" Reformed evangelicals: fully accepting of the supernatural and miraculous in Scripture and theoretically open to contemporary miracles and use of charismata but limited in experience and expectation. In Hopewell's terms "canonical" with "romantic" aspirations.

- *Central Chapel:* "Non-expectant" evangelicals or mild cessationists: accepting of the miraculous in Scripture but non-expectant of contemporary experience beyond conversion and interior transformation of the believer. Fitting Hopewell's model of the "canonical" worldview.

Focus Groups Findings

New Life

Taking up an average of 18 percent of their discussion, the New Life groups' consideration of the supernatural was the most in-depth and reflected their charismatic spirituality. None of the three groups expressed any doubt that the textual accounts were anything other than historical events, and it was clear that they believed God still engaged in such activity—although, surprisingly they demonstrated little by way of personal testimony.[41] This might suggest that the supernatural remains a relatively abstract concept. However, Sarah expressed surprise and was emphatic that supernatural experiences, including healing, were widely discussed and occurred on a semi-regular basis. Their reluctance may be attributed to the artificial nature of the group and uncertainty about how the researcher would respond, but Sarah was adamant that tangible experience of the angelic, demonic and both *miracula interior* and *exterior* were not uncommon at New Life and she had recently started "prayer lock-ins" to encourage this passion for spiritual engagement. Their discussions fell into two categories: belief and the miraculous and participation in the supernatural.

1. Belief and the Miraculous

ORDINARY AND PROPER MIRACLES

Two New Life groups distinguished between what they described as "ordinary" and "proper" miracles. Both referred to *miracula exterior*. The healing of Naaman was described as "not so spectacular or miraculous," "unimpressive-looking," and "simple." Rather than focus on the outcome of the event (a supernatural healing from an incurable disease) they appeared to recognize Naaman's disappointment that the method of healing was mundane and categorized the miracle as such. Comments revolved around the idea of God's actions not matching one's expectation.

---

41. Testimony is a key part of charismatic praxis. Moore, "Pentecostal Approach to Scripture," 12.

> Mandy: "It's his [Naaman's] pride that's stopping him from do-
> ing what God is telling him to do. . . . I think that's something
> I'm quite familiar with. When you want God to step in, you want
> him to do it like, blazing fanfare and flashes of lightning. You
> want it to look impressive!"

> Thomas: "God does miraculous things but he doesn't make a
> show out of it. That's something I've learnt in the last couple of
> years when amazing things happen but it's never made like a
> show. You expect something big and showy and flashing light
> and thunderbolts and all that sort of thing, but it doesn't have to
> be that by a long way. God works in the ordinary."

Clearly personal experience is significant in their understanding of God's actions; their experience, worldview, and reading mutually inform each other.[42] Both have an expectation of contemporary supernatural experience but have learnt to interpret God's hand at work in other ways too, which they still refer to as miracles. They are using the language of miracle loosely, based on personal reflection rather than public acclamation, but this implies that any act of God can be described as a miracle.[43] It would appear that charismatics do not all have dramatic supernatural experiences but rather a framework that allows them to interpret ordinary events as divine in origin. This matches Moberly's description of Hebrew attitudes: God performing his will through both ordinary and extra-ordinary events.[44] It is also noteworthy that a healing should be described as "ordinary." It suggests that these western emerging adults understand health as normal and healing from disease as an unremarkable. Sarah agreed that perhaps an older group who had more experience of chronic or life threatening illness might have seen Naaman's healing as more significant. Similarly, those without access to modern healthcare might have empathized with the desperation of the situation and identified a remarkable, life transforming act of God.

By contrast, Peter's angelic liberation was described as "a proper miracle" a "big, fantastic event." Groups recognized this sort of supernatural activity as unusual, but possible.

> Mandy: "So, sometimes God does stuff in powerful . . . and does
> do big, miraculous things—which I think we come not to expect
> so much in our culture today."

---

42. Village notes this among Anglican charismatics, *Bible and Lay People*, 147.

43. Basinger argues that a miracle must be public or widely observable. *Miracles*, 20.

44. Moberly, "Miracles in the Hebrew Bible," 57.

Felicity: "Yeah, nothing's impossible for God and he does send angels to guard us."

Mandy was overt about her lack of experience and recognized the rationalism of contemporary British culture. However, both women were enthusiastic about the possibility of experiencing dramatic divine activity. Sarah attributed this partly to the teaching of an American, Bill Johnson, who emphasizes a theology of "Heaven invading earth," raising the expectation that Christians should regularly have dramatic experiences of God and challenging a low anticipation of *miracula exterior*.[45] Felicity's comment demonstrates a romantic worldview, associating the angelic protection of Peter with God sending angels to guard us.[46] It is unclear whether she considered this as normative—an ever present guardian angel—or as the presence of the angelic in extreme situations. Either way, she identified modern believers with the apostolic generation, referring to both as "us" and assuming God's actions towards both are comparable.

The Angelic

With regard to the presence of an angel, there was surprisingly little discussion. Felicity commented, "It could be quite easy to read over the fact that there was an angel there because we read about angels so much in both parts [Old and New Testaments] of the Bible, but it's miraculous that there's an angel there." She demonstrates both familiarity and unfamiliarity with the angelic; her frame of reference appears to be solely the text. This is in contrast to the pilot groups run at Hope Community who explored the angelic more widely:

> Caroline: "I think I would be more surprised at an angel turning up than someone being healed or coming back to life. . . . Oh, that's weird isn't it?"

> Hattie: "I think the other way. I'd be more accepting of an angel coming than someone being raised from the dead. You know you were saying about word of mouth? Well, my mum says that she's had an experience of an angel, and because mum is very close to me I'm more likely to believe her."

---

45. Johnson, *When Heaven Invades Earth*: www.ibethel.org/offering-readings

46. Hopewell describes it as frightening and thrilling, involving encounters with evil. *Congregations*, 76.

The tension that western charismatics experience is explicit; their education and experience inclines them to be cynical of supernatural activity, but their evangelical and charismatic faith inspires a worldview where the divine is present and active. Caroline (a science graduate) demonstrates some confidence in supernatural medical activity, but a sense that she should be more expectant of angelic intervention. By contrast, her mother's testimony has convinced Hattie of the existence of angels. This is common among charismatics: second-hand or anecdotal experience provides sufficient evidence to legitimize belief in supernatural events. Rather than a theological acceptance of the angelic as presented in Scripture, it is the experience of someone she trusts that has convinced Hattie, a form of common sense realism.[47] A second Hope Community pilot group discussed the same points:

Joseph: "But we don't see angels now."

Rachel: "You hear stories of angels."

Joseph: "Yeah but not, not stuff like getting bust out of prison by . . ."

Miriam: "I have a friend who can see angels in every room she goes into."

Joseph: "Hmm . . ."

Rick: "My dad has been on like mission trips in Siberia and Mongolia and places like that, and he's had times when he's been lost in a busy airport and this man has come up to him and has spoken good English to him and helped him carry his bags and shown him the way to go, "Go through this checkpoint, that checkpoint," and he's turned round to thank him and he's just disappeared. So you don't realize necessarily while you're with them . . . but . . . there are various stories that go round like that."

Here, two individuals cited specific second-hand experiences, while a third made generic comments about "stories." Joseph's scepticism was outweighed, although Rick did acknowledge, "I think it is like a rarity to have angels, but this was at a time just after Jesus' death and we see one story of an angel. I find myself sometimes thinking why aren't I seeing more of such things as well? When so many other people have seen things [but] just cos I haven't seen something myself doesn't mean it's not happening."

47. Marsden, *Understanding Fundamentalism,* 165–68.

He is explicit that his lack of experience is not conclusive evidence either way but considers that perhaps he *should* be experiencing the supernatural. Miriam had an alternative explanation, "I think we have a perception of what an angel is and what it should look like, when really we don't know; it could be a person you see on the street. Like the two men that eat with Abraham and Sarah, they're angels but they look like ordinary people."[48]

This speculation that perhaps they have met angels without knowing illustrates Miriam's belief that divine actions are taking place around them. The group also linked miraculous experience to persecution and, since they had not suffered for their faith, concluded they had not needed angelic intervention. If they were to face persecution, perhaps God might similarly intervene?

Returning to the pattern of accepting second-hand evidence, sufficiency of testimony as convincing evidence for the miraculous has a long and disputed history.[49] There is social scientific evidence of a hierarchy of credibility for information based on personal anecdotes, and for these emerging adults it appears to convince them that such events *are* still occurring.[50] This is significant because, while it may well be true that older charismatics experienced spiritual renewal in the 1970s and 80s, and the "Toronto Blessing" of the 1990s, emerging adults are unlikely to have any memory of these phenomena.[51] Much of their expectation may well come from the testimony of older generations; their theology is vicariously experienced. Although the practice of tongues and prophecy may still take place, many churches that experienced the charismatic renewal have reverted to a moderated form of traditional liturgy and a routinization of charismatic spirituality.[52] Wilson suggests this is inevitable: "Movements must balance the ecstatic (in however a dilute form is permitted to persist) . . . with the imperative of the orderly."[53]

The New Church networks (to which New Life and Hope Community belong) have typically maintained a higher emphasis on charismatic worship, but there is caution around claims of healing and demonic activity, which critics argue have often been anecdotal and exaggerated.[54] Fifteen years ago, Guest found young adults to be disillusioned by charismatic reviv-

---

48. Genesis 18:2.

49. Brown, "Miracles," 282.

50. Kitzinger, "Focus Groups," 115.

51. Percy, *The Toronto Blessing*.

52. Guest, *Evangelical Identity*, 130; Coakley, *God, Sexuality and the Self,* 165.

53. Wilson, *Social Dimensions*, 212; Wright, "Signs and Wonders," 40.

54. Hilborn, *Toronto in Perspective*, 21; Thiselton, *The Holy Spirit*, 487.

alism.[55] It may well be that today's church leaders are cautious about raising expectations, having been disappointed themselves. Sarah was explicit in describing supernatural expectations in a non-inflammatory manner:

> We have something called "encounter," which is when people get stuck with fear, anxieties, lies, all the spiritual and emotional baggage that comes along the way. The team who are doing it would probably feel that part of what they are doing would come under the term "deliverance," but we wouldn't use that term because it's too loaded. We'd probably use the terminology of "seeing people set free."

She claims there have been significant transformations in the lives of those involved and that supernatural experiences do occur at New Life—although the groups were reluctant to share them in the research context.

BELIEF AND DISBELIEF

There was a lot of discussion within the New Life groups around the belief and disbelief of the early church in Acts 12. All were reassured by Peter's confusion; if even the Apostle was overwhelmed, then it was fine for them to be. The younger groups were sympathetic about the church's confusion but the older group were frustrated.

> Josie: "The people who are here are people who have seen ridiculous stuff. These are the people who may well have seen Jesus rise from the dead. Lots of them will have been around on that whole like, 'They're drunk, no it's only 11 o'clock in the morning,' Holy Spirit going mental kind of phase! But the idea that it's Peter standing outside the door—despite the fact they've been praying for it all night—that's too much to bear?"

Josie placed value on experience as evidence and implied that, if she had had such experiences, she would have believed. Another woman in the same group speculated as to how many miracles one might need to witness before immediately believing in events such as Peter's rescue. Their expectation appears to be that living during this period would have undoubtedly exposed believers to dramatic divine acts, and thus their faith should have been strong. Once again, experience and faith are intertwined for charismatic evangelicals.

---

55. Guest, *Evangelical Identity*, 131.

2. Participation in the Supernatural

The Power of Prayer

Participation with God was a highly developed theme among the charismatics, and prayer was particularly significant. A number said that they were personally challenged by the fervency of the believers' prayer, implying them as an admirable model but also suggesting disappointment in their own spiritual practices:

> Linda: "I always find it a real challenge that the church was earnestly praying for him. I earnestly pray for a couple of days and then it slips off my radar. So I find it a real . . . they were praying and this amazing thing happened. Like, YES! That's exciting!"

> Leon: "It makes me think of the power of prayer. It you pray enough and you earnestly pray then God will do it even though how unbelievable it is. But without prayer, that wouldn't have happened . . . it's encouraging—the power of prayer—there's nothing too big!"

Leon's certainty that sufficient, fervent prayer will cause supernatural events to occur was singular, perhaps illustrating his Pentecostal background.[56] No one else voiced this certainty; their reticence clearly distinguished evangelical charismatics from those influenced by the "Word of Faith" movement. Sociologists suggest this employs a form of magic involving ritual incantations known as "positive confession" and certainty that spiritual powers, including God, can be commanded into compliance for the health and wellbeing of believers.[57] Discussing the execution of James one woman commented,

> Elsa: "Maybe the intention was for him [Peter] to be beheaded, but maybe it was the result of the church praying that he was released and so we are really important in God's plan. Prayer makes things happen and maybe the church wasn't praying for James in the same way? I don't know, but the fact that prayer is mentioned, . . . it's a key part of the story perhaps?"

Elsa suggested that Christians have genuine power to alter or subvert events through prayer. Her speculation that fervent prayer could have saved James was tentative—she was unwilling to reject entirely his death as part of

56. He previously attended a church which teaches a doctrine of positive confession, critiqued in Perriman, *Faith, Health and Prosperity*.

57. Hunt, "Magical Moments," 275; Coleman, "When Silence Isn't Golden," 42–54.

God's sovereign plan—but she was demonstrating a more open view of the will of God.[58] This understanding, that without prayer God would not act, was unique among the churches and suggests a genuine sense of responsibility and relational cooperation between God and his people. It echoes the views of open theists:

> There is no absolute best, God always has options which can be limited by human response and action. Given that, God may well be influenced by the request of one of his children with regards to which possible action to pursue. Our submission to God gives him choices and actions that our rejection or disobedience closes off to him.[59]

This sense of a flexible, open universe was also implied by the younger group, who affirmed the importance of praying, "even if you don't believe it." Clearly, a willingness to try to change circumstances through prayer was more important than a certainty of divine intention; it was worth praying just in case God might answer.

The older group explored God responding to the prayer of the church in parallel with the Exodus narrative: an act of mercy to those under oppression. However, they were also certain that God was "bigger than the power of the day," ultimately sovereign even though terrible events might befall believers. Their reading was an optimistic one; having completed his role in God's plans, martyrdom and death were a fast-track to glory for James. It was striking that the group was determined to present James' death in a positive light and demonstrated one of the widely noted criticisms of the charismatic movement—that of triumphalism.[60] It is possible that this may be a naïve perspective due to the age and experience of the participants, but it does reflect an instinct to hold together God as sovereign and the suffering of believers—again matching Hopewell's romantic model.

Prayer and Spiritual Warfare

The theme of human agency was also part of a theology of spiritual warfare:

> Felicity: "Sometimes things don't come to fruition, sometimes things experience blockages, sometimes things experience intense prayer and breakthroughs happen and I don't think we can ever pinpoint it as a, 'That didn't happen because of a lack

58. Forster, God's Strategy in Human History.

59. Ward, Divine Action, 158.

60. Warner, Reinventing English Evangelicalism, 84.

of faith' or, 'That didn't happen because of a lack of prayer.' I feel like it's bigger than that."

Like Elsa and Leon, Felicity was confident that human participation was significant in divine action, but she introduced another spiritual dimension: "blockages"—alternative spiritual forces thwarting the actions of God and his people.[61] Hers was a lone voice, and she did not expand her position, which suggests a caution to embrace the concept of believers confronting the demonic. These groups were not guilty of an excessive divine/demonic duality or a paranoid preoccupation with demonic forces.[62] A moderate form of spiritual warfare was a background note in the theological worldview of at least some of the participants. Sarah observed, "We don't use the term 'spiritual warfare' that much just because I think it's quite a loaded term, but in reality I think we probably practise it. Our main warfare is worship and we keep our eyes fixed on Jesus, but as we're doing that we're bringing more of the Kingdom in darkness that gets dealt with along the way."

PROACTIVITY IN PARTICIPATION

New Life discussion of participation with God emphasized the need for human proactivity:

> Leon: "Naaman gets really miffed off, like 'Oh why do I have to do that? Can't you just put your hand over my head and cure me like that?' So I think there's a lesson of patience you know, it's not going to come, your prayers are not going to be answered just like that, you actually have to do something . . . shake a leg a bit and go to the river Jordan and get healed."

Individual autonomy and choice to participate with God—or not— was a significant component of their worldview. God did not simply act upon Naaman; he had to be proactive. Similarly, the mid-aged group extensively discussed reversing curses. They discussed "generational curses" and the power of the cross to end such effects.[63] Elsa stated,

> "I don't think it [curses] stopped at the cross, I think through the cross, that's given a path to ensure it can be stopped. But I

---

61. Wimber and Springer, *Power Evangelism*, 21–27.

62. Hunt, "Magical Moments," 275; Walker, "Demonology," 53–72.

63. A doctrine whereby whole families, or subsequent generations, can be oppressed by spiritual forces. Kraft, *Defeating Dark Angels*, 74–75.

do think there's something powerful in working in partnership with God to end this rather than it just happening. I see it more as now we can say with confidence, 'Get off you, in the name of Jesus,' and it happens."

This articulates the necessity for human participation both in divine action and in spiritual warfare. Elsa was articulating a theology of *Christus Victor* (an understanding of the atonement as Christ's victory over hostile powers that hold humanity in subjugation), popular in some sections of the charismatic church, while emphasizing the authority delegated to his people in spiritual matters.[64] Felicity added,

> I'm just astounded by how much power God entrusts to us; we could all curse people and I'm sure some of it would stick, do you know what I mean? In terms of the power that we've been given and had entrusted to us, I just think that it's phenomenal, and I don't get it! I don't get how God trusts us so much—but that's his heart, and he likes working in partnership and he's fine with us carrying the power of his kingdom.

This is more than just a belief that humans can ask God to act through prayer; rather, He has delegated power for which they now have responsibility. This comes close to the anthropological understanding of magic as supernatural power which an individual can wield for good or evil.[65] However, Felicity was describing authority delegated to believers in order to function in *partnership* with God rather than rituals given to control him. Although she did imply the power of Christians to do harm as well as good, this had a conscientious tone: believers should be careful with the power they carry. Sarah again cited external influences. "I think the majority of the congregation, influenced by Bethel stuff, [believe] we are far more powerful than we realize and that we are bearers of the divine image and that we have got a high amount of spiritual authority invested in us."

New Life emerging adults had been told that they are spiritually powerful, and some overtly articulated that. Citing 2 Kings 2:23–25, where Elisha calls down bears to maul youths who taunt him, one participant was extremely concerned that he was abusing his authority and, by implication, that power over the bears and leprosy was delegated to him.[66]

64. Popular interpretations draw on Aulen, *Christus Victor*: e.g., Boyd, *Satan and the Problem of Evil.*

65. Hunt, *Magical Moments*, 275.

66. Keener, *Miracles*, 47. Scholars have noted this ambivalence. E.g., Marcus, "The Boys and the Bald Prophet," 49–51, 64–65; Gray, *I & II Kings*, 479; Moberly, *Miracles*, 64.

One final area of discussion for the New Life groups revolved around the violent or negative supernatural events described in all three passages. These caused considerable consternation and are discussed at length in chapter 6. In short, New Life groups employed a different rationale to explore such events, including scientific explanations, blaming humans, the demonic, or ignoring them entirely. They appeared to be comfortable with God performing benevolent miracles and were confident that he still did so today, but wanted to find an alternative explanation for the judgements or punishments the text attributed to him.

Summary

Overall then, the charismatic groups from both New Life and Hope Community read events in the texts as accurate descriptions of historical events, but also had expectations of supernatural events in contemporary life. Experience of "proper miracles" appeared limited; most of their interaction with the divine had come in much more mundane forms, which they had interpreted as supernatural. Nonetheless, they were committed to the idea that God acts in dramatic and powerful ways today and were prepared to accept second hand testimony to validate their belief. They also held a high view of human participation in supernatural events, particularly through prayer, but understood believers to be endowed with supernatural authority. This sense of responsibility included a moderate openness to dealing with evil forces. Their confusion over negative supernatural events and the interpretative strategies they used to resolve them were also striking. In short, God appeared to be a romantic figure, a powerful, benign deity, offering blessing and partnership to his people rather than being the omnipotent creator and judge of humanity.

Central Chapel

Although minimal amongst the youngest group (11 percent of their discussion), overall there was more discussion of the supernatural in the Central Chapel groups than Ken had anticipated. Their views were significantly different from those of the New Life groups and have been divided into three sections: 1. Scripture, personal experience, and the miraculous; 2. mission and the miraculous; and 3. the Sovereignty of God.

1. Scripture, Personal Experience, and the Miraculous

FACTICITY OF SCRIPTURE

As with New Life, all the Central Chapel groups understood supernatural events as accurate historical accounts. Alan, in the mid-age group was emphatic:

> There's so much in this story that is clearly the work of God, there's just no argument that Peter escaped, there's *no argument* that Peter got free of his own strength, there's *no way* that people could dispute what the Lord has done here. People always want to argue this miracle can be explained in this way or this miracle can be explained scientifically. This story—there's no logical argument with chains falling off wrists and prison guards being blind to a prisoner escaping, because the prison guards were executed because of their part in this! [Emphasis his]

It was implausible to him that the guards would risk their lives or look the other way in allowing Peter to escape and thus he concluded this was indisputable evidence for a plain reading. Another participant also commented, "It's perfectly feasible to be blinded to what's going on . . . that's done again and again [in the Bible] isn't it?" The identification of this pattern (e.g., 2 Kings 6:18; Acts 9:8; 13:11) situated 2 Kings 5 within in a line of miraculous events, all of which she accepted as historical fact.

PERSONAL EXPERIENCE OF THE SUPERNATURAL

In contrast to their accepting of *miracula exterior* in Scripture, when it came to contemporary experience, the discussion was significant only in the mid-aged group. Reflecting Ken's expectations Charles stated,

> I think it's actually amazing, the miracles, 'cos it doesn't really happen very often nowadays, . . . but [these are] clearly supernatural things. I feel like those kind of miracle things happen really, really rarely nowadays. I never really experienced God's answer to prayer in a dramatic, like miracle way. For me, my experience of my faith is more about gentle, little, subtle things, like answers [to] prayers, and in far less dramatic [ways]. Mundane things that you suddenly realize that God *did* answer the prayer for this, God *did* answer the prayer for that. For me, I feel that God uses situations; little gentle things. [Emphasis his]

Charles was describing ordinary workings of grace; events that could be rationalized but which he understands as God's hand at work.[67] Echoing the Reformers, he ascribed New Testament supernatural activity as a validation of the gospel message but had little expectation of God performing similar actions today. This matches the mild cessationist views of the church. The older group also briefly explored the idea of living in a time of apparently dramatic and frequent supernatural activity. "Peter obviously had some real visions if he thought that this was just. . . . The visions he must have [already] had from God must have been so real, clear for him, to have thought that this could be a vision and not an actual happening event!"

Again, no one testified to any sort of overt supernatural experience, and the consensus was that the early believers had a set of experiences they were unlikely to have; God now worked mostly in the ordinary. However, both older groups were self-critical of their lack of expectation, speculating about their ability to recognize the supernatural. There was also conjecture that lack of faith created an inability for non-believers to interpret events as supernatural. The implication was that faith gave perspective to see divine action which might otherwise be understood as coincidence. This is distinct from Tillich's understanding that "the miracle is mainly in my mind."[68] Rather, it mirrors Calvin's "spectacles of faith" which suggest that the Bible allows certain levels of reality to come into focus for the believer that non-believers might miss.[69]

Both groups also explored the idea of seeing God's actions as internal. For example: "God was at work in Naaman's heart, the Spirit prompted him to follow what people were telling him." "God just wants to work in your heart." "God is slowly working on our hearts. His Spirit is working in us to prompt us to do the right thing." Internal transformation was their priority and, they apparently believed, God's. Similarly, contemporary divine activity was described as a slow, transformative process rather than a dramatic external one: *miracula interior* over *miracula exterior*.

Discussing the early church, a mid-age participant distinguished between the Spirit, "Really being on them" and "I've got the Bible to refer to." Although he did not explicitly deny the agency of the Spirit today, the implication of his (extensive) speech was that the New Testament text should be a sufficient source of confidence for contemporary Christians. However, in his and other's comments, there was a wistful tone and a sense of disappointment at their lack of supernatural experience. They felt that

---

67. Del Colle, *Miracles*, 236.

68. Ward, *Divine Action*, 177.

69. Vanhoozer, *Remythologizing Theology*, 353.

they were cautious, lacking faith and experienced God only in mundane, gradual things. However, this caused debate in the mid-aged group. Mary remarked, "I think they [miracles] do happen. I just don't think that they happen in our part of the hemisphere, because you hear about stories in Africa and China and Russia and whole continents where the message of God is spreading." This demonstrates an interesting link between evangelism and supernatural events, but also concurs with second-hand stories as evidence of the miraculous. Members of the oldest group cited a popular Christian biography.[70]

> Miranda: "Reading it made me think of that Chinese guy."
>
> Lewis: "Brother Yun. I was just thinking the same thing. . . . He just walked out of prison!"
>
> Miranda: "Cos God just opened all the doors. But he had two broken legs. Both his legs were broken and he was able to just walk out of prison!"

It was clear that they were prepared to believe in divine, miraculous activity supported by the testimony of others or generalized hearsay but happening only in places where widespread evangelism, church growth, and proselytizing in the face of persecution took place and cultural expectation or need was higher.

2. Mission and the Supernatural

In line with a strong conversionist ethos, all three Central Chapel groups linked supernatural activity to mission: a sign of God's power to unbelievers.[71]

> Scott: "Maybe the LORD wants the Arameans to know, and maybe the LORD in this story wants the King of Israel to learn something too? To learn that Elisha is his man on earth, working for him and showing the power of God and showing that, yeah, he can heal leprosy and he can heal even the future enemies of Israel."
>
> Lewis: "It also shows Israel being a blessing to the surrounding nations doesn't it? Which was part of the plan."

---

70. Hattaway and Yun, *The Heavenly Man*.
71. Carelton-Paget, "Miracles in Early Christianity," 135.

They understood Naaman's healing as part of God's evangelistic strategy: to demonstrate his power both within and outside Israel. Likewise with the Acts 12 text Alan commented, "'But the word of God continued to spread and flourish'. Just sums up maybe why the story happened, why the whole situation took place—for the spread of the word of God."

Their understanding of Peter's supernatural rescue was linked to his necessity for the mission of the early church. Similarly, Herod's death was seen as a witness, a warning to believe only in "The God of Heaven." Thus miraculous events functioned as signs to show the power of God and lead to conversion. The implication was that where Christians are proactive in evangelism, and possibly facing persecution as a result, God was more likely to act in overtly supernatural ways. These were "other" places. In their ordinary western lives, where they did not see the gospel spreading dramatically, they did not anticipate such activity. Instead, they expected the Holy Spirit to be inspiring moderate internal rather than miraculous public transformations. This has parallels with the Hope Community perspective, but the Central Chapel groups were far more explicit in the link between mission and the supernatural. It was also linked to their disappointment; several individuals expressed self-criticism at their lack of courage to proselytize. This fits Hopewell's canonic worldview: prioritizing obedience and the need for individual repentance and salvation. Although they did expect personal transformation by the Spirit of God, there was little anticipation that this would take place in a dramatic spiritual encounter such as charismatics might expect.[72]

3. Sovereignty of God and the Supernatural

Rather than the human participation New Life had emphasized, all three Central Chapel groups focussed on divine orchestration of events.

> Charles: "This story [2 Kings 5] is showing that every bit of the story God's hand is always on it, like God's pretty much the director behind this story and God is saying where the story's going, like where Naaman's going and how Elisha responds and how things develop and how from the very beginning to the very end, God's hand was on it."

> Miranda: "This was all part of God's plan for Naaman to actually recognize God and come to serve God. Give him leprosy so he

72. Hopewell, *Congregations*, 70.

would go to see Elisha so Elisha would heal him and then he'll be converted."

Charles saw God's hand micromanaging every part of the narrative, and Miranda expressed no qualms about God inflicting leprosy on Naaman as part of a greater plan. Indeed, the groups went so far as to ascribe the role of actors in God's plans to the human agents involved. Similarly, they emphasized direct divine action in Peter's rescue:

> Scott: "The fact that an iron gate opened by itself . . . that's God's power over creation."

> Alan: "It doesn't say the angel of the Lord opened the gate. God sent the angel of the Lord to rescue Peter, to save him and tell him what's going on, but then he doesn't use the angel to open the gate, it opened for them by itself, so the two of them needed the gate opening by God."

They understood these events not as God delegating Peter's rescue to an angelic messenger, but instead being actively involved in blinding guards, removing chains and opening doors. This reading placed a lot less significance on other agents and far more on direct divine intervention.

The sense of God's active involvement to achieve his plans (no matter what) creates an interesting dichotomy with the sense of responsibility they expressed in terms of evangelistic activity. Is conversion of the unbelieving their responsibility or God's? No one explored the dichotomy, but it illustrates some level of uncertainty and ties in with their final significant subject of conversation around the area of supernatural activity, which was that of prayer. This was less developed than the New Life debates but, nonetheless, questions were raised.

> Joel: "I find it interesting how when Peter was in prison it says the church was earnestly praying to God for him, and yet when their prayers are answered and Peter comes knocking they think 'God can't have answered our prayers, don't' be silly! You must be mad woman!' What have they been expecting? It's strange you can pray for something so much but not just believe it's going to happen."

> Jimmy: "Sounds a little bit familiar don't you think?"

This theme of doubting answered prayer was picked up all the groups, but Joel went on to commend the earnestness of the church explaining, "I think that's just a really good practice of praying and even if they're not faith-filled in thinking that it's actually going to happen, they're still doing it and thinking something might happen. I think that's a good example for today's church in praying for people all round the world who are in Peter's position in prison because of what they believe."

His understanding seemed to be that sincerity, rather than faith, is the key to effective prayer. This again tied in with a high view of the immutability of God, who will hear those with little faith and act according to his plans.

A question with regard to the responsibility of believers was raised by Karen in the mid-aged group. "So they were earnestly praying to God to do something. I wonder whether if the Church didn't pray this would have happened?" However Charles held a different view. "Prayers without faith don't work, faithless prayer doesn't do. . . . Miracles happen because you pray and I would say if you are praying things that you don't believe in, then prayer won't work. If you pray without faith it is not a heartfelt prayer, it's not what you really want to happen."

Charles seemed to understand faith to be not only vital for prayer to be effective, but synonymous with what you *really* want. This contrasts with Joel who distinguished between what one might really want God to do and an expectation that he will do so. Karen was questioning how significant prayer actually is. This sense of uncertainty was further unpacked by Alan, who considered that the Holy Spirit had inspired fervent prayer in Acts 12, again, attributing events to God's sovereign actions. Echoing the findings of Luhrmann,[73] he was highly critical of his own prayer life:

> Sometimes I do earnestly pray for something, but maybe not the right thing. Maybe I pray earnestly "God can you help me in my life at the moment? Can you help me get a job? Can you help me in my relationship?" But I don't pray earnestly "God can you help me be Jesus to the people that I meet? Can you help me tell others about you today?" Perhaps the prayers that I pray earnestly aren't the prayers that matter as much? I think that's what this passage challenges me to do, to pray earnestly for the spread of the gospel.

Alan had returned to the theme of the supernatural and evangelism but also to frustration and self-criticism. His speculations that his own prayers were self-centred or trivial seemed an explanation of why perhaps he did not experience God's divine actions and that instead he should be focussed on what he perceived as God's priorities (i.e., evangelistic mission).

---

73. Luhrmann, *When God talks Back*, 156.

Summary

Once again, the groups understood biblical supernatural events as accurate historical accounts. Although there was limited conversation in the younger group, the mid-aged and older group demonstrated a low expectation of contemporary supernatural experience. Their main expectation was that it would take the form of an internal transformation, like conversion, or little "mundane" answers to prayer rather than a dramatic, external experience. They did not entirely dismiss *miracula exterior* but linked them with proactive evangelistic activity in other parts of the world. Their understanding of prayer seemed uncertain rather than existing within a coherent framework. However, in general, they demonstrated a high view of God's authority and direct involvement in events and a lower sense of the significance of human activity.

The conversations did largely match Ken's expectations: mission as the priority and low expectation of *miracula exterior*. However, there was more interest in the subject than he had anticipated. On the whole, they were less inclined towards mild cessationism but rather identified miraculous activity in other parts of the world as being primarily linked to evangelization and church growth. Finally, although it was not explicit, there was a sense of frustration at their lack of expectation of how God might act, as well as self-criticism of their own participation in evangelism and prayer.

Trinity Church

Trinity church discussions about supernatural activity were varied. The younger and mid-aged groups were moderately engaged (14 percent and 17 percent of their discussions), but the older group barely discussed any related themes. Given that two of the texts contained miraculous events, it is striking that only 5 percent of their conversation was related. They did not deny or reject the events; they simply did not reflect on supernatural themes. It is difficult to conclude why this might be but, given their Reformed background, it may indicate a low expectation regarding contemporary miraculous events, or even a cessationist reading. One individual repeatedly raised strong criticism of "Word of Faith" preachers but there were virtually no other comments. Will doubted that cessationism was the cause:

> The elder group has a lot of medics and healthcare people who I think find the whole healing thing really difficult because of the nature of their work. So they see all of this everyday all the time, some people get better and some people don't and sometimes

you don't know why they get better and is that miraculous or not? It's just too difficult, so we do our jobs and don't think about it too much.

He explained that within the city was a church with an assertive healing ministry. Thus his congregation had "heard very shallow answers from the worst sort of parts of the healing movement, and if you work in healthcare you just know that's nonsense." He also described the recent death of a young child in the congregation, which had shaped their thinking, and suggested that their "strong view of God's sovereignty" left miracles as mysterious. His conclusion was that the oldest group, who were peers of the bereaved parents, probably avoided the subject for pastoral reasons, but also out of uncertainty. The younger and mid-aged groups did have more to say, although there was no obvious pattern in their theological priorities. Their discussions revolved around the angelic and attitudes to prayer.

1. The Angelic

The younger group were curious, discussing their uncertainties around the angelic:

> Jenny: "It's just very hard though, for me to imagine an angel coming. What did it come like? What was the angel like? Could you see the angel or was it a spiritual thing? I don't know, I just find it very hard to get my head around."
>
> Jim: "It makes we want to see it, what did it look like?"

Clearly, no one had experiences to share on the subject, nor did they reflect in detail on other biblical examples. They did, however, distinguish between their own experiences and those of the early church:

> Jim: "They seem quite normal with angels. When he's [Peter] knocking, they're like, 'Oh it's an angel, it must be his angel,' or something. So they're quite . . . angels are around kind of thing."
>
> Simon: "And they truly believe there is the supernatural and things don't they?"

References to "they" imply an understanding that supernatural experiences were a normal part of early church experience, presumably in contrast to their own. This suggests that perhaps Simon did not "truly believe" in the supernatural, or at least he was unclear about spiritual beings. He did not go as far as rationalizing away the angelic, but there was an implied scepticism and cessationism in their conversation. However, Jenny countered this stating, "I believe [in] it too, it's just that the supernatural obviously, I don't know, I just find it quite hard sometimes to imagine."

As with the other churches, their rationalist education was conflicting with historical reading of the text. Angels were real because of their occurrence in Scripture, but the readers were torn, uncertain whether it was feasible for them to rationally believe in intelligent non-human entities. Vanhoozer observes, "The existence of invisible beings does not sit well with modern thinkers who can find no place for angelic activity in a world explicable by scientific law."[74] Jenny was nevertheless prepared to overrule her scientific background (as a medical student), although her belief in angels was based entirely on the authority of the biblical narrative.[75] Similar to groups from other churches, the younger group briefly referred to secondary supernatural encounters, but this too seems to have been confusing rather than confirming or clarifying for them. "You hear of angels and [the] like in the Bible and then people's encounters now-a-days. Sometimes it's just seeming like a normal person. Was it like that? Do they look normal?"

Where groups from other churches had discussed alternative biblical stories of the angelic, contemporary literature, or personal experience, the Trinity Church group left these questions unresolved, remaining confused and curious.

2. Prayer

The most significant related conversation among the mid-aged group was about prayer in Acts 12. They acknowledged the fervency and urgency of the early church's prayer and commended them for their vigilance and determination but, based on their surprise at Peter's release, wondered if they had actually been praying for that to occur?

> Sophie: "I wonder what they were praying for. Were they praying for him to be released or . . . ?"

> Bridget: "It doesn't say 'The church was earnestly praying to God that he might be released.' It was for him, so it's recognizing that God will keep him strong, but they're praying for him as a person."

---

74. Vanhoozer, *Remythologizing*, 228.

75. Ibid.,

The younger group also speculated on the faith of the church but assumed they were praying for Peter's release. They identified with this, recognizing the limitations on their own expectations of God. Simon stated, "I think God's power can still shock us, it's like . . . we can't fully comprehend God. So even though we are praying, we think 'It can't be fully done.' I think, you're still going to be 'Wow, this actually does work!' Like it's still going to be pretty amazing if he does show up."

The phrase, "If he does show up" implies that God is distant or even absent, only occasionally intervening—a somewhat dichotomous view. It suggests that God can sometimes be persuaded, through prayer, to show his power but that this is not a frequent experience for believers. The older group also sympathized with the early church and commended them that regardless of their faith levels they were earnestly praying. "They didn't believe that God had answered when it happened, but they were, you know, doing what they should do!"

These discussions also included reflections on their own prayer habits. Bridget commented, "We can expect God to answer our prayers, but still do it in our way. So that there will be a fair trial and they will let him go, not [that] an angel will come and guide him out of prison at night time."

She voiced a critique of her own rationalization of how God might act. Indeed, the group speculated that their prayers were limited by a lack of expectation of the supernatural. James asked, "Are we expecting God to work thought the natural? So if someone heals the ill through the wonders of the NHS . . . or are we expecting him to work, potentially miraculously? I think English people in general are very good at being sort of middle-line conservative. Being like, 'Lord, help them, heal their body with good drugs from the NHS.'"

This was expressed with a critical tone, a sense of irritation that English people did not have higher expectation of the miraculous. It is interesting that James here partially distinguishes between God working through the natural and acting in a miraculous manner. His frustration appears to be with a rationalized form of faith that has little confidence to pray for *miracular exterior*. Other self-criticisms included, "Praying throughout the night, they're all together! I've never prayed like that!" Will was disappointed at this attitude, commenting, "I'm not surprised, but I'm slightly discouraged that people fell into self-flagellating about it."

The group were particularly concerned about striking the right balance of faith and fervency in prayer with not limiting God. They explored how to discern between their will and God's, citing Daniel chapter 3 and prayer for rescue, held in tension with the fact that God might not do so. Sophie was explicit (and self-critical) in explaining her strategy for prayer. "We play it safe don't we? I do [that] a lot when I'm praying. Ask for the reasonable, ask for what is possible, you know, so you won't be disappointed."

Once again, a high view of God's sovereignty meant that the group was concerned to pray in line with his will without being certain as to what that might be, but Sophie recognized that she limited her prayers for fear of damaging her own faith. This tension between wanting high faith levels for God to do the miraculous and yet not wanting to make assumptions about his will seems to have manifested itself in a form of rationalistic prayer which closely matched their limited experience of divine action. The group was self-aware enough to recognize the tension they were experiencing. They were far less certain of their own influence than the New Life groups had been but still felt a weight of responsibility and concluded their discussion by agreeing that earnest prayer, even if faith was limited, was still a good thing and that God would achieve his will despite weak human faith. This mirrors Will's view:

> It seems very clear in the New Testament that we would see God do more if we prayed more and yet God is still sovereign and not dependent on our prayers in order to do stuff. And well, . . . I find that difficult. I think that confusion is probably as it should be in that we emphasize both things. It matters that we pray, there is a call to pray, prayer is both real in its effect on history and in its effect on you *and* God is sovereign. [Emphasis his]

He concluded that perhaps the congregation needed some teaching about prayer adding, "I guess my pastoral hope is that [this] drives us to pray because we are uncertain. My pastoral fear is that what it drives us to do is go 'It's too difficult [to understand] I'm not gonna bother.'" The final comment in the group's discussion suggested his hopes were more founded than his fears. Jim believed that Acts 12 is "[a] great glimpse of God answering prayer, of people praying earnestly, he answers it. It's an amazing bit of God working, despite [what] we pray!"

3. Other Supernatural Themes

Beyond these two discussions, a number of lesser themes were explored. The negative miracles were mentioned only in passing; Herod's death was described as "another miracle." It was unique to describe a violent act as a miracle and this contradicts definitions of miracles as benevolent events.[76] There was also some linking between the supernatural and mission though

76. Basinger, *Miracles*, 20.

in nowhere like as much detail as the Central Chapel groups. The youngest group saw a link between the supernatural and the word of God continuing to spread and flourish, considering Peter's rescue as designed to testify to the validity of the gospel message: "So that people will come to believe." Likewise, the older group speculated, "Some people must have become believers from hearing Peter's story." Conversionism was therefore one of their priorities.

There was also limited discussion about Naaman's healing, but as with other churches, they focussed on the method of healing rather than the outcome. Attention was on his healing as *miracula interior*—an inner transformation. When explicitly asked, "Are you surprised at God healing people?" the response (in its entirety) from the youngest group was,

> Jim: "No."

> Simon: "He has the power to do anything doesn't he?"

This did not provoke a discussion of contemporary healing. There were no personal anecdotes or secondary testimonies. One possibility is that they were focussing on interpreting the specific text, staying on topic rather than exploring themes within it. Will explained that objectivity in reading a biblical text was modelled as a priority within the church. Another explanation is an avoidance of a confusing theological issue (as Will suggested), a third is that it was not of any real interest to them; other themes, such as conversionism, were simply a higher priority.

Summary

Once again, the groups read the narratives as accurate historical accounts, with no questioning of the authenticity of the events. Similar to Central Chapel there were some parallels drawn with mission, although they were far less explicit about God's sovereignty. In reality, only two significant themes were raised in the Trinity Church groups: the younger group's confusion about the angelic and disappointment at their lack of experience, and the mid-aged group's discussion on prayer, demonstrating self-criticism at their lack of expectation. Both groups appeared to demonstrate the frustration, that Will had anticipated, and a sense of disappointment with their own rationalism or reluctance to embrace the supernatural. The sense was a desire for greater faith and experience of miraculous events with a simultaneous uncertainty about them. Open but cautious is an accurate description for the younger groups, while the older group expressed virtually no interest in supernatural aspects of the texts at all.

Comparisons and Conclusions

As anticipated, the subject of the supernatural showed theological distinctives between the three participant churches. The charismatic groups showed the greatest interest and expectation of contemporary supernatural experience. In reality, they appeared to have limited personal experience but were prepared to accept second-hand testimony as authoritative in proving a continuation of the kinds of supernatural activity described in the Bible. Hope Community groups showed the greatest interest in the angelic, while New Life participants showed the greatest sense of confidence in engaging with the supernatural. They held a high view of human participation and responsibility in seeing divine supernatural actions come about—whether through prayer or directly delegated authority. They also demonstrated considerable concern about negative supernatural events.

There was greater similarity between the Central Chapel and Trinity Church groups, who accepted events described in the text as historically factual but were uncertain about contemporary occurrences. The Central Chapel groups had a sense that in other places (particularly in places where the gospel was spreading or believers were persecuted) such events occurred but that, in Britain, God typically acted in mundane or internal ways. Their focus was on mission and the supernatural signs and wonders for this purpose. There was, however, a sense of disappointment which they articulated as self-criticism; perhaps if they were more engaged in evangelization they would have a wider experience of the supernatural. The Trinity groups were the least engaged with the subject, their oldest group essentially ignoring it. Discussions demonstrated curiosity, confusion and frustration. They articulated uncertainty about the angelic and the function of prayer in the light of God's sovereignty.

With regard to their leaders' expectations, Will, from Trinity, was closest to the findings—having expected confusion and some disappointment. The Central Chapel groups were more engaged than Ken had anticipated, and the New Life groups less so than Sarah had expected. There was little discussion of supernatural healing and, overall, it would appear that few members of any group had significant supernatural experiences—or at least not that they articulated. Given that one member of the eldest New Life group claims to experience the angelic on a regular basis and healings are semi-regular occurrences (according to Sarah) it is interesting that these were not reported in the discussion—perhaps inhibited by the presence of a researcher.

Only a few members of charismatic groups articulated theologies of spiritual warfare, rather than it being a widespread assertion. Two decades on from the Toronto Blessing it would appear that mainstream and conservative young adults are prepared to accept the existence of the supernatural in Scripture, rather than rationalize it, and to entertain the idea in principle for contemporary faith, but have little personal testimony or expectation of such occurrences. The charismatics have a higher expectation but distinguish between different sorts of supernatural event, interpreting ordinary circumstances and coincidences as orchestrated by God. Second-hand stories are largely believed, but these are largely "other" to the faith of the majority (things that happen to other people, in other times or places). It may be that stories they have heard from older generations have encouraged (or deterred) such expectations, but even in the two "canonic" churches there was a sense of wistfulness amongst participants; they wished that they did experience dramatic supernatural events. For some this was transferred into criticism towards their own prayer, mission, or faith lives: if they took their faith more seriously then perhaps they would see more dramatic divine intervention. They do indeed appear to be caught between a rationalist wider culture and evangelical belief in supernatural scriptural accounts. Although scholars suggest experience as particularly significant in shaping the faith of Generation Y, it would appear genuine encounters of *miracular exterior* are infrequent.[77] However, many aspire to this sort of dramatic experience, while charismatics, whose spirituality tends to be more emotive and expressive, are most confident that they might encounter such divine activity.

77. Savage, *Generation Y*, 22.

6

Evangelical Theological Distinctives: Wrestling with the Violence of God

Introduction

THE SECOND THEOLOGICAL THEME under examination is the attitude of participants towards acts of violence attributed to God in the texts under discussion. These include the striking dead of Nabal (1 Samuel 25:38), the cursing with leprosy of Gehazi and his descendants (2 Kings 5:27), and the striking of Herod by the Angel of the Lord (Acts 12:23). This chapter will also consider participant responses to other deaths in the text, such as the martyrdom of the Apostle James (Acts 12:1) and the execution of Peter's guards as a result of his escape (Acts 12:19). These deaths have been categorized:

1. The antagonists' punishments (Nabal, Gehazi, Herod)

2. The innocents' suffering (Gehazi's descendants, Peter's guards)

3. The believer's death (James)

This was the most widely discussed theological subject across seven of the nine groups. New Life groups discussed it for an average of 29 percent of their time (the topics of gender and the supernatural averaged at 16 and 18 percent). Central Chapel averaged at 27 percent (as opposed to 13 and 16.6 percent) and Trinity Church at 19.6 percent (compared to 16 and 14 percent). Admittedly, there were examples of deaths or divine punishment in all three narratives but this was clearly a subject of real concern to the majority.

Leaders' Expectations

The church leaders had a variety of expectations on this subject. Sarah anticipated that New Life groups, "Will wrestle with that. That will definitely cause discussion, potentially some angst—some kind of confusion trying to add [this] up [with] a God of love." Ken suspected a diversity of responses from Central Chapel groups:

> I suspect some of them will just go, "We trust that God is going to do the right thing and if God thinks they needed to be killed then they'll be killed. And if you're in the way of what God wants to do then that's going to have implications. If you're getting in the way of his redemption plans for history . . . He's got a world to save and you may find yourself collateral damage but that it's going to be just and fair." Some might be struggling with the justice of God and how can a God of love and grace act in these kind of ways? I doubt many of them would.

Will, at Trinity Church anticipated,

> Most people will not flag that as a big issue. Some may but most won't. And I think that's because most people are comfortable with that idea rather than because they want to avoid it. So I think probably, especially among the better thought out people, [there's] actually a quite solid theology of suffering (partly because of events that have happened at church this year). A sort of recognition that God is both good and brings disaster. [But] I think there will be people who've never thought about that who might then be a bit disturbed when it gets pointed out to them.

These comments are telling. Will anticipates a majority will have resolved the issue based on being forced to face hardship as a community. Ken cited these events within a metanarrative of God's character and wider actions, reflecting an evangelistic ethos and expecting groups to adopt a "greater good" approach.[1] Sarah explained that much of New Life's energy went into evangelistic activity for emerging adults from unchurched backgrounds. "We've had a big emphasis on the Father heart of God and the unconditional love of the Father: the kindness, the grace, the acceptance. So perhaps that's why people struggle with the angry God who sends leprosy."

A deliberate strategy to present a humane, friendly God to those with no religious frame of reference means that they have emphasized his mercy and avoided making non-believers feel judged. It might be possible to argue that in presenting a benign God they are playing into the happy-midi

---

1. Seibert, *Disturbing Divine Behaviour,* 77.

narrative of today's emerging adults, presenting God as benevolent and domesticated; a "divine butler and cosmic therapist."[2] Alternatively, their understanding of the cross as a means of reconciliation rather than judgement is a legitimate historic interpretation.[3] By contrast, those from more Reformed or mainstream evangelical backgrounds continue to use the language of God's judgement in their presentation of the gospel, emphasizing penal substitutionary atonement and thus it was anticipated that God's anger and violence would be less controversial for their emerging adults.

Contemporary Evangelical Context

This issue is set within a long history of evangelical discussions about the wrath of God. In recent decades the crucifixion and existence of hell have become flash points for inter-evangelical division. In the face of growing liberalism, British evangelicals united around these two issues in the 1930s and, despite the longstanding tradition of multiple interpretations of the crucifixion, IVF (later UCCF) and the Reformed wing of British evangelicalism presented penal substitutionary atonement as the definitive (and even only) legitimate understanding.[4] This became the norm for interpreting the cross in the same way that conscious eternal torment was the norm for the evangelical understanding of hell.[5]

However, recent shifts within trans-Atlantic evangelicalism have reopened historic discussions. In 2003, British Baptist minister and social activist Steve Chalke, with scholar Alan Mann, published *The Lost Message of Jesus Christ*. This attempted to demonstrate the ministry of Christ as a vehicle for social transformation and presented multiple images for understanding the cross, challenging the dominant conservative framework.[6] The crucial point of contention was, "The fact is that the cross isn't a form of cosmic child abuse—a vengeful Father, punishing his Son for an offence he has not even committed. Understandably, both people inside and outside of the Church have found this twisted version of events morally dubious and a huge barrier to faith."[7]

---

2. Collins-Mayo, *Generation Y*, 18; Savage, *Generation Y*, 20; Smith "Moralistic Therapeutic Deism," 41.

3. Green and Baker, *Scandal of the Cross*, 97.

4. Wood, "Penal Substitution," 70.

5. Acute, *The Nature of Hell*, 2.

6. Green, *Scandal of the Cross*, 97.

7. Chalke and Mann, *The Lost Message*, 182.

This caused considerable conflict. The then Bishop of Durham, N. T. Wright, and popular figurehead for the emerging church movement, Brian McLaren, supported Chalke. Conservatives such as Piper, Carson, and Grudem roundly denounced his position.[8] An individual's understanding of the atonement became, in some circles, a test for the soundness of evangelical faith and inflamed existing tensions between conservatives and the evangelical left—amongst whom the *Christus Victor* model of the cross had gained popularity.[9] Repercussions across evangelical networks particularly affected emerging adults. The rift centred on the support of the Spring Harvest group for Chalke (a member of their steering group) and caused UCCF to withdraw from their fourteen year alliance, the Word Alive Bible teaching conference. In partnership with the conservative Keswick Convention, UCCF set up the alternative "New Word Alive" conference. Simultaneously the charismatic Momentum conference saw an increase in attendance, thus charismatic and conservative emerging adults found themselves (often unknowingly) pushed into two theological camps.[10]

A second recent debate has centred on the subject of hell. In a pluralist society with an increased anathema to religious violence and absolutism, hell as a place of conscious eternal torment for the unbeliever has become increasingly unpalatable to many evangelicals.[11] Recent surveys confirm a visible nervousness about hell.[12] Contributing to this debate was the American Rob Bell. Bell's earlier works had made him popular in progressive evangelical circles, but *Love Wins* caused a storm of controversy.[13] Despite support from some progressives, Bell was widely accused of universalism and denounced in many evangelical circles.[14] His "Mars Hill" mega-church haemorrhaged three thousand members, and he stepped down from its leadership.[15]

Current British evangelical discussion about the character of God is also shaped by other American writers. Bill Johnson has produced fifteen popular books which have had a profound influence on some charismatic groups.[16] Johnson's emphases on experience of the Divine, physical healing

8. John Piper, www.desiringgod.org; Warnock "Grudem Retracts".

9. Wood, *Penal Substitution*, 113.

10. www.momentum.co.uk.

11. ACUTE, *The Nature of Hell*, xiii.

12. Holmes, *Evangelical Theology*, 32.

13. Bell, *Velvet Elvis; Sex God;* nooma.com, Accessed June 16, 2014.

14. McClaren, "Will Love Wins Win?"; Deyoung, "Rob Bell Love Wins Review."

15. Weber, "Rob Bell, Tells," www.christianpost.com. Accessed June 16, 2014.

16. Johnson, *Face to Face with God*; Johnson, *When Heaven Invades Earth*.

and the power of prayer have raised accusations of prosperity theology but attracted eighteen hundred international students to its School of Supernatural Ministry in 2012/13.[17] Alternatively, coming from the New Calvinist grouping, Mark Driscoll and Tim Keller have been widely popular in the UK (although Keller has been criticized for not being outspoken enough on hell and Driscoll has now stepped down from leading his Mars Hill megachurch following accusations of bullying.)[18] This diversity of theological views and the ease of access to sermons via the internet mean that while some evangelical emerging adults position themselves in one theological camp or another, others are relatively indiscriminate.

Participating Churches and Contemporary Evangelicalism

Given that it was planted by former UCCF staff members, unsurprisingly Trinity Church participants reported a tendency to engage more conservative theological resources. They attended Christian Union and UCCF sponsored conferences and listen to podcasts from Driscoll and MacArthur.[19] New Life has close links with Fusion, and its participants cited attendance of charismatic events such as New Wine, Momentum, Spring Harvest, and Greenbelt. Some had been involved in the Christian Union movement but their preferred podcast listening was from Holy Trinity Brompton, Bill Johnson, Rob Bell, and Shane Claiborne.[20]

Central Chapel, true to its diverse nature, had participants involved across the evangelical spectrum. Significant numbers had been involved in the Christian Union movement and its associated conferences but also cited Soul Survivor, Momentum, Spring Harvest, and New Wine as significant in their faith. Some attended the Keswick convention, but they reported listening to both Johnson *and* Driscoll. Central Chapel emerging adults were genuinely eclectic in their evangelical theological input.

Although none of the texts under discussion made any reference to either the cross or hell (and the latter was mentioned only once in the focus groups) this context illustrates the tensions within contemporary evangelicalism about God's character and attitudes towards acts of judgement or

17. www.bssm.net. Accessed May 27, 2014.

18. www.newcalvinist.com. Accessed May 19, 2014; www.christianitytoday.com/ct/2014/october, Accessed 16 September 2016.

19. John MacArthur is a prolific preacher, writer and public figure for conservative evangelicalism in the United States. http://johnmacarthur.org. Accessed May 12, 2014.

20. Shane Claiborne is a social activist and writer. *The Irresistible Revolution* and *Red Letter Revolution*.

violence attributed to him. The conflicts of the last decade have framed, and are likely to have influenced, the understanding of God's nature developed by these emerging adults. They will therefore have shaped how they engaged with the narratives under discussion.

Historic Understandings of Divine Violence

The subject of divine violence has always been difficult for Christians. Seibert notes that the Chronicler made "minor adjustments in his version of events so that acts of evil were no longer attributed to God."[21] The church fathers produced a variety of interpretative strategies: Marcion rejected the Old Testament and its God entirely, while Origen and Gregory of Nyssa proposed typological or allegorical readings.[22] Cassian appealed to Paul's view that Israel's experiences were written for our instruction.[23] Irenaeus, however, "extolled the virtues of simple faith" and proposed that "there were many questions that should simply not be asked."[24] Following this trajectory, Calvin responded to God's instruction of annihilation in Joshua 10:8 with, "It would have been contrary to the feelings of humanity to exult in their ignominy, had God not so ordered it. But as such was his pleasure, it behoves us to acquiesce to his decision, without presuming to enquire why he was so severe."[25]

His plain sense reading called for an acceptance of such events as part of a humanly unintelligible yet divinely good higher purpose, and for many Protestants this became "the only kind of sound Christian voice."[26] Alternatively, "most of the traditions (academic and confessional) believe God to be good and limitless in power and knowledge. Therefore, any biblical story that implies otherwise must be either ignored or aggressively interpreted so as to force it to agree with more acceptable theological views."[27]

Scholars have adopted a wide range of models for interpreting such texts. Among the most recent of these are Penchansky, Moberly, and Seibert.[28] Volf distinguishes between the right of God to use violence and New

21. Seibert, *Disturbing Divine Behavior*, 54.

22. Ibid., 57–61.

23. Moberly, "Is Monotheism Bad for You?" 103.

24. Seibert, *Disturbing Divine Behavior*, 73.

25. Calvin, *Joshua*, 157–58.

26. Earl, *The Joshua Delusion*, 7.

27. Penchansky, *What Rough Beast*, 5.

28. Moberly, "Is Monotheism Bad for You?" 94–112; Seibert, *Disturbing Divine Behaviour*.

Testament insistence that his people may not.[29] He remarks that a just, loving God *must* get angry and that, "A 'nice' God is a figment of Liberal imagination, a project onto the sky of the inability to give up cherished illusions about goodness, freedom and the rationality of social actors."[30] He goes on to explain the importance of divine justice, including acts of violence, for those who have suffered.[31] However, despite such arguments, outside of academia, "People who read the narratives read them as they are, not as scholars or experts would like them to be read and interpreted. History is no longer with us. The narrative remains."[32] The interpretative strategies of ordinary readers are not usually widely informed by academic techniques, and they often struggle to reconcile the violent acts of an allegedly loving God. Seibert may well be right in describing contemporary Christians as behaving like "functional Marcionists" by ignoring difficult passages, but he also summarizes a series of interpretative strategies that are adopted by contemporary ordinary Christians.[33] These include:

- *Divine immunity* (God is always good and right because he is God, even if we cannot understand).

- *Just causation* (his violent acts are justly deserved punishments).

- *Greater good* (God's actions are legitimate because they are justifying a higher purpose).

- *Progressive revelation* (God used violence with primitive peoples but has gradually revealed his true nature as humanity became more sophisticated).

- *Permissive will* approach (God allows rather than causes bad things to happen, thus he is not culpable—other forces are).[34]

Some of these arguments were evident in the ordinary readings represented here but, interestingly, there are also echoes of earlier interpretative models.

---

29. Volf, *Exclusion and Embrace*, 301–3.

30. Ibid., 297.

31. Ibid.

32. Warrior, "A Native American Perspective," 290.

33. Seibert, *Divine Disturbing Behavior*, 67.

34. Ibid.,71–83.

Findings from Focus Groups

1. The Antagonists' Punishments

The death of Nabal in 1 Samuel 25 was discussed by all nine groups. For some there were no qualms; Nabal deserved the judgement he received. Others were extremely uncomfortable about God acting in this manner and raised extensive questions about it. Gehazi's leprosy in 2 Kings 5 was somewhat less contentious. Four of the groups considered it entirely fitting, three considered it harsh but recognized it as self-inflicted and only two groups were uncomfortable. The third protagonist to be struck by God was Herod in Acts 12. Here only one group expressed concern, eight considered this a fitting, even humorous, end.

Trinity Church

NABAL

The most noticeable pattern amongst the Trinity Church groups on the subject of God's violence towards the antagonists was that the older the group the less concerned they were. The younger group, who were newest to the church, wrestled at length with the idea of God killing.

> Simon: "Why did it take ten days for Nabal to die? Why didn't He [God] strike him straight away once she'd told him it was bad? I don't get that bit."

> Jenny: "I don't mean to be controversial, but if God, through the Holy Spirit could empower her [Abigail] to do all that, then why didn't he do the same for Nabal? God could have empowered Nabal to do it and saved the whole thing!"

Jenny, a new believer, repeatedly asked why it had been necessary for Nabal to die. She was not alone in this, and the group wrestled with possible answers for a considerable amount of time. One option was to distinguish between it being a divine or medical death (i.e., heart attack or stroke). This initially appeared to absolve God of responsibility but on examining the text it was accepted that God *had* done the killing—although perhaps as an act of mercy to put Nabal out of his misery after giving him time to repent. His failure to do so apparently justified his death. Others argued that Nabal had already "had his chance" and "paid him [David] with evil." God's actions were justified, since a rejection of David was a rejection of God himself. Jenny, however, responded, "That's one thing I find it quite difficult to get my head around, because God can choose. He can change us, there's no depth of sin God can't work on in your life, and change, and save you. So it just confuses me why he chooses some people and not others?"

She was wrestling with a question larger than Nabal's fate, questioning the doctrine of election. Despite their Reformed background, the group responded with confusion. Vague references to this being "in the Old Testament, pre-Jesus time" were made; others agreed, "Nabal never had the chance, but I guess we don't know!" Naomi argued, "I guess it all comes down to freewill, because we don't know the whole story. God gives free will so obviously he [Nabal] might have chosen not to follow Him or something."

This is moving away from the immutability of God and echoing free-will theism, such as that propounded by Wesley or C. S. Lewis, more than classical Calvinism.[35] The confusion is interesting because, although it was driven by the questions of a new believer, a group of established Reformed emerging adults were unable to give her a satisfactory response. Ultimately, the conversation moved on to God's striking of Ananias and Saphira in Acts 5, Simon adding, "He's still pretty brutal in the New Testament!" He concluded, "It's still the same God, he's not changed his mind or anything. Jesus has come and his love is expressed a lot more, but it's still if you reject God you're still ultimately going to die . . . and Nabal basically rejects him. I think, in a way it's showing if you reject Jesus you will die."

The conversation moved from the death of an individual to penal substitutionary atonement. To reject David was to reject not only God but also Jesus, and rejection of Jesus had one outcome—death. This was no longer an episode in the rise of the Davidic kingdom but a warning of the consequences of rejecting the gospel. This mirrors some aspects of the typological readings proposed by Origen. Although the entire narrative is not spiritualized, at one level Nabal is. He represents the unrepentant sinner and functions as a warning.[36] It is interesting that this pre-reformation interpretation appears to fit comfortably within a Reformed evangelical framework. It might have been expected that the groups would adopt a Calvinist plain sense reading but in negotiating this issue, they accessed other interpretative resources. The group seemed content to conclude their conversation with this analogy. They had not resolved all their questions, but concluding the conversation with Jesus appeared to be a satisfactory response.

The mid-aged group also had an extensive discussion around Nabal's demise. There was initial confusion about why God should have acted in this way given that it was David who was insulted. They explained this in

35. Sanders, "Divine Suffering," 115.
36. Moberly, "Is Monotheism Bad for You?" 103.

two ways: firstly, by exploring the idea of humans trusting God to bring justice rather than avenging themselves. Similar to Volf, they were clear that David's violent response was not a model for humans to follow but that God could be trusted to bring about justice on behalf of his people.[37] Their second method of resolution was deciding that David represented the line of Christ and thus it was actually Jesus who was being rejected. James articulated, "You're either with David—you're on God's side or you're against. There's no middle ground, in the same way, sort of, the gospel is you believe or you don't."

As with the younger group, the narrative was read as a metaphor for Christian conversion. Nabal was positioned with unbelievers and thus deserving of his fate. However, the group did have some qualms about God's violence and posited a number of alternative readings. They speculated at a medical diagnosis for Nabal's heart failing and explored cultural taboos or Jewish laws that he might have broken in refusing hospitality to David. This, they suggested, legitimized God's actions. They also suggested that, "He's a wicked man and maybe he doesn't deserve redemption?" This is an interesting statement given that they understood the narrative as pre-empting the gospel. Since a traditional understanding of the gospel is that undeserved forgiveness is available to all, that Nabal should be excluded as "undeserving" seems incongruous. It suggests at some level, even if it is unconscious, a misunderstanding of grace and a framework that suggests good people deserve God's mercy and bad people his judgement.

A final justification for God's action included his averting a massacre of Nabal's household, that Nabal's death was the lesser of two evils (a greater good approach).[38] This received some support but was questioned. Sophie asked, "But God does allow this to happen in the Old Testament doesn't he? When they're going into new territory, and its people that don't believe in God, he asks them to wipe out whole cities doesn't he? One might argue in that case young children . . . young babies who don't know anything about God . . . I often struggle with that thing . . . ."

In referring to instructions to annihilate the indigenous peoples of Palestine in Joshua 20:13, Sophie's dilemma was left unresolved, as was the suggestion of Nabal's death being the alternative to whole-scale bloodletting. The group were uncertain but, as with the younger group, resolved the tension by concluding that Nabal's actions were like all those who reject Jesus and thus his death was the inevitable outcome of siding against God, who was perfectly entitled to pass such a judgement.

37. Volf, *Exclusion and Embrace*, 301–3.

38. Seibert, *Disturbing Divine Behaviour*, 77.

The oldest Trinity group were least conflicted about Nabal's demise. Initially there was some speculation as to why, when he so often used humans to bring about his judgement, on this occasion he prevented David from doing so. This was understood to be part of a learning point for David to trust God for justice. They had no qualms about whether Nabal deserved death.

> Suzi: "Nabal's holding a banquet like a king. So you see Nabal's heart and he's rejected God as king and put himself in that place. [His death] is the Lord saying "No!" He's obviously thinking 'Look at me, I've got away with this!'"

> Charles: "And the good thing at the end [is that] justice is done. So David wanted to take justice into his own hands and God prevented him through Abigail. But that didn't mean justice wasn't done. God did it!"

Although they too speculated about a medical condition, they ultimately viewed Nabal's death as an appropriate punishment for his physical and spiritual actions. He rejected David's request for hospitality and rejected God in doing so.

GEHAZI AND HEROD

With regard to the other antagonists, Gehazi received unquestioned hostility. His leprosy was entirely deserved as far as the Trinity groups were concerned. The younger group stated, "Yeah, Gehazi knew exactly what he was doing, that it was wrong." The mid-aged group were equally unsympathetic, although they recognized the severity of the punishment. Joss, a member of the older group stated, "I mean, how stupid is Gehazi? Even though he's just seen this whole thing happen. He knows who Elisha is, knows he's just cured this man, all this power from the Lord and yet he thinks he can hide something like that?" They saw his crime as "robbing a brand new believer." No one questioned his receiving leprosy; they considered it an appropriate punishment, given the severity of his crime.

Similarly with Herod, the older group raised no concerns, certain that a human accepting worship was something God would not tolerate. The mid-aged group concurred, "As if we need a sort of explanation for why Herod deserved to die!" They were mildly perplexed that his accepting of worship rather than his execution of believers was the final cause of his judgement, but they had no concerns that God should strike him down. The youngest group recognized that his death "sounds horrible!" and there was some concern that God might have tortured rather than just executed him, but this was not a major problem; Herod was an enemy of the gospel and, in a power struggle with God, was inevitably going to lose.

Central Chapel

As Ken had suspected, the response of the Central Chapel groups to God's acts of violence were diverse. The older group's responses demonstrated a conservative and relatively relaxed position. The mid-aged group expressed concern in some narratives and ignored it in others, while the younger group, who spent 37 percent of their time on the subject, presented diverse opinions; it being the sole point of discussion on 1 Samuel 25 yet virtually ignored in the other two texts.

Nabal

The primary query of the older group was whether David's response had been justified or not? Their interest was in the cultural norms of hospitality and Nabal's crime in violating them, and their concern was primarily at David's seemingly disproportionate threat to slaughter Nabal's entire house-hold. They repeatedly stated, "God provided a way out" for David, adding, "God deals with it himself," "God stepped in and struck Nabal," "It's God's place to take vengeance," going so far as, "And they all live happily ever after . . . ish!" God's actions raised no ethical concerns at all.

The mid-aged group's discussion primarily focussed on whether Nabal's death was the result of a medical condition.

> Mary: "It's hard isn't it? Especially with the Old Testament be-cause so many things are attributed to God, its like 'God made this happen' and 'God made that happen,' but actually in that culture so many things are attributed to the will of God. It's hard to know if there was actually a supernatural occurrence, where clearly a man was struck down by God visibly or if a natural cause happened?"

Notwithstanding Mary's dualistic understanding of something either being caused by God *or* being natural, this statement is interesting in that she is questioning the author's interpretation of events. It reflects a wider uncertainty as to whether God would do such a thing or whether this is a primitive misinterpretation. The group discussed Nabal's crimes at length, making it clear that they considered his judgement deserved. However, there were some notes of uncertainty. Alan could see that God was teaching David a lesson in self-control but stated, "I don't understand God's will towards Nabal. I mean God strikes down Nabal, in the end, God takes his life." He clearly felt concerned that perhaps Nabal, for all his crimes, had been harshly treated. Charles added, "There are passages, really difficult passages, especially in the book of Joshua, like God just wiped people out! And it's sometimes maybe judgment is what a whole household deserves. But God is saying in a way that there's justice and there's also grace."

He cited alleged "genocide" texts of Joshua 10–11 but was unwilling to doubt God's motives and proposed a Just Cause approach, assuming that even though it is not apparent why, those groups must have deserved such action. He concluded by distinguishing the justice of Nabal's death from the mercy of God's protection on his household. This group recognized the theological difficulty but, as Ken suspected, were willing to give God the benefit of the doubt.

For the youngest Central Chapel group, the question of Nabal's death was the first point raised, and the allocated time was almost entirely devoted to trying to make sense of it:

Joel commented, "Well, the bit about Nabal getting killed, err . . . dying, getting stricken down, just struck me as an example of where God shows his justice and his plan in quite sort of . . . severe . . . blatant way that we don't often look at."

Joel's language shows his inner conflict. "Getting killed" is altered to "dying" and then rephrased as "stricken down," suggesting that he is even uncertain what vocabulary to use. He was uncomfortable with God's action describing it as "severe" but could not avoid the fact that the text was explicit about it. He also noted this as a subject Christians often avoid.[39] Other conflicted language such as "the killing thing" was used. Various strategies were adopted to try to resolve the tension of God acting violently, which was described as "quite alien to us." One option was to assign such actions exclusively to the Old Testament, although this was refuted; speculation about Ananias and Sapphira in Acts 5 raised a New Testament example of God's violent judgement. Joel asked, "It's interesting how some people get struck down and some don't even though we're all just as bad as each other. I suppose you wonder why? And I don't know. Does anyone else know?" Jackie responded by challenging his right to question God's actions:

> It's funny that we ask "why?" every time God seems to strike
> people down or punish them. We're like "Why does he do that?"
> Should we ask why he does it? I mean it's good to question men's

39. Seibert, *Disturbing Divine Behaviour*, 67.

teaching but if God is high and mighty above all then he does it because he does it, and it was the right thing to do. And our little minds don't have to always understand it—because we have little minds.

This articulates Calvin's arguments almost word for word: finite humans cannot understand and should not challenge the reasoning of a supreme God.[40] Joel went on to postulate that it was a sign of God's grace that he didn't kill everyone immediately. "Just the very act of allowing us to continue living is an act of grace that we don't deserve. I suppose if God wants to strike someone down to show us that we shouldn't lie, it's his call."

It is interesting that their conversation had moved away from the particular instance of Nabal and had become about all human sin. The use of "we" peppered the conversation, with the group identifying themselves as guilty of God's judgment but living under his grace. This appears to illustrate a particular trait of contemporary emerging adults: a rejection of judgementalism.[41] Guest suggests that contemporary pluralism and emphasis on tolerance have affected the attitudes of emerging adults, and here Joel is illustrating this tolerance, emphasizing that he, and the group, have no right to consider themselves superior to "sinners."[42]

Questions about free will and Nabal's culpability were also part of the conversation. Jimmy identified examples of "God hardening people's hearts" but wondered if he ever "softened them." A confused explanation about law and grace in both Testaments was attempted and there were some vague comments about faith in Jesus saving those in the Old Testament. However, ultimately these questions were left unresolved. As with the Trinity groups, this group presented Jesus, and penal substitution as the answer to their concerns about God's violence. Nabal's rejection of David was seen as synonymous with a lack of faith in God and thus a rejection of Jesus, which marked him out for judgement. Others, like Abigail, had placed their faith in God and his anointed and had been included in the forgiveness offered by Christ's death. Once again, the narrative was given spiritual meaning and a messianic theme.

40. Earl, *The Joshua Delusion*, 7.

41. Savage, *Generation Y*, 7.

42. Guest, *University Experience*, 98.

GEHAZI AND HEROD

With regard to the other antagonists, discussions were more uniform. Gehazi was barely discussed by the older group beyond, "He should have known" not to disobey Elisha. The younger group were entirely disparaging, accusing him of "wanting glory for himself," misrepresenting both God and Elisha, and concluded, "It's a really horrible thing Gehazi does." They considered his punishment a fitting end for someone who had exploited Naaman's new faith. The mid-age group had some concerns, but they read it as a story of how his selfishness and greed caused him to lose his faith. They were particularly concerned that "ultimately Gehazi was almost corrupting the message of grace because he was demanding some kind of payment." They also attempted to minimise the seriousness of leprosy, suggesting that "the actual psychological effect of leprosy is far worse than the physical one." They based this on their understanding that the main effects were social isolation and exclusion from the temple, a "separation from the presence of God." This may be a naïve understanding of the seriousness of the disease, but the group felt Gehazi deserved divine judgment.

Likewise, Herod's demise was considered by Central Chapel groups to be an appropriate act of judgement. The mid-aged group ignored it entirely, while the younger and older groups felt it was a fitting ending to an arrogant ruler who lost a power struggle with God. They identified his death as humiliating and appropriate given his acceptance of worship. The older group's only qualm was over why God had not acted sooner and saved the Apostle James. Overall, the group agreed that a grisly, public execution by the angel of the Lord would have been a salutary warning to those watching not to oppress God's people. It was an act of violence not only to bring about justice but also for the greater good.

New Life

New Life discussions were distinctly different from those of the other two churches. Rather than decreasing with age, the amount of conversation increased. The greatest proportion of their time was spent on the subject and, rather than showing the diversity of the other churches, they were unified in their discussions. As Sarah had anticipated, they were highly distressed by divine violence and struggled to reconcile these episodes with the God they worshipped.

Nabal

All three New Life groups were disturbed by God striking down Nabal. The oldest group discussed,

> Jason: "I assume that these days not many people would pray 'strike down my enemy!' That's pretty much what God did and wanted. It's not an element of God one expects these days."

> Josie: "It's one of those passages isn't it, where it's hard to reconcile the God we know, of mercy and love and that kind of stuff, with a God who's like, 'He was a bit rude to you so I'll kill him!' that's what it looks like on the face of it!"

Similarly, the mid-aged group considered it extreme. Marcus commented, "I still find it hard when it says stuff like 'The Lord struck Nabal and he died.' I've been looking for God showing love. Because God doesn't want to kill people—it's a last resort thing."

The younger group were concerned but concluded that Nabal's death was an act of mercy not judgement. Nadine stated, "I find it really hard to see whether this is something that he was supposed to die, that God wanted him to die or whether it's pity? God struck him out of pity; that he was a stone, in and pain and withering." The others agreed that Nabal had probably had some sort of medical episode and that whether he had had a stroke, heart attack or was in a coma, God's killing him ten days later was an act of kindness. The other two groups used a similar strategy in an attempt to remove hostility from God's action. The mid-aged group suggested that he was a "big drinker," not "the healthiest guy in the world" and that his death was the result of a hedonistic lifestyle. One referred to his alternate Bible translation, which confirmed this interpretation:

> Thomas: "So my version here, in the Good News Version says, "Then after he had completely sobered up she told him everything, he suffered a stroke and was completely paralysed. Some ten days later the Lord struck Nabal and he died."

> Mandy: "Oh, like a stone—that makes sense! He literally shocked himself to death!"

There was considerable relief that God could be absolved of violence and the death be attributed to his mercy. However, Marcus did return to the text remarking, "I certainly think God kills people though, but as much as he had a stroke and that is probably what killed him, it still says the Lord struck Nabal and he died. Why does it have to say that? Why can't it just say 'He had a stroke and ten days later he died'?" He wanted to allow the text to have authority rather than their comforting interpretation; however, he also resorted to questioning the passage itself: "I'm almost thinking the version's been changed from what it originally said or something? Maybe an extra word there that made it make more sense or something?"

This tension between wanting to accept the text at face value and speculating that it might be in error presents an interesting interpretative strategy. Clearly, Marcus was aware of textual issues and used them as a way of reducing the authority of a difficult passage in order to absolve God. He went on to demonstrate a permissive-will approach, distinguishing between God killing and God allowing someone to die.[43] The sense of internal conflict was however evident in rationales given by all three groups.

The older group's discussion extended to the theme of God using warfare to bring about his will in other Old Testament narratives. One participant described her frustration that a senior figure in the church had been unable to answer her questions on the subject. Josie reasoned that violence was legitimate in such situations. "I know that was a thing at that time. You had to kill absolutely everybody otherwise they would come back later, so it was. . . . I'm struggling to remember the details, . . . but I think it was almost a thing of mercy. Like killing everyone so they were all wiped out then it wasn't kind of leaving them."

She was uncertain of her argument that annihilation was preferable to leaving women and children vulnerable, and the others did not respond with any sort of affirmation. The group appeared to accept that God killed, or instructed killing, since it was in Scripture, but they were uncertain about it, and their discussion contained a number of extended periods of silence, as they appeared not to know what to say.

Some individuals did speculate about Nabal's death being a punishment:

> Nadine: "I find it really easy to read 'Oh God's punishing people, God wants people to die in the Old Testament but not in the New [Testament].' It's not something that God does. It's taught in church that God is not punishing, that's not what God is about. So it's really weird to hear anything like that. But it's easier to hear when we're thinking Old Testament."

Nadine was overt in articulating a dichotomous view of the two biblical Testaments, although she recognized the incongruity in this. What is most interesting is her sense that the God who approves of human death as punishment is not presented in the church settings she has experienced.

43. Seibert, *Disturbing Divine Behavior*, 83.

Indeed, on attending New Life services this complication became evident to the researcher.[44] However, it seems unlikely that Nadine's confusion is entirely the result of New Life teaching. Although their emphasis on demonstrating God's mercy and love is in play here, so presumably is the teaching of other theological influences Nadine has been exposed to—many of which appear to emphasize God as benevolent.

Gehazi & Herod

The New Life concerns extended, to a lesser extent, to Gehazi. The younger group considered leprosy as "a pretty hard deal" although self-inflicted, but the two older groups were both concerned that this was an unfair judgement. Although some group members were prepared to argue that Gehazi had undermined the principle of grace, and that this was a serious crime, others struggled to accept that God might cause disease. One removed culpability from God by suggesting Elisha had abused his power in pronouncing the curse. Another defended Gehazi, arguing that it was hard to know when it might be appropriate to take financial reward for acts of ministry.

Herod's death was less confusing. It was evident to the two younger groups that his crimes were significant and he was deserving of judgement. The mid-aged group asserted, "I'm sure Herod deserved it" but also speculated that it was a medical condition that caused his death. The younger group found Herod's death amusing but were uncertain "what it means to be struck by the Lord." Ultimately, they viewed him as "a kind of hindering block" to the gospel and saw the public nature of his demise as significant in God showing his authority.

Comparisons and Conclusions on the Antagonist's Punishments

Overall then, the Trinity Church groups presented a mixture of responses to divine violence inflicted upon the antagonists. As Will had anticipated they were largely unconcerned about Gehazi and Herod, seeing their punishments as justified. Nabal's fate was more complex, partly because they were uncertain as to why his actions were so reprehensible. The youngest group, including a new believer, were most concerned, raising questions about predestination and free will. Although they attempted to wrestle with

---

44. As reported in chapter 3, a preacher responded to 1 Samuel 18:10 stating "God is good, He doesn't do anything evil. He didn't do this." She did not explain why the text might report such an untruth or what an alternative understanding might be. She simply dismissed it as not fitting with her understanding of God.

them they found few answers and ultimately concluded that Nabal was the equivalent of an unbeliever who rejected the gospel of Jesus. They did not discuss the fate of such individuals. This may be the result of a strong theology of election, although this was not postulated in any of the discussions. Alternatively, it may be a subject too contentious for this context, with the group unwilling to engage in a conversation about the post-mortem fate of unbelievers. As a strongly conversionist community, Trinity Church puts considerable time, effort, and resources into proselytization and exhorts its members to do the same. It seems unlikely that these groups were unconcerned about the fate of "the lost" or lacked compassion for the future of their non-believing friends and family. Instead, the response seemed to function as a form of theological "full stop," which tied up the conversation and allowed them to conclude on a point of agreement. It appears that age made a difference: the older the group the less it troubled them. This may be the result of ongoing education within a Reformed tradition; those who have been part of it for longer have accepted teachings on God's judgement and predestination. It seems likely that those who had found Reformed teachings unpalatable had left the church and thus were not represented in the older groups. Alternatively, it may be that those who have continued to follow this particular evangelical tradition have, over the period of their twenties, resolved their difficulties with such issues and no longer feel the need to raise them. Either way, the older group appeared to have no doubts that God did use violence, that it was used for reasons of justice and that this could be trusted as fair. The mid-aged group added that humans should not emulate such behaviour; vengeance belonged to God alone.

Central Chapel discussions on God's violence were mixed, as Ken had anticipated. Both Gehazi and Herod were seen as deserving of their fate and few qualms were raised about God bringing disease or death. It would appear that when they perceived an individual's crimes as serious enough, groups accepted violent divine judgement. However, uncertainty about the seriousness of a crime caused a different response, thus Nabal's demise was more complicated. The older group were unconcerned, seeing it as just. The mid-aged group voiced concerns but concluded that God's violence could be trusted as appropriate. The younger group were highly confused. Various avenues were explored (unsuccessfully) to resolve this, and ultimately they concluded that all humanity (themselves included) deserved judgement and that only faith in Christ and God's mercy prevented that violence from being seen more often. All the groups understood divine violence as real and justified but, once again, the older they were the less concern they demonstrated. It would appear that this is a serious issue for younger evangelicals but, as they grow up into the tradition, violence attributed to

God becomes something they reconcile with their understanding of him as loving and just.

Although the New Life groups demonstrated considerably more concern about the violent actions of God than groups from the other churches had, and adopted a variety of mechanisms to absolve God of responsibility, it is interesting to note that, at some levels, they had similar internal processes for judging these acts. Essentially, it depended on whether they considered an individual's crimes as deserving of judgement or not. Herod's actions they condemned, thus God's violence towards him was justified. Gehazi's crimes were more serious, his punishment was less severe and so although they were concerned they were far less so than in the case of Nabal. His crimes were, to their minds, negligible and not deserving of death. They did not resolve this tension by identifying David with Christ and seeing Nabal as an unrepentant non-believer. Rather, New Life groups read this as a story of interpersonal conflict in which God apparently took a side and acted in an extreme manner. They could not reconcile this with God, as they understood Him, and so attempted (largely unsuccessfully) to resolve this.

It would appear that the more progressive forms of evangelicalism to which they have been exposed had not equipped them for dealing with these texts. An emphasis on love and mercy had made God's judgement and anger unacceptable in all but what they understood to be the worst cases of human sin. Sarah's reflections on this were twofold. One was the effect of New Life's propensity to describe God as an accepting father but the second was the influence of Bill Johnson's teaching; an adoption of the idea, "God is always in a good mood."[45] She did not entirely endorse this and had attempted to address it informally with members of the congregation. However, she speculated that an emphasis on God's desire to bless, emphasized by Johnson, had created a particular framework amongst the congregation for understanding the nature of God.

2. The Innocents' Suffering

The second category of individuals in the texts who were indirect recipients of divine violence were Peter's guards (who were executed after his escape) and the descendants of Gehazi (who inherited his curse). These groups differ from the antagonists because their actions do not make them culpable for any violence, divine or otherwise. It might legitimately be argued that the focus of the text is not on these individuals, that they provide background detail to a bigger narrative. However, many of the groups focussed on them

45. www.ibethel.org. Accessed February 2, 2014.

and showed concern for their suffering. The variety of responses largely followed the trend of attitudes towards violence against the antagonists.

Trinity Church

The Trinity Church groups were predominantly unconcerned about the suffering of "innocent" characters. The mid-aged and older groups made no reference to the death of Peter's guards, while the youngest group attributed this to the crimes of Herod. Likewise, the younger and eldest group ignored the leprous fate of Gehazi's descendants. The mid-aged group did distinguish Gehazi's punishment from the consequences on his descendants, briefly describing it as "harsh" but simply Gehazi's fault. Although they had been concerned that God should protect the innocents of Nabal's household, the fate of these innocents was not of interest to them.

These responses tie in with other reactions of the Trinity groups to the texts. Firstly, they focussed on the primary characters in the narrative; minor characters were of little interest. Secondly, they expressed that those who oppose the gospel (such as Peter's Roman guards) will experience the negative consequences of that, and, thirdly, that God's violence is largely accepted as justifiable.

Central Chapel

The Central Chapel groups showed marginally more concern about the fate of these characters. The two younger groups ignored the execution of Peter's guards, although the older group compared them with the Philippian jailer in Acts 16, considering them "unlucky." With regard to Gehazi's descendants, the younger and older groups ignored their suffering but the mid-aged group were concerned. Scott stated, "His descendants would be leprous forever. I always really struggle with such things. 'And so your entire household and all your descendants will be cursed' and I'm like, 'Hang on a minute!'"

Various members of the group speculated that Gehazi's crime of "corrupting the message of grace" was sufficiently severe to deserve this, explaining, "He could have ruined everything" (by which they meant God's salvation plan for humanity). Others tried to minimise the seriousness of leprosy as a disease, implying that the severity of the curse was minimal. Scott was not convinced, and Alan agreed. "It's really hard to understand why God made all his descendants lepers forever. Are Gehazi's descendants still around? Are they still under this [curse]? It's really hard to get your head around." He went on to expound the sinfulness of all humans, including himself but concluded that,

> We need to reflect on how serious our actions and our wrong doings are, so like our actions and our wrongdoings led to Jesus going to the cross. So what Gehazi did—the punishment may seem bigger than the sin but what we've learnt from the New Testament is that sin is sin and that every sin we commit leads to Jesus dying. But everybody is under the original curse from Adam and Eve, . . . but all the curses of God upon people go back to the cross.

Rather than address this specific curse of leprosy, Alan invoked a governing meta-narrative by extending God's justified anger at sin across all humanity. Even though God's response might seem disproportionate, Alan asserted that it was not. He asserted instead that sin is more serious than we understand and thus deserves punishment. He concluded that the crucifixion had broken all the curses anyway. Once again, penal substitution was a sufficient concluding response; human depravity was dealt with through Christ's death.

New Life

New Life groups showed most concern for the fate of the "innocent" characters. Given their struggles with judgement on the antagonists, concern for those who appeared to be collateral damage was not surprising. Although the youngest group ignored the fate of Peter's guards, the oldest group expressed sympathy:

> Paul: "It's the first time it jumped out to me that the two guards were executed. It struck me. Poor guys. You think they did what they were asked to do and . . ."
>
> Carla: "But Herod's never going to believe they just . . ."
>
> Paul: "Oh yeah, yeah, I totally see the consequences of it but if the angels turn up and save Peter and these two guards now get executed, and they're completely oblivious . . ."

They were convinced the blame lay squarely with Herod but recognized that God's actions provoked this response. The mid-aged group also had concerns, comparing them to the Philippian jailer in Acts 16. Marcus asked, "Yeah, but he [God] saved that guard. So it's like why do these guys not deserve it but that guard did? I struggled with that. I'm pretty sure God knew what was going to happen to them but he allowed it to happen still. He didn't save them. He could have transported them out of jail to some random place and they're like 'Where are we?' but they're safe."

Marcus' confusion seems to stem from his perception that God is showing favouritism. He speculates that God could have performed a miracle of divine teleportation similar to events in Acts 8, yet chose not to, condemning the guards to inevitable execution. Another participant suggested that perhaps the guards were already Christians, and thus death was not the end for them, but the group was sceptical. Finally, with regard to Gehazi's descendants, all the groups were extremely concerned at what they perceived as unfair judgement: a curse based on ancestral, not personal, culpability. Linda commented, "I really struggle with 'Leprosy will cling to you and your descendants' or whatever. When there's other places in the Bible where it says 'And your descendants' I'm like 'Harsh!' but then I guess your actions don't just affect you. But I . . . that is something I just can't get my head around." The older group also discussed this:

> Carla: "I don't like the bit where it says 'Your descendants for ever' it's a bit harsh! Like you said, do his descendants still have it now? There's still leprosy in the world isn't there?"
>
> Kat: "Well he [Gehazi] was trying to cheat ultimately."
>
> Carla: "Yeah, I get that, I just don't get why he [God] needed to . . . or is that just an exaggeration when he says 'And to your descendants forever.' Does he literally mean that or is it just an exaggeration or a thing they said?"

The groups rehearsed various options to resolve this apparent inequality. Since they understood leprosy to be contagious by touch, perhaps it was inevitable that the disease would be passed on. Another medical explanation was that the illness was a hereditary or genetic problem explained as a divine judgement. Mandy speculated, "In which case, when he says 'It will cling to you and your descendant forever' it's not that 'I'm going to curse each of your descendants individually and it's your fault [but rather,] You have leprosy therefore any descendants you have are going to have leprosy because it's hereditary.'"

This seemed comforting to the mid-aged group; however, the younger group were not convinced by the same explanation. The older group attempted to put the phrase "descendants forever" into literary and cultural context by referring to a study Bible.

Kat: "There's something about, in the Old Testament, about three generations. So it might have been the three generation thing?"

Carla: "This says that when Elisha said that he's referring to something about the Ten Commandments about to the third and fourth generation. Oh, that's interesting. It says he will punish to the third or fourth generation but show love to a thousand generations if they still love me. Because a lot of number stuff isn't literal is it?"

The group appeared relieved that the curse would be limited in duration and were mollified by understanding it as a figure of speech. God was judging, but his severity was limited.

One final rationale was linked to their charismatic spirituality. An individual in the younger group, from a Pentecostal tradition, was familiar with the terminology of generational cursing. He speculated that the severity of Gehazi's crime was such that God's judgment needed to be on more than him as an individual. The idea of contemporary cursing also resonated with individuals in the mid-aged group. They concluded that all curses were voided with the new covenant of Jesus. Elsa articulated her belief that the breaking of curses is not an inevitability but rather part of the blessing believers can receive; multiple generations need no longer be subject to cursing or spiritual oppression brought on by the actions of their ancestors.

Summary of Attitudes to the Innocents' Suffering

Overall, Trinity and Central Chapel groups showed little interest in these characters—the mid-aged group at Central Chapel being an anomaly. However, the New Life groups showed considerable concern about the indirect consequences of divine violence. They paid particular attention to the wellbeing of minor characters. This appears, in some way, to be an unconscious form of resistant reading. Rather than focussing on the main characters, whom the author emphasizes, they are concerned with incidental figures caught up in the events. They were concerned that God might be showing favouritism and neglecting the wellbeing of minor innocent parties. This democratic reading was not unique to them but was a consistent priority; little people mattered a great deal. Their individualism was also clear: people should receive the consequences of their own actions, not be culpable for someone else's. However, no one was willing to overtly attack or criticize the character of God. Confusion and concerns were often articulated with the phrase, "I really struggle with," suggesting the tension between their understanding of the nature of God and the evidence of the biblical text. They were not willing to reject the text; instead they speculated, discussed and looked to extra-biblical resources for answers that would allow them to maintain their image of a benevolent, merciful deity. The New Life groups clearly felt able to question and were open and honest about their difficulties with the texts but often, ultimately, left them unresolved.

3. The Believer's Death

The death of the Apostle James in Acts 12:1 is described in contrast to the rescue of Peter. The text gives minimal attention to it, presenting it as background information for the escape narrative. It was, however, of considerable interest to two thirds of the groups.

Central Chapel

Although the youngest group ignored it, the older two Central Chapel groups had difficulty understanding why God might choose to rescue Peter but not James. Mary commented, "For me it raises the age old question, why did one person survive and one die? Why is one healed and one not? Why do we see God's miracle in one person's life and not in our lives?" None of the group had answers; they left this unresolved. The older group raised the same question and rejected a simplistic understanding of Peter as favoured although they had no immediate answer. They concluded,

> Catherine: "I think the answer is we don't know why God did that."
>
> Helen: "Yeah, these are wider questions. The church is being persecuted and some people are spared of that and some people take the hit."
>
> Catherine: "God is still in control."
>
> Helen: "He doesn't promise us an easy ride [that] life's going to be fine."

Persecution was not a sign of negligence on God's part. They understood it to be something believers, both then and now, might experience. Even though they did not understand his actions, they reaffirmed their certainty that God was still ultimately in control.

Miranda: "I guess don't give up on . . . you might feel like you're in an impossible situation and that there is no way out, but don't give up because God can always find a way. If it's in his plan then he'll always find a way and you should trust him 'till . . . well, always trust him. I was going to say until the end but the end is really the beginning isn't it?"

Miranda's certainty that God can resolve any situation is tempered by the qualification, "If it's in his plan," which presumably might include suffering and death. This she rehabilitated by asserting her belief in the resurrection of Christians. Thus martyrdom is not a tragedy but rather the beginning of a new existence without pain and suffering. This comment was met with silence—atypical for the group. Although this was a somewhat comforting resolution, the group treated it with a serious, reverent attitude.

New Life

All the New Life groups made a point of discussing James's martyrdom and had a clear understanding of why God allowed him to be executed.

Leon: "James has done everything that God needed him to do so he could just die."

Thomas: "Yeah, because that's the ultimate gift really. It seems like quite a nice death—struck with the sword. It sounds better than worms and crucifixion! Yeah, God was probably like 'You've done everything, your plans have been fulfilled.'"

Nadine: "Yeah, I think God was OK with that."

Betty: "I think it might have been OK with James too."

This discussion was rehearsed in both the other groups. Essentially, James had completed his tasks for God's kingdom and was rewarded with a fast track to glory via a humane death. Peter, by contrast, still had responsibilities and was rescued. This is a somewhat romantic reading of the brutalization of the early Christians and resonates with Hopewell's model of charismatic spirituality.[46]

Thomas was not alone in speculating that this was a merciful death. Other groups postulated that eventually all twelve of the disciples became martyrs, thus James was simply the first and Peter's reprieve was only temporary. Others speculated that "James was destined to be a martyr." They

46. Hopewell, *Congregation,* 59.

noted that "Jesus had warned [about] the coming suffering; death by the sword." Persecution they understood as prophesied and to be expected, thus, although this was a difficult experience, it was not a disaster and certainly did not suggest that God's plans had gone awry.

> Marcus: "I don't think God favours anyone. I don't think he favours Peter more than James but I think there's also a time to come back into the Kingdom for each of us, and God has a plan for that. It's not always a bad thing, like going up to Him. We see death as the worst thing, but I think what we all want is to get to heaven one day."

> Mandy: "I agree with Marcus. We tend to think that death is the worst possible thing that can happen to a person but it reminded me of what Paul says that 'To live is Christ and to die is gain. While I live I'm useful to God which is brilliant and when I die I get to go and be with God, which is brilliant.' I don't know if James had this perspective but after hanging round with Jesus I can't imagine that he was too far from it!"

Mandy here cites Philippians 1:21, the response of the Apostle Paul to persecution, but all the groups held a strongly eschatological perspective on human life. Its purpose is to serve God and then, task complete, to be with him in heaven. Although they recognized a fear of death as innate in human beings, they also articulated that faith gave one a different perspective on both life and death. Thus, James dying as a believer, even at the hands of a tyrant, was not a disaster but a victory.

There was, however, concern with this perspective. One mid-aged participant, Felicity, speculated that perhaps if the church had prayed harder God might have rescued James too. This was at odds with the majority, but again illustrates open theism: human behaviour influencing God's actions.[47] She also rejected that it was God's desire for James to die. "I don't read that and say 'He died because it was the plan for him to,' because I don't necessarily think that was the heart of God. But we're certainly on this earth for a fairly short time. I don't know." She was more inclined to understand James' death as a victory for Satan due to the negligence of the church in prayer. She did accept that there was an eternal destiny for James and that either way this was not a disaster, but she was unwilling to attribute the death of the Apostle to God's plans. She concluded, "That doesn't mean the grief doesn't happen, mourning doesn't happen. It does—it's the most horrific

---

47. Sanders, *Divine Suffering*, 112.

thing, but if you zoom out it's part of an extraordinary big picture and it's not all plan A."

Felicity was one of the few members of New Life who articulated the suffering endured by those under persecution. Her throw away comment, "It's not all plan A," suggests that she holds a position of weak immutability.[48] Ultimately, God will be victorious, but along the way, because of his partnership with flawed humans and the evil forces at work, battles are lost as well as won. However, hers was a lone voice in an otherwise somewhat triumphalist reading of the text.

Despite a few minor concerns, New Life groups articulated a real confidence that the death of a believer was not a tragedy. God's plans for each would be fulfilled and even James's death was ultimately under God's control and God had fast-tracked him to glory. This demonstrates an interesting mixture of attitudes towards God's sovereignty. There are elements of classical theism (God's plans are established and immutable) but also elements of open theism (human actions are genuinely free and significant). The New Life groups leant towards open theism in terms of the significance of believers (including themselves), but fell back on the comforting idea that God had their lives and futures preordained.

Trinity Church

As Will had anticipated, the mid and older Trinity Church groups did not discuss the martyrdom of James. It is difficult to speculate on the significance of this but they were groups who spent least time discussing the wider theme of God's violence. Perhaps, since they understood God as just and sovereign whomever he allows to live and die, he is simply to be trusted. Alternatively, it may be the case that, for a community where a small child recently passed away, the issues of a believer dying are too raw and the groups avoided them. However, the youngest group processed the death of James in an interesting manner. Simon speculated, "James's work is done? What the Lord wants him to do has been done? 'Right you've done what I asked you to do. Come and be in glory with me.' That's where we'd all rather be [isn't it?] Whereas Peter still had work to do for the Lord. The Lord still had a plan for him?" The framing of this response as series of questions highlights Simon's hesitancy and contrasts with the certainty of similar sentiments held by New Life groups. It was affirmed by Naomi who added, "I think that God has plans for everyone. And no two people's plans are the same." Other suggestions included James' death inspiring faith in others. Simon

---

48. Sanders, *Divine Suffering*, 116.

commented, "James would obviously become a martyr, so he's showing that it's [the gospel] worth dying for. By James dying he shows he's willing to die for it so it has to be taken seriously. Because you're not going to die for something that's false are you? So if one of the pillars of the church is willing to die for what he's saying, I think it adds an element of validity to it."

He is making the assumption (as did the New Life groups) that James had some sort of choice about his execution. Presumably they believed he was given the chance to renounce Christ or face execution, something the text does not specify. But, once again, James is cast as a hero rather than a victim, and triumph is salvaged from his murder. The group did, however, conclude their discussion with Jenny's comment, "That's the thing. You don't really understand why something's happening, you just have to have faith. That's the hardest thing isn't it sometimes?" They were far less certain than the New Life groups, recognizing the challenges of faith and, like the Central Chapel groups, asserting that sometimes the believer just has to trust God, even in the face of confusion.

Conclusions

Overall then, the death of James produced a variety of responses. The older Trinity groups were either disinterested or avoidant, while the younger group were concerned and presented a number of potential rationales, concluding that it was difficult to understand such suffering although they believed God was sovereign. The Central Chapel groups were also uncomfortable and uncertain. They made vague references to eternal life and God's sovereign plans for believers but were not definitive in their conclusions, articulating the need for faith in the face of persecution. The New Life groups demonstrated an almost triumphalist reading of the text. James was cast as a hero who had been rewarded with a quick death and eternal glory. Although one participant voiced an alternative reading, the general sense was of God being in control. His faithful servant had completed his task and thus Herod was an instrument in God's hands. It is fascinating that the death of believers was so much more palatable to them then the punishment of those portrayed as his enemies. Perhaps this is based on their certainty that the fate of believers is an eternity with God while their discomfort with judgement on non-believers implied an unhappiness at the idea of hell. The closing comments from the mid-aged group were,

> Mandy: "It brings up the whole issue of, what happens to people that haven't met God yet? But that's a big discussion!"

Thomas: "Yeah, what about the lives of the innocent?"

Time prevented this theme from being explored but their uncertainty was evident. The fate of those who follow God is safe; as for those who don't, they are uncertain or at least unhappy about what the future holds.

Conclusions on the Violence of God

Overall participants showed considerable interest and concern about this issue. Among the two more conservative churches, a pattern emerged: the older the group the less difficult they found it. The younger and mid-aged groups had questions and demonstrated uncertainty as to whether events were justifiable or even acts of God at all. For the main part, these went unresolved, although penal substitution appeared to relieve the tension. No one speculated that God might still act in such ways today; this behaviour appeared to be largely relegated to the Old Testament with the occasional (confusing) outbreak in the book of Acts.

Various schema were used to defend God. These included "just cause" and "greater good" motifs as well as Calvinistic responses of Divine immunity. The death of James was treated with sober uncertainty. Overall, the oldest groups appeared to have resolved the issues younger groups wrestled with, and this was one occasion when age appeared to be a significant factor in their reading. They were more inclined simply to trust God's actions as just and demonstrated the theological understanding their leaders anticipated, presumably because they had been educated into these frameworks but also because those with these beliefs are more likely to remain part of a community that shares them.

The New Life groups had a distinctly different set of concerns and interpretative strategies. They held a triumphalist reading of the death of James, but were extremely concerned at the death of "innocent" figures, adopting a variety of strategies to absolve God of responsibility. These tended to emphasize a permissive will approach, although they also recognized the specificity of the text in attributing deaths to God, using just cause and greater good approaches on occasion. A key factor appeared to be their personal opinion of whether an individual deserved such a fate. Herod, they were sure, deserved to die, Gehazi's leprosy they had mixed feelings about, but Nabal's fate seemed pernicious. It appeared that their concern was really at God acting violently when they thought it was inappropriate. None of them were prepared to abandon their belief in the text as authoritative, and their confusion came largely from their understanding of God as benign. It seems that their framework for understanding the gospel did not contain, or at least emphasize, God's judgment on humanity, thus they struggled when faced with episodes of it. Sarah did identify this to be result of the emphases the church placed in its presentation of the gospel, but also expressed frustration at some of the online teaching her congregation were absorbing. Nonetheless, she was certain that presenting the gospel in a positive light was culturally appropriate and that they were seeing results in terms of conversions and the transformation of individual lives.

It could be argued that New Life groups were most typical of Generation Y. Certainly, they were individualists and their concern for minor characters and fairness suggests that they were altruists.[49] Their level of resistance to God's actions implies that while they were evangelical and unwilling to reject the text, they also demonstrated a willingness to challenge traditional explanations.[50] All of the groups were prepared to wrestle with difficult questions and they tended not to resolve dilemmas with default responses. In this way, they were less compliant to evangelical orthodoxy than groups from the other two churches (although the youngest Central Chapel and Trinity groups demonstrated some of the same traits). This could be age-related, undergraduates not having resolved these conflicts yet. Alternatively, it could indicate that the younger end of Generation Y are more open to questioning authority, while older members have more in common with established evangelical resolutions.

It is also worth noting that there was little evidence of participants demonstrating a happy midi-narrative[51] (with personal happiness as the goal of life) or moralistic, therapeutic deism (which orients God around the desires of individuals).[52] Clearly, without further exploration it is not possible to conclusively state how far evangelical spiritualties reflect these priorities, but these emerging adults were not deists and firmly believed that their function was to serve God as partners in his kingdom mission. However, it is evident that acts of violence attributed to God in the Bible continue to be a significant problem to some portions of the British evangelical community, and for younger emerging adults these dilemmas are particularly difficult to resolve.

---

49. Beck, *Individualization,* 27.

50. Woodhead, "Epilogue," 239.

51. Collins-Mayo, *The Faith of Generation Y,* 18.

52. Smith, "Moralistic Therapeutic Deism," 41.

7

Evangelical Theological Distinctives: Gender, Postfeminism, and the Faith of Generation Y

THE FINAL THEOLOGICAL DISTINCTIVE under consideration is that of gender. Women's leadership is currently one of the most obvious distinctions within British evangelicalism and the participating churches illustrate that diversity. A number of factors are likely to contribute to ordinary discussions on the subject, including church practice, conflicting theological understandings, and sociocultural expectations. These are briefly explored before ordinary discussions are analyzed.

Issues around Gender and Leadership

Theological Issues

Theological issues centre on understandings of gendered authority or "headship" in marriage and the authority of women to lead and teach men within the church.[1] These range from complementarian readings, espoused by Reformed groups,[2] through to the egalitarian views of some Anglicans and New Churches.[3] Much of the debate centres on key texts, primarily: 1 Corinthians 14:34–36, Ephesians 5:22–23, and 1 Timothy 2:11–15.

Complementarians argue for an essential distinction between male and female based on traditional readings of Genesis 1–3 and an understanding of marriage as demonstrating the relationship between Christ and

1. This language is adapted from 1 Corinthians 11:3 and Ephesians 5:23.

2. Bebbington, "Evangelical Trends," 102; www.reform.org.uk. Accessed February 26,2014; www.proctrust.org.uk. Accessed February 26, 14

3. www.fulcrum-anglican.org.uk./about, Accessed February 26,2014; Kay, *Apostolic networks* 115; Forster and Forster, *Women and the Kingdom*.

his bride (the church).[4] The male role is to sacrificially love, protect, and provide while the female one is to submit, honor, and respect.[5] Based on this intrinsic hierarchy, they understand the Epistles as laying down "timeless prescriptions for male authority and female silence" rather than addressing specific first-century pastoral issues.[6] However, complementarians hold a variety of positions. In some cases, women may not speak at all in church while in others they may perform public duties but not undertake roles that involve teaching men.[7] Others allow women to teach and lead, as long as they are under the oversight of a male pastor.[8]

Egalitarians typically base their position on Galatians 3:28, "There is no male and female in Christ Jesus," arguing for equality in marriage and church leadership.[9] Some suggest that, although there are inherent gender differences, Jesus showed counter-patriarchal honor to women and that the Pauline texts are culturally specific. They also cite biblical evidence of female leadership, arguing that the church should reclaim its egalitarian roots and feminist heritage.[10] The efforts of biblical feminists in challenging patriarchal interpretations of Scripture have influenced some theological institutions and contemporary Bible translations.[11] Evangelical Christian feminist arguments are believed to be significantly responsible for persuading the Church of England to vote to ordain women in 1992.[12]

Evangelical commitment to Scripture as authoritative means that arguments on gender must be rooted in the biblical text.[13] Rather than rejecting it as irredeemably patriarchal, evangelical feminists, "Use biblical exegesis in the manner accepted in their subculture. They turn gender theology on its head, but they use traditional methods to do so."[14] Indeed, issues around gender have become intrinsically linked with questions of hermeneutics and scriptural authority. "For conservative evangelicals there

---

4. Grudem, *Systematic Theology*, 454–71.

5. Based on Ephesians 5:22–23.

6. Gallagher, *Evangelical Identity*, 34–35. Grudem, *Systematic Theology*, 937–44.

7. Aune, "Marriage in a British Evangelical Congregation," 645.

8. Ingersoll, *Evangelical Christian Women*, 16.

9. Gundry, *Heirs Together*; Bilezikian, *Beyond Sex Roles*; www.cbeinternational. org. Accessed June 16, 2014.

10. E.g., Forster and Forster, *Women and the Kingdom*; cbeinternational.org.

11. E.g., Baukham, *Gospel Women*; Osiek, *Families in the New Testament World*; Trible, *Texts of Terror*; The 1989 *New Revised Standard Version* and 2005 *Today's New International Version* were launched as gender neutral translations.

12. Redfern and Aune, *Reclaiming the F Word*, 155.

13. Bebbington, *Evangelicalism*, 12–14.

14. Ingersoll, *War Stories*, 19.

appeared to be only two positions: abandon a high view of Scripture in an effort to defend egalitarianism or uphold a high view of scripture and defend the anti-egalitarian, countercultural notion that gender hierarchy in marriage and in the church are non-negotiable."[15] Particularly in the United States, attitudes towards women's roles can function as a litmus test for the legitimacy of one's biblical understanding, and in Britain they are a source of contention.[16] Even amongst groups who hold an egalitarian view, few British churches are led by women. The 2013 Evangelical Alliance survey of 17,000 members reported 73 percent agreed women should hold senior positions within the church and 80 percent believed women should preach and teach. However, 84 percent of senior leaders in affiliated churches were men, thus even those who claim to be egalitarian rarely have female leadership.[17]

Theology in Practice: Benevolent Patriarchy?

Given the current sociopolitical climate of the UK, complementarianism is increasingly perceived as arcane and sexist by those outside the church.[18] However, the popularity of American complementarian preachers online provides an assertive source of theological instruction among emerging adults.[19] Even among churches in this project—two of which endorse women's leadership—individuals cited the influence of the strongly complementarian preacher Mark Driscoll.[20]

Research shows that while few western women will tolerate overt discrimination, many will collude with benevolent sexism, embracing the idea of being nurtured or protected.[21] A number of scholars conclude that late-modern evangelical women cooperate with patriarchal systems, negotiating within them, and believe themselves to be "empowered by submitting."[22] Stacey and Gerard observed a blending of feminist and traditional attitudes

15. Ibid., 51.

16. Ibid., 15.

17. Many Reformed churches are not affiliated to the Evangelical Alliance thus its findings are more likely to be from egalitarian congregations.

18. Kimball, *They like Jesus but not the Church*, 115–35.

19. E.g., Grudem, www.beliefnet.com. Accessed March 26,2014; Driscoll, www.marshill.com. Accessed March 26,2014; www.theresurgence.com. Accessed March 26, 2014; Piper and Grudem, *Countering the Claims of Evangelical Feminism*.

20. Driscoll stepped down in 2014, accused of bullying and sexism. His 11,000-member church subsequently closed. www.christianitytoday.com/gleanings. Accessed January 27, 2015.

21. Glick et al., "Beyond Prejudice," 780.

22. Brasher, *Godly Women*; Griffith, *God's Daughters*.

functioning as "patriarchy in the last instance."[23] Research into British Reformed marriages suggests a contentment on the part of evangelical women
with their submissive status since it is primarily symbolic and their marriages are functionally egalitarian.[24] Gallagher suggests that despite official,
theological language "family is most often a blending of symbolic headship
and pragmatic egalitarianism."[25] Wilcox calls this "soft patriarchy," noting
that the patriarchal bargain, "[s]eems to have some success in domesticating
men; that is, it prompts them to make greater investments in the practical
and emotional dimensions of family lives, especially in ways that appeal to
the ideals and aspirations of their wives."[26]

The benefits for women of submitting appear to include a sense
of protection and security in a pressured and uncertain world.[27] Aune
summarizes, "Evangelicalism remains an arena towards which women
who want defined roles and the patriarchal bargain of protection may
gravitate."[28] However, she also notes dissatisfaction and isolation among
women who do not comply with the model of heterosexual marriage and
family, noting that women are currently leaving the British church at three
times the rate of men.[29]

Even if it is benevolent, the traditional patriarchal model is not feasible
or desirable for all evangelical women.[30] Ingersoll argues that benevolent
patriarchy is only part of the picture because loyalty to their churches means
women are unlikely to describe their negative experiences to outsider researchers.[31] She found evidence of discrimination, oppression and ridicule
suffered by those who challenged the norms of male leadership.[32] Also
challenging "patriarchal benevolence," Maddox criticizes profound gender
differentiation within the Australian Pentecostal Hillsongs movement. This,
she argues, encourages men to take authority and discover their similarities to God, while women "are exhorted to diet, exercise, use makeup, get
pampered and even resort to plastic surgery."[33] She describes the infantalisa-

23. Stacey and Gerard, "We are not Doormats," 108.

24. Aune, "Marriage," 649–62.

25. Gallagher, *Evangelical Identity*, 155.

26. Wilcox, *Soft Patriarchs*, 13.

27. Woodhead, "Gender Differences," 572.

28. Aune, "Evangelical Christianity," 285.

29. Ibid., 286–86.

30. Collins-Mayo, "Evangelicalism and Gender," 105.

31. Ingersoll, *War Stories*, 9.

32. Ibid., 80.

33. Maddox, "Rise Up," 13.

tion of women through a highly marketed "Princess Theology" of beautiful women waiting to be rescued by a dashing hero.[34] This theology is typified in the New York Times bestsellers *Wild at Heart* and *Captivating*, which have also been popular in the UK.[35] Evangelical women (who outnumber men) are often encouraged to acquire a husband and can find themselves ostracized, pitied and given less responsibility than their male or married female peers.[36] It may be the case that, for those who embrace a lifestyle of marriage and children, benevolent patriarchy functions well, but this is not a universal rule. Despite claims that evangelicals marry young, in this study only 30 percent of participants were married and only four had children.[37]

Postfeminism

Models of Postfeminism

The complex picture of evangelical attitudes is also shaped by wider societal phenomena including postfeminism. Debate exists around its existence and definition, the popular conception being that younger generations frequently reject the label "feminist."[38] There are at least three possible definitions of postfeminism. Firstly, there is a proclamation of feminism as irrelevant, a backlash against one's mother and grandmothers. These so-called second wave feminists often berate younger women, arguing that postfeminism "suggests not only that women have arrived at equal justice but have moved beyond it, and are simply beyond even pretending to care."[39] However, Redfern and Aune emphasize that 25 percent of young British women surveyed *did* self-describe as feminists stating, "Most young people are feminists without realising it. In theory at least the principles of equality, fairness and non-discrimination are burned on younger people's brains."[40]

A second form of postfeminism is as a revision of second wave feminism recreated for a new generation.[41] Although challenging the metaphor

34. Ibid., 19.

35. Research into *Wild at Heart* showed male enthusiasm, while young women rejected its gender essentialism. However, huge sales of *Captivating*, its female counterpart, suggest widespread popularity within evangelicalism. Gallagher and Wood, "Godly Manhood," 147–48.

36. Aune, "Singleness and Secularization," 61–65.

37. Ibid., 58.

38. Douglas, *Where the Girls Are*, 7.

39. Budgeon, "Emergent Feminist (?) Identities," 12.

40. Redfern and Aune, *Reclaiming The F Word*, 5.

41. Ibid., 12.

of generational waves, Llewellyn notes that so-called "third wave" feminism takes many rights for granted but "deals with issues facing contemporary women that second wave feminists couldn't have envisaged."[42] Third wave feminists tend to use online platforms and music, rather than public political protest, to communicate their ideas.[43] However, they are shaped by powerful cultural forces of individualism which "overshadow notions of sisterhood and solidarity that are arguably central to previous feminisms."[44] Research confirms individualism and self-determinism amongst young British women who had embraced a form of popular feminism or "Grrrl Power."[45] They recognized problems of inequality only when they personally experienced sexism and believed individual women needed to defend their own rights rather than be part of a collective movement addressing systemic problems.[46]

A third view is that postfeminism is a "both and neither" movement. [47] Ambiguous in its values and aspirations, "it demonstrates the simultaneous avowal of feminist ideals and nostalgia for a non-feminist gender order."[48] Feminist values are both endorsed and rejected simultaneously, young women having high expectations of self-actualization, informed by feminist values of gender equality, which are seen as common sense. However, aspirations are highly individualistic focussing on "my rights" rather than wider sociopolitical systems.[49]

Evangelical Christians and Postfeminism

Despite an historic tradition of feminism, where for their first-wave foremothers (social reformers of the nineteenth century) "feminism was a natural expression of their religious faith," few evangelical emerging adults today self-describe as feminist.[50] Books such as Storkey's *What Right with Feminism?* and Merrill-Groothuis's *Women Caught in the Conflict*, written

42. Llewellyn, "Across Generations," 181.

43. Ibid., 181.

44. Ibid., 185.

45. This originates with the 1990s feminist punk movement but was popularized by the Spice Girls and fictional female warriors like Buffy the vampire slayer. Genz and Brabon, *Postfeminism*, 42.

46. Bugdeon, "Emergent Feminist (?) Identities," 16.

47. Genz and Brabon, *Postfeminism*, 3.

48. Aune, "Marriage," 641.

49. Bugdeon, "Emergent Feminist (?) Identities," 18.

50. Redfern and Aune, *Reclaiming The F Word*, 154.

to educate evangelicals on positive aspects of feminism are two decades old and organizations such as the Sophia Network avoid using the language of feminism despite actively endorsing women's ministry and leadership. Gallagher suggests a complex attitude towards feminism among evangelicals. Many consider feminism as hostile to them and show sympathy for liberal feminism alongside silence, ambivalence and ambiguity.[51] Findings amongst British Christian students confirm, "Wariness and negativity towards the term feminism and a perception that feminism has gone too far in ignoring legitimate gender difference."[52]

Aune also found a negative correlation between feminist attitudes and religiosity. Within the British evangelical church, single women are more likely to hold feminist views than married ones, and they are more likely to disaffiliate.[53] Ingersoll found that those raising even a morally conservative biblical feminist agenda in the United States were viewed as radical, even subversive, although younger women were most inclined to address issues of sexism.[54] During this research one participant commented, "Girls of my age don't see what the problem is. They've just grown up assuming men and women are equal and don't really think about stuff being sexist. Not until we're faced with the true facts anyway!" This articulates a postfeminist mind set; equality is a given, but any sense of pursuing wider justice or rights is negligible. She also acknowledged this assumption of equality does not hold up under close scrutiny but, as Collins-Mayo notes, the tendency for many young adults is not to scrutinize anything too closely. Their happy-midi narrative encourages them to focus on what is fulfilling and pleasant rather than to engage in difficult reflection or debate, presumably unless it directly affects their aspirations, at which point the problems of sexism are theirs to resolve.[55] Smith's findings of emerging adult passivity and belief that structures and systems cannot be changed may also play into this.[56] Perhaps young adults feel powerless to change anything, and thus they avoid conflict rather than worry about injustice or the theological issues surrounding gender? Alternatively listening to multiple, conflicting voices both within and outside the church may create a sense of confusion. This, combined with post-modern political correctness, which largely forbids overt displays of

51. Gallagher, "Where Are the Antifeminist Evangelicals?," 458, 470.
52. Guest *Christianity*, 186.
53. Aune, "Singleness," 66.
54. Ingersoll, *War Stories*, 41, 133.
55. Collins-Mayo, *The Faith of Generation Y*, 18–19.
56. Smith, *Lost in Transition*, 78.

sexism, means that, for many emerging adults, issues of patriarchal oppression may well remain unaddressed.[57]

Participating Churches and Policies on Gender

New Life

The churches involved in this project represent a wide spectrum of positions on this subject. New Life, part of the egalitarian Pioneer network, was established by and is led by a mixed team. Their senior leader, Sarah, is in her forties and married, with a young family. She wryly described experiences of opposition to her ministry. This included relating to a local New Frontiers pastor. "He's a good guy. Probably has to do all sorts of mental gymnastics because he really rates me! He's brilliant! We've had some good chats, I've challenged him a bit to lay down our own agendas, honor each other, play to our strengths . . . and he goes, 'You do my head in!'" Her husband, another man, and two other women (all aged under forty-five and married) make up the leadership team. Women preach at least as often as men do, based on their ability. Sarah explained, "We had someone join New Life about six months ago. She'd gone through some horrendous stuff in terms of male leaders in her church and there was a run of nine weeks and every week it was a different woman speaker. It was an anomaly, it wouldn't normally happen, but she couldn't believe it!"

New Life then, actively models female leadership and functions as a form of sanctuary for some who have experienced patriarchal oppression in the church.

Trinity Church

Trinity Church is at the other end of the evangelical spectrum on gender. Led by two men in their early forties, who are both married with children, the church holds a complementarian position. Its staff team of ten contained one woman (the administrator), although a number of women volunteered, playing significant roles in church life. Occasionally elder's wives taught alongside their husbands at the more informal evening meetings. Will thought the congregation were happy with their practices.

---

57. Redfern and Aune describe principles of equality, fairness and non-discrimination as being part of the underlying world view of young adults. *Reclaiming the F Word*, 5.

I would say that on the whole the church is content with our practice on gendered roles in the same way that they are happy that the church is well led and they mostly don't want to do it themselves! I know of some churches where one of the reasons some of the women want to be in leadership is because the men are rubbish. And I don't think many of the women at our church feel like that. A significant number of women are ministry experienced and they are very positive about a complementarian approach and feel like that liberates them to do the things the Lord has called them to do. They are often more vehement than any of the men in defending that view but will be quite comfortable with the idea of assertive, authoritative women with power because on the whole the way in which we approach those issues is affirming.

Will was slightly defensive on the subject (perhaps in response to the gender of the researcher), but it was interesting that he chose to emphasize not his theological reasoning but rather how he believed women in the church felt. He subsequently explained that those who were uncomfortable were encouraged "that they might be happier worshipping somewhere else." It is interesting that Will understands women's desire for leadership as being about the quality of oversight rather than one of vocation, gifting or principle. However, in a subsequent interview he qualified the church's position:

We seek to empower women to do ministry in whatever way they feel—within our framework—is appropriate. And we push our framework as far as we can to be accommodating of that. So that is basically Sunday morning preaching and being an Elder where there are issues of headship—not leading services, small groups, [public] praying, reading. But for missionary reasons [we] try and push the envelope as hard as we can and say "Given that our culture finds women not doing things offensive let's not try and offend our culture as far as we can within the bounds of Scripture." And we push that envelope so that we do have women at the front.

Although there are non-negotiables, Will recognizes that their complementarian position is countercultural and can cause offence. Therefore he is willing to be as flexible as he feels able in allowing women public ministry roles, for evangelistic reasons. His multiple references to pushing boundaries suggest a desire to distance the church from accusations of misogyny. Clearly, Trinity aims to be perceived as moderate and pro-women within a complementarian reading of the Bible.

Central Chapel

Central Chapel has an unusual history in this area. Established as a Gospel Hall in the nineteenth century it followed a traditional Brethren complementarian position until 2009. Ken explained, "The catalyst for change was a growing conviction on the part of the leaders that our current understanding of Scripture was not the best understanding. And that therefore our theology and our practice needed to be reconsidered."

Change had come through leaders "staying abreast of contemporary thinking and publications," combined with "fairly vocal egalitarians" who persistently made their case. The leaders had discussed and prayed about the issues, held multiple open meetings with the congregation and ultimately reversed the theological position and begun to implement a pro-women policy. Few people had left in reaction; the majority were convinced by new biblical interpretations. Four years later, the leadership team was made of six men and one woman. Seven of their fifteen staff were women (although primarily in administration, pastoral care and children's work roles) and of their ten regular preachers, three were female. Ken hoped, when it came to the texts under discussion, that the Central Chapel groups would believe, "Women have an equal status to men and in a patriarchal society these were the kind of examples that were signalling that's the case. I hope we've won that battle! I'm not expecting anybody to be going, 'Look at the women in this passage, look at the women!' because I think they will just be taking for granted that women are playing valid and important roles."

Focus Group Findings

Findings have been structured into three areas which were of interest to participants:

1. The character and actions of Abigail in 1 Samuel 25.

2. The issue of marriage in the same text.

3. Engagement with minor female characters in 2 Kings 5 and Acts 12.

Each congregation is considered in turn with regards to these themes.

Trinity Church

Trinity Church participants showed a number of interesting attitudes in their discussions. Given the church's complementarian position, I was interested to see how texts including influential female characters would be received. The oldest and youngest groups discussed issues of gender at some length: 20 percent and 18 percent of their time respectively, although the mid-aged group spent just 10 percent of their time on the subject. It should be acknowledged that the more extensive discussions were influenced by researcher interaction. In their discussions both the older and younger groups approved of Abigail so enthusiastically that it seemed appropriate to probe whether they had *any* reservations. Thus conversations were somewhat extended, although this had minimal impact on their opinions.

Abigail

As Will anticipated, all of the Trinity Church groups approved of the actions of Abigail. They described her as "godly," "bold," "wise," "eloquent," "tough," the "hero" and having "good judgement." Regardless of their age, groups made the same two points about her: Firstly, she was perceived to have grasped "the bigger picture" of David's anointing and future destiny. They heavily emphasized a spiritual dynamic to her actions suggesting that it was her faith in YHWH and recognition of his chosen king that motivated Abigail. "She's looking at David being appointed king over all Israel, like, God's on David's side. It's like she's showing faith in God." They believed that "the LORD is acting through her," some suggesting that she was intentionally saving David from himself. They also rejected proposed accusations of her as a manipulator, based on their belief that she was a godly woman who "had the Spirit of the LORD" and was empowered by him—thus her motivations were positive rather than self-seeking.

The second point made by all three groups was a repeated understanding of her having a messianic function.

> James: "I suppose it's under the story of redemption in the Bible. We've got Esther and all these other characters actually, like Abigail, as a redeemer of sorts. That you know, David doesn't come and kill all of them, through Abigail's actions they are saved. So she's a mini-Jesus."

> Nadine: "Abigail has been the go-between, between the guy who needs forgiveness and the guy who doles out punishment. It's

really interesting how Abigail seems to be like, the Christ-like figure in this? Like the real hero!"

Notwithstanding her perception of God as an insulted figure with a short temper who "doles out punishment," it is significant that both Nadine and James had no qualms with a woman paralleling Christ. None of them expressed any surprise or criticism of her usurping male authority. They seemed comfortable with an assertive woman, empowered by God, bringing about resolution in a difficult situation. The only criticism came from two men in the mid-aged group who, in a slightly disparaging tone, referred to Abigail as "the wife." This was immediately addressed by a woman who pointedly referred to her by name after which they followed suit.

Despite reading the events as historically factual, there was little evidence of them understanding Abigail as a woman in a desperate situation acting to protect her household. The older group was willing to grant her mixed motives in "trying to save her own skin," but only the youngest group focussed on the urgency of the situation. Readings tended to spiritualize her actions, centring them on the destiny of David rather than on her being a woman acting to protect her family from imminent slaughter. They also rejected suggestions of her as manipulative, preferring to describe her actions as "clever" or "persuasive," although they made interesting observations on how they perceived women's power:

> Simon: "You've got to show respect haven't you? Back then women weren't viewed as equal to men. So, if she's going to a man—when basically the man who represents her has hurled insults at David—for her to be listened to. She sort of has to kiss up to him a bit, because a bloke wouldn't normally just listen to a woman in that sort of culture, because men thought they were above women."

Simon was clear that the idea of male superiority is archaic rather than contemporary. His support for Abigail's actions was based on his belief that women, oppressed by a patriarchal society, had to behave in certain ways to have influence. His assumption that women no longer need to "kiss up a bit" suggests that Simon believes gender equality has been achieved; contemporary women would not need to go to these extremes. That women experience restriction on holding positions of leadership in the church did not appear to contradict this view, no one raised the church's complementarianism at all.

Marriage in 1 Samuel 25

A second recurring discussion around gender related to marriage. Surprisingly, given the theology of their church, the older group had no qualms about Abigail usurping Nabal's authority: "Taking over the role" (of head of the household). This they understood as a wise, necessary, and diplomatic intervention inspired by her faith. Their only concern appeared to be,

> Joss: "It's quite shocking just how Abigail speaks about her husband. To me it's not how [women] speak about their husbands in the Bible is it?"

> Suzi: "The fact that she goes on about her husband quite a bit . . . she probably takes that a little bit far!" (Laughs)

It is striking that the two female members of the group were the ones who vocalized qualms about Abigail's attitude towards her husband, but even then they were unwilling to criticize her for it. Rather they were surprised at what they perceived to be a counter-cultural response for a woman of her time. The same occurred in the mid-aged group, although one woman noted, "It doesn't seem very respectful to her husband." The group were uncritical, suggesting, "She recognizes he's a wicked man." Despite the complementarian emphasis on headship in marriage, these comments suggest that this view is not strongly held. Clearly Abigail's obedience to God (as they saw it) was more important than honoring her husband. The women had only mild censure for her criticism of Nabal, and the men voiced no concerns at all. There was however considerable concern about Abigail marrying David at the conclusion of the narrative. One older woman read it in a romantic light.

> Suzi: "How gracious is that actually? Again, it's just a beautiful picture of this woman who intervenes, who saved the day and then potentially is a widow."

> Charles: (Interrupting) "A very rich widow!"

> Suzi: "Still beautiful! For David to take her in, she hasn't been tainted by her husband's—you know—actually David takes her in, and gives her a future."

She sees David as a chivalrous, a forgiving benefactor of the tragic, courageous widow who now has a wonderful destiny as a royal wife. However, as Charles's interruption suggested, he was more cynical of David's motivation adding, "David had a weakness for beautiful women, but I also wonder whether by marrying her he inherited all the property and stuff? Which would come in handy!"

He implies a sense of Abigail being something of a victim in David's machinations. This willingness to criticize David's attitude towards women combined with concerns about his polygamous marriage.

> Joss: "But then we have this little one [verse] 'David had also married this one and then this one,' which is completely going against what God's intention for marriage was. Which it says in the law, that you should have one wife, and that's always the sign (being married to more than one person) of bad news isn't it, in the Old Testament?"

Joss understood heterosexual monogamy as "God's intention," and thus David's acquisition of multiple wives was in defiance of God's law and a sign that all was not well in the Davidic camp. However, only the oldest group were concerned. The mid-aged group, described it as "a little bit greedy," and the younger group expressed mild surprise that the Lord's anointed would engage in polygamy. However, it is pertinent that all three groups made reference to this marriage as a reward, either for Abigail's loyalty or David's restraint.

2 Kings 5 and Acts 12

With regard to female characters in the other two narratives, none of the groups engaged in any significant discussion. The slave girl in 2 Kings 5 was acknowledged but little was made of her role. One man in the older group acknowledged that she was used by God but her identity, suffering and faith were ignored. The mid-aged group briefly acknowledged her compassion in helping those who had caused her suffering, and one of the younger men, affirmed, "It shows, I think, a lot of compassion from the girl . . . to say, 'look, you've taken me captive but yet I'm still going to tell you how to get rid of this horrible disease.' How many slaves would do that? It's like quite wow!"

The women in the group speculated that her relationship with Naaman was sweet and that perhaps she was well treated, an orphan who was grateful to him. The men however were adamant that as a captive it was remarkable she should help her oppressor. The only other reference to her was an unexplored comment that she "seems to have more faith than the king!" Just as the text gave her attention for only one verse, so did the majority of the Trinity Church readers, and Naaman's wife, the presumed intermediary of this message, was ignored entirely. Feminist commentators have noted female characters can often be invisible in established biblical readings, and this appears to be the case among the Trinity Church groups.[58]

The same was also true for the female characters in the Acts 12 narrative. Mary, wealthy homeowner and host of the church, was only mentioned once as a point of clarification. Her leadership in the early church community was ignored. Rhoda was referred to with some condescension:

> Darren: "It's strange though. She's so excited that rather than opening the door she legs it back and tells them. So, he's knocking on the door and, 'Got to be quick, one sec—he's here!' If she's so excited . . . ?"
>
> Suzi: "Girls get excited like that! It's comical!"

Darren's confusion at Rhoda's error is answered with a gender stereotype. Her determination in the face of the church's doubt is ignored; instead, she is seen as hysterical and irrational—like other girls! The mid-aged group referred to her only twice as "poor, unfortunate Rhoda" and "poor little Rhoda," although one woman, Sophie, did empathise with her. "That's because she's overjoyed! That's so me, if I'm so excited about something, I forget what you actually have to do and just sort of start running around!" She again presents the hysterical girl stereotype which fits a well-researched pattern of women belittling themselves.[59] This image of an amusing, silly girl who made a mistake was universal among the Trinity groups but, again, neither Rhoda nor Mary was of any real interest to them.

Trinity Church Summary

Overall, these discussions present some interesting findings. Firstly, all the Trinity groups read *with* the text, accepting, unquestioningly, its version of the female characters and giving them proportional attention in their discussions. Abigail they accepted as a heroine: beautiful and intelligent. Rhoda they read as a comic character. Naaman's slave girl was incidental, a small cog who put larger wheels in motion. This compliant reading was also demonstrated by the amount of discussion each character received.

Secondly, a Christocentric hermeneutic was evident; all of the groups described Abigail as being like Jesus in some way. However, in emphasizing her faith, at least one group removed any sense of peril from the narrative; Abigail became less of a real woman and more idealized. There appeared to

---

58. Schussler Fiorenza, *Bread Not Stone*, 16.
59. Campbell, *A Mind of Her Own*, 118.

be no conflict between the complementarianism of the church and a woman usurping male power in this situation. Indeed, the younger group were explicit in their view of women and men as equal. Either the groups did not see the incongruity between their church's position and their support for a dominant woman or were unwilling to open a theological "can of worms" with a (female) researcher present. This may have been to avoid conflict. Alternatively, it may have been an example of postfeminist assumptions of equality as obvious, and an unwillingness to engage with contemporary gendered issues.

A third, possibly age-related, pattern was that of concerns around marriage. There were no serious concerns about Abigail's lack of submission to her husband. It would appear that, despite their complementarian theology, if one's husband behaves badly Trinity Church emerging adults consider it acceptable to overrule him. This reflects findings on functional egalitarianism within Reformed marriages.[60] Only the oldest group explored polygamy in any meaningful way. It is possible that, given their age, they were more thoughtful about how marriages should work and the challenges of either an unhappy or polygamous one. However, all age groups appeared to view marriage as a reward. Despite their concerns about polygamy, the general tone was that this was a positive outcome for Abigail, who had gone from being a strong, married (if unhappily so) wife to being a vulnerable widow in need of male protection and finally being rewarded with an anointed husband. Only three of the seventeen participants were married and, other than cynicism on the part of two older men about David's motivation, there was a sense of marriage being a happy ending.

This mirrors Aune's findings on marriage as the desirable life-course amongst young British evangelicals.[61] It also paints a picture of them understanding God as using it as a reward for the obedient. By implication then, those who are left unmarried are unfortunate, possibly even disapproved of by the divine matchmaker. However, this is not simply a reflection of Christian attitudes, among young western adults, marriage is often viewed as proof of success or prestige.[62] The Trinity Church comments suggest that they subscribe to this view; to marry is to succeed in some way and to attain status.

A fourth, and final, note is that, overall, any voices of criticism aimed at the actions of female characters came from women themselves; typically the men were likely only to commend them, although they were more than

60. Aune, "Marriage," 650.

61. Aune, "Singleness," 62.

62. Cherlin, "American Marriage," 586.

happy to criticize male characters. It may be that these men have learned not to be critical of women for fear of censure as sexists. Indeed, there was some evidence of this. However, there was also some condescension, for example, "poor little Rhoda," which women colluded with, even referring to themselves in similar language. However, on the whole, men were often the most positive about the actions of the women in the texts.

Central Chapel

The discussions around issues of gender among the Central Chapel groups were diverse and distinctly different from those of the other churches.

Abigail

The youngest group consisted of six men and two women and this is possibly the cause of the minimal discussion (9 percent) of female characters in the text, or gender related issues. Even Abigail, a predominant protagonist, was barely discussed. One younger man referred to her briefly as "Nabal's wife." Unlike Trinity Church, there was no voice of censure, it would seem that, for him, she was defined by her husband and neither of the two women (or indeed men) picked up on this. Other men acknowledged that Abigail pursued peace, prevented violence and demonstrated admirable humility but there was no further discussion of her actions, attitudes or motivation. She appeared to be merely a minor player in the Davidic narrative who did not warrant discussion. It is possible that the young men were demonstrating patriarchal reading, reducing women to negligible figures and that the young women lacked confidence to challenge this. However, little was said about the male characters either. Rather than discuss characters or the narrative itself the group were unique in focussing almost entirely on theological questions around the actions of God. This discussion was extensive and occupied most of the allotted time. It appeared that this was more pressing, and the neglect of other themes was not intentional.

The older two groups were markedly different in their attitudes. Ken noted diversity within the congregation as both a positive and challenging factor, and it was evident from the discussions that a wide breadth of evangelicalism exists within the church. In the mid-aged group, an individual woman voiced strong opinions, expressing a clear pro-women agenda. Mary, a literature graduate (and presumably informed by her studies) demonstrated awareness of authorial intent and gendered issues in the text.[63] "I think what always strikes me about stories about women in the Bible—because there are so few of them—is that this must have been an incredibly exceptional circumstance for an author to write about it, to even bother to include [it], because women weren't seen as anywhere near as important as men and events directed by women just very rarely occurred!"

This reflects the view of a number of feminist scholars who focus on and reclaim female biblical characters.[64] Although Mary did not describe herself as a feminist, she demonstrated affinity with both second and third wave feminism.[65] She demonstrated an intentional hermeneutic of identifying women whom she believed would understand her, almost as if she were making friends with women in the text.[66] Mary was unusual in the Central Chapel groups, and it was evident that this was something others found uncomfortable. Although no one directly challenged her or voiced contradictory opinions, the body language and avoidance of eye contact when she raised such issues suggested that this was something they were unwilling to engage.

This mirrors Gallagher's findings on evangelical ambivalence towards feminism and a tendency to avoid conflict.[67] Mary was a forceful influence on the discussion and made a point of remaining after the session to discuss issues with the researcher. Unsurprisingly, she was effusive in her affirmation of Abigail. "I find it interesting that in a book about David, Abigail is the main character as it were, she drives the turn of events. She completely changed the course of the future which could have meant loads and loads of lives lost." She also described Abigail as a replacement for Samuel, the voice of wisdom and moderation to curb David's excesses. Charles agreed, seeing the hand of God behind her actions and Alan stated, "I think that this introduces Abigail and her qualities and maybe why the Lord put her in David's life. I think Abigail was probably a big factor in David's life after this and . . . maybe it's an Old Testament way of saying God puts people in our lives to factor on us . . . to be that intelligent and wise and loving person."

Rather than reading Abigail as central (as Mary had), Charles and Alan read this as a Davidic narrative with Abigail as a supporting character. Alan's speculation of her future influence on David was not substantiated

---

63. This modifies findings that academic studies do not make significant impact on the faith of British students. Guest, *University Experience*, 131.

64. Schussler Fiorenza, *Bread Not Stone*, 12, 54; *Searching the Scriptures*, 339. Slee, *Faith and Feminism*, 18–20; Perrin, "Inspiring Women," 7–8.

65. Llewellyn, "Across Generations," 182–83.

66. Perrin, "Searching for Sisters," 114–15.

67. Gallagher, "Antifeminist Evangelicals?" 451–72; Guest, "Friendship," 71–83.

by any biblical evidence, and he also added a romantic note, understanding her as a loving wife. Projecting his late-modern ideas about marriage, Alan believed that, even in this ancient patriarchal context, marriage to a wise woman was bound to have a domesticating influence over male excesses.[68]

The older group's conversations around gender took a moderate amount of their time (14.6 percent). The group consisted of three men and five women, several of whom held positions of responsibility within the church. Their extensive discussion of Abigail was entirely positive. They defended her from accusations of manipulation by constructing four arguments: Firstly, that the text was "not written that way." Secondly, she had planned to save Nabal's life and could not have known he would die. Thirdly, as an agent of God's will, her motives could not have been devious. Finally, they contrasted her with Esther who intentionally bathed to seduce the king, whereas she raced to David without physical preparation. They explored and discredited an alternative scenario where Abigail had beautified herself hoping that David would kill Nabal, see her beauty and marry her. Likewise, they created a scenario where Abigail motivated all the women of the community to "protect your menfolk!" presenting her as a positive and powerful leader. They did not speculate about her theological understanding of David's role, although they identified that God was using her to control David's behaviour. Neither did they draw messianic parallels but rather saw her as a remarkable woman who "set out to avert disaster on many households."

Marriage in 1 Samuel 25

As with the other churches, marriage was a common topic of discussion. The younger group articulated confusion about "Old Testament marriage stuff" but left it unexplored. In the mid-aged group, however, most of the discussion revolved around criticism of polygamy. Instigated by Mary, the group spent considerable time discussing whether David was following the example of Jewish or pagan monarchs in taking multiple wives. Scott saw David's actions as misguided but altruistic. Mary, however, understood his motivation as one of possession, to advance his prestige and status.

The older group had a unique reading of Abigail's second marriage. Where other groups largely reduced Abigail to a powerless widow, by the end of the narrative, this group continued to describe her in the language of empowerment:

68. Wilcox, *Soft Patriarchs*, 8; Bartkowski, *Remaking the Godly Marriage*, 162; Stacey and Gerard, "We are not doormats," 106–8; Brasher, *God's Women*, 168.

Helen: "Do you think in that culture that David taking Abigail as his wife was him looking after her and being able to provide for her now her husband was dead?"

Catherine: "Presumably."

Miranda: "I think also, obviously, because of what she did he could see an immense amount of strength of character in her, that she would be an asset to his family as well as being able to protect her."

Gary: "Plus she had good judgement in that she obviously did quite a good thing, a brave thing, and maybe he wanted someone around him who was quite good in that way."

They were explicit about this being a mutually beneficial arrangement. It was not her beauty, or even her wealth she brought to the marriage, but rather her character, courage and judgement. Abigail was not rich, beautiful and defenceless but rather a significant authority figure who David wanted as part of his entourage. One man stated, "She swapped a clearly mean-spirited git for the guy who was about to become king!" He saw her as having choice and, by implication, control and influence over her own destiny. Abigail, to this group, was a powerful figure whom both genders admired, from start to finish.

2 Kings 5 and Acts 12

Despite their lack of interest in Abigail, the younger group did pay attention to Naaman's slave girl. Here one woman overcame her reticence and voiced positive opinions, explaining that she had heard a sermon on her. Young men repeatedly voiced admiration for the girl.

Jimmy: "The band of raiders from Aram have gone out and taken captive a young girl from Israel and yet she's serving her master wholeheartedly. She's not saying 'I hope you die!' This girl is being humble and she is loving these people."

Joel: "A slave girl captured has set in motion this whole thing. I mean it just shows what the weakest person can do!"

Louise (who had heard the sermon) commented, "She still had enough faith in her God, in our God, to speak up and offer the guy hope, when actually she had no reason to do that because she was a slave, but she offered him hope!" Previous teaching appeared to give her the confidence to voice this opinion—perhaps because it was her pastor's view she was repeating. Evidently, this sermon had captured her attention and, although she did not explain why, it seems likely that she follows in the pattern of girls and women being drawn to female characters in the text.[69] The mid-age group expressed minimal interest in the slave girl. Mary articulated admiration for her, while Charles noted that Naaman's other servants had also been significant in the narrative. They too agreed that those of low status were used by God to bring about positive transformation. Ken explained this as influenced by their Brethren background.

> We place a massive emphasis on servant leadership and I hope on humility in leadership—the sense that "God is made perfect in my weakness."[70] So it doesn't matter who you are, you are gifted and you have the potential to serve and there's an expectation that you will serve. I suspect the Brethren heritage [helps]: the very flat leadership structures—maybe that's behind it? I hope so!

The oldest group paid most attention to the girl, praising her faith and courage despite her age and suffering. They also noted, "Here's another case of the underdog being used by God. Like the servants and Abigail. They're not the strongest characters in the story but yet they're the ones that help bring about God's will." There was an affectionate tone towards this child, perhaps influenced by the fact that a number of the group were mothers or taught Sunday school. This affection was similarly raised by a mother in the oldest New Life group, and it suggests that women were identifying her with little girls they knew and were proud of her actions.

Finally, the female characters in Acts 12 were of minimal interest to the Central Chapel groups. In the youngest group, Jimmy acknowledged Rhoda's faith, contrasting it with the unbelieving church, and seeing it as part of the pattern of the value of the weak, but beyond this there was no discussion of her or Mary. In the mid-aged group, Karen, who had said little up to this point, affirmed Rhoda's faith and joy, which she contrasted with the disbelief of the gathered church. "She just heard his voice and was like 'Wow!' and 'I believe and I'm excited' and she was overjoyed but everyone inside was saying 'You're out of your mind, this can't be happening.'"

This was in contrast with the condescension articulated towards Rhoda by the Trinity Church groups. As women from Trinity Church had done, Karen articulated a clear identification with Rhoda but saw her as a positive role model. Following this hermeneutic of identification Mary inserted an

69. Perrin, "Searching for Sisters," 114.

70. 2 Corinthians 12:9.

extra female character—the mother of the martyred James—with whom she felt a sense of empathy. Although it was quite common for groups to envisage a back story to texts, it was rare for extra characters to be created. However, it was evident that Mary felt strongly for a woman she had extrapolated from the gospel narratives.[71]

Amongst the oldest group it was specifically the men who were sympathetic towards Rhoda's faith. They focussed not on her error but on the evidence that she was disbelieved. One identified with her, describing how he felt about being mocked for his faith, while another stated, "It's like the Lord Jesus being raised on the third day. They didn't believe the report of females again then." As with the other Central Chapel and Trinity Church groups, the conversation of minor characters was minimal, proportional to their inclusion in the text, this group were positive and aware of the faith of female characters in the text and of the courage and suffering they experienced.

Central Chapel Summary

Central Chapel discussions on this theme were varied. The male dominated younger group showed little interest, the mid-aged group, driven by a feminist participant, discussed issues of gender at length, and the oldest group were entirely positive about the female characters, discussing them in some depth.

This only partially reflects Ken's expectations that gendered questions would be of little interest. It may be that he is correct and that the younger group had little to say on the subject because they hold egalitarian views. However, the (unfortunate) gender imbalance and initial silence of the two women suggests that this may not have been the case, but rather that the young men became engaged in an in-depth theological discussion on the subject of judgement, ignored any gender-related issues.

The mid-aged group's domination by an individual with a pro-women agenda seems atypical for the church, and the group's response suggested a discomfort with a feminist agenda. Nonetheless, Mary clearly felt comfortable to voice these views, and Ken commented that, although she was not unique in her views, she was particularly vocal about them.

The oldest group, where dynamic women with leadership roles were in the majority, expressed enthusiastic support for female characters. Clearly, the church was successfully encouraging its community to embrace a positive attitude towards gendered issues. Many of this group had lived through its policy transition, and it is not surprising that both genders were

71. She appears in Matthew 20:20.

conscious of and positive towards the female characters in the texts. Indeed, the contributions of older male participants were markedly different from the conflict avoidance of the mid-aged group, suggesting a genuine egalitarianism.

New Life

The New Life discussions raised unique responses on this theme. This is unsurprising given their active encouragement of women's leadership. Discussion of the topic in the younger two groups took 19 percent of their time while oldest participants made least reference to it (11 percent).

Wider Gendered Issues

The first noticeable difference was that the mid-age group overtly noted tensions around gendered questions. The opening observation was that 1 Samuel 25 described a situation where, "A woman was used by God to minister to men." A number of groups had commented on Abigail being used by God, but on this occasion the gendered language was significant. As the opening response to the text, it suggests that for this individual it was the most striking thing about the narrative, implying an awareness of wider issues around women's ministry. Having a woman leader may well make this a live issue for the congregation, not least in their interactions with those from other churches.

The second significant observation was around the treatment of women as commodities. Thomas suggested, hesitantly and somewhat apologetically ("I don't really want to say it, but . . ."), that perhaps in this cultural context women were a form of political currency. Rather than engage in any serious discussion of this idea, there was nervous laughter, an expression of female outrage, "You did not just say that!" and the subject was swiftly changed. The man involved was not expressing his approval, if anything the opposite, but his level of anxiety at raising the subject and the female voice of censure suggest that a male voice raised on female oppression was considered inappropriate. This parallels a similar reluctance by some younger Central Chapel men to express opinions on gendered issues or engage with feminist discussion. It would appear that political correctness and a fear of being accused of sexism silences some male voices, even in criticism of patriarchy.

Abigail

There was an unexpected range of opinions within the New Life groups on the actions of Abigail. Among the mid-aged group she was described as "courageous," "wise," and an "intercessor" who had perspective on the ramifications of the wider situation. She was also considered to display "grace" towards David, "negotiating properly" and "calming him down." There were also comments about her being used by God, acting as a saviour and functioning as a protector of her household and David himself. Their overwhelming attitude towards her was one of admiration as a leader and peacekeeper.

However, this was not entirely uncritical. The group was prepared to reflect on her actions towards Nabal as disloyal, understanding her criticism of him as an attempt to ingratiate herself with David. When presented with the possibility of Abigail as manipulative, they were far more open than the Central Chapel or Trinity Church groups to consider this alternative reading. While some rejected the idea, others described her as a "sweet-talker." They considered that, given the cultural context, a woman doing obeisance was probably appropriate although they speculated that her actions were extreme, motivated by a need to protect herself and her household. However, Mandy commented,

> I think it's really easy to divide Bible people into heroes and villains and that's how you're taught in Sunday school. I [prefer] to think of people as real people. So I used to think of Abigail as a heroine but now I'm seeming that she's smart, beautiful and is married to a rich guy who is obviously horrible. And maybe she is trying to get out? *Maybe* she's the puppet master behind the household? She's the one making peace with David! But there's so many things about her that we don't know so I don't want to say outright that she's manipulative but I also don't want to say that she has completely pure intentions. [Emphasis hers]

Mandy intentionally engaged with Abigail as a real woman, caught in difficult circumstances doing her best to save her household from disaster. This is significantly different from members of other groups who insisted that the text presented her as a heroine or a messianic type.

The oldest group spent the least time discussing issues around gender, and most of their conversation about Abigail was in response to the accusation of her as manipulative. Interestingly it was the women in the group who were most critical of her while at least one man defended her. The group were open to consider the idea of Abigail as having mixed motives, speculating that self-preservation was her primary motivator. They concluded that protecting her household would justify manipulative behaviour. However, they also speculated that in order to escape an unhappy marriage she had gone beyond appropriate custom to ingratiate herself with David.

Kat stated, "It says that she sent out her servant before herself. So it's almost like 'You guys can get killed first then I can tag along at the back.'" She reiterated that she considered Abigail to be brave and that her willingness to challenge David and be a peacemaker was admirable. What was most striking about the conversations of these two older groups was their willingness to allow Abigail to be a real, flawed, pragmatic woman with mixed motives and yet still demonstrate approval and support for her. One explanation for this unique viewpoint is the female leadership of their congregation. Sarah's preaching often includes anecdotes about her own struggles and mistakes, and it is possible that this has created a culture where women can be respected, given authority and yet allowed to be flawed humans rather than saintly caricatures.

The response of the youngest group was entirely unique. They embraced the suggestion that Abigail was manipulative and read *against* the text. Led by a female participant, they described her as "saving her own skin," "getting on David's side," and "detaching herself from her husband" in order to "retain her dignity." They also described her as "a bit selfish" and "trying to cover her own back," although they were prepared to concede that she was trying to save the lives of her household too. Rarely did they refer to her by name but rather as "she" or on a couple of occasions as "Nabal's wife". Their criticism seemed to centre on what was or was not appropriate behaviour for a wife in this context.

Marriage in 1 Samuel 25

Amongst this younger group, there was tentative speculation about the nature of marriage in the ancient world, and this appeared to be at the root of their criticism of Abigail. They were highly critical of her breaking what they considered the cultural norms of how a wife should behave towards her husband.

> Leon: "She goes against his point of view, so that's pretty big at that time, to disagree with your husband."

> Betty: "She should try and make good of him, even though he's the meanest person."

Nadine: "I think it's really dodgy that she goes off and does any of this at all!"

They went further in their criticism:

Nadine: "She's almost wishing it [Nabal's death]. I think [if] she cared about her union with Nabal then she wouldn't ever be going off alone anyway in that culture."

Leon: "Instead of going up to David as saying, 'He's a good man, don't kill him,' she goes, 'He's a terrible man, he's no good, kill him! Get rid of him.'(Laughing). 'Get rid of him and marry me and I'll be fine!' She doesn't do a good job of backing her husband up at all!"

Leon is putting words into Abigail's mouth based his speculation of her motives. It bears little resemblance to the text, but the group's agreement on Abigail's motives as primarily self-seeking escalated to a point where they saw her as plotting her husband's murder. The escalation of critical perspectives among focus groups is not without precedent in scholarly literature but was unique amongst the groups involved in this project.[72]

There is no obvious reason as to why this particular group should have argued for this reading, particularly as it was led by female voices that, in subsequent discussion, showed sympathy and support for the female characters. It might be that this group were naïve or idealistic about the nature of marriage, or that they held a strong theology of female submission, though this seems unlikely given the church they attend. Another possibility is that, given an initial reticence to contribute and self-confessed lack of confidence with Old Testament narrative, the group took an idea proposed by the researcher as automatically correct and interpreted the text in light of that thesis. It may reflect the findings of research, that focus groups can create a synergism that emphasizes and exaggerates a critical view through members reinforcing each other's negativity.[73] No one referred back to the narrative or checked the details of the text, they effectively jumped to conclusions based on an emotional response to Abigail's actions as a wife. It is fascinating that a group, who clearly had no issues with female empowerment and leadership, should, on this occasion, extrapolate an idea to extreme lengths. Sarah, was also bemused by this response and suggested it was an anomaly, agreeing that lack of confidence probably caused acquiescence to the researcher's proposal.

72. E.g., Jobling, 1 *Samuel*, 158.
73. Kitzinger, "Introducing Focus Groups," 300.

Concerns about Abigail's marriage from the older groups were far less pronounced. The mid-aged group's main criticism was the speed at which it took place after Nabal's demise. One woman did suggest that marriage was a reward for her submission to David, but there was uncertainty about Abigail's future security and resistance to a romantic reading.

> Mandy: "As a woman, I wonder what would happen to her? Will she end up married to someone she has no choice over? In the end after Nabal dies and David asks her to marry him, is that the better option than staying here and trying to defend the line by herself?"

> Thomas: "I think it's not so much that he fell in love with her on the spot, but that he recognizes someone with skills he should probably have on his side!"

They speculated that the only way for David to have Abigail as a strategist and advisor was to marry her, suggesting, "She's speaking sense and I think he appreciates that." The older group suggested that ancient marriage was a trade transaction, women being bartered for financial or political gain. They were critical of David's polygamy, comparing it with a scathing critique of Abraham's actions in Genesis 12. "It seems an awful lot like Abraham presenting his sister to the king [saying] 'I'm in your hands so marry my sister—why not?'" The idea of women being used as pawns in male machinations was clearly disapproved of, but it is noteworthy that a man voiced this criticism of the treatment of women. Unlike the hesitancy of men in the mid-age group, Paul was clearly confident to speak out against the oppression perpetuated by his gender. Perhaps his confidence had grown with age, or perhaps different group dynamics allowed him to speak, but it would appear (unsurprisingly) that the older men who have chosen to be part of this church community hold pro-women views which they articulate more than the women do themselves.

2 Kings 5 and Acts 12

None of the groups discussed Naaman's Slave girl, or issues relating to gender from this text in any depth. The mid-age group described her actions as "something quite special," and in the younger group one woman expressed approval. "Naaman is like a big man so . . . the message for him to go to the prophet was from a servant girl and that's humbling. A young girl who is basically a slave tells him to go, and he goes." The older group also made only minor observations. One woman commented that Naaman's slave girl "took herself seriously," noting her courage and recognizing that she was "a slave, and female, and young. The last person you'd listen to in the house!"

Finally, with regard to Rhoda, the youngest group drew parallels with the women disciples in the gospels. Nadine suggested that the Acts 12 narrative was, "A countercultural thing. It's a culture where women's words don't mean anything but in the Bible—in Acts and in the Gospels—there are examples laid out there. And I don't think it's an accident when it says that a woman reports something happening."

She understood the Bible as valuing the testimony of women and ascribed a pro-women agenda to the author of Acts, which certainly reflects the church's policy. The mid-aged group did not mention either Mary or Rhoda at all, and in the older group there was minimal discussion but an affectionate tone towards Rhoda. Rather than condescension or an emphasis on her faith, they were entertained by her excitement and being "in a flap."

New Life Summary

Overall, the New Life groups were most aware of wider gender-related issues and engaged positively with female characters in the texts. Like other churches, two of the groups read with the text but the youngest embraced an alternate thesis on the actions of Abigail. Groups were most likely to perceive Abigail as a real woman, with mixed motives, rather than as a messianic figure or committed to David's kingship. There were also moments when female participants censured (sympathetic) male contributions, although it was evident that older men were confident to voice egalitarian views and challenge patriarchal attitudes.

As with the other two churches, readings tended to be proportionate, attention being given to characters based on their appearance in the texts, but the overall tone was positive whilst allowing the female characters to be real women and girls rather than figures in a wider narrative.

Conclusions on Gender

It must be recognized that the subject of gender is an emotive one for many evangelicals. Even within this sample of churches, women's leadership is a defining feature of their self-description. All consider themselves to have a specific agenda, underpinned by their understanding of Scripture. It is therefore a contentious topic, and a female researcher, often introduced as a Bible teacher, potentially creates a set of perceived assumptions as to what views might or might not be acceptable. If the groups had been asked for their views directly or presented with controversial texts on women's roles, the findings might have been different. The conclusions that may be drawn from their discussion of these narratives are often inferred rather than explicit, but they are diverse rather than homogenous, even within the same congregation.

For the most part groups read with the texts and gave approval to the actions of female characters. The New Life groups were most open to alternative readings, but still eight of nine groups expressed overwhelming approval for the actions of Abigail. The Trinity Church groups described her most frequently in messianic terms, basing her actions on faith in God and his anointed, while New Life groups treated her as a real woman making pragmatic decisions rather than as a theological type. Central Chapel groups ranged from ignoring her to vociferously defending her actions and motives.

There were also concerns about ancient marriage, primarily from mid-aged and older groups, and a clear sense of heterosexual monogamy as a biblical mandate for relationships. Where patriarchal marriage customs were discussed, it was often older men who were most critical of them, while some women were inclined towards a more romantic reading of the texts. On several occasions, the language of reward was used with reference to the marriage, but groups were divided between those who saw Abigail as powerless once widowed and those who understood her to have real choices as a leader in her community. On no occasion did these discussions spill over into any meaningful analysis of contemporary marriage or questions of women's leadership. Perhaps the groups did not see this as an appropriate setting to discuss these issues. Alternatively, they were asked to discuss what struck them from the text, and the majority stuck to that task. It may also have been the case that a mixed gender group inhibited their conversation. Whatever the cause, although they expressed opinions on ancient patriarchy, there was almost no discussion of contemporary patriarchal or feminist themes. It appeared to be the case that, amongst all the groups (even those from a complementarian background), gender equality was taken as a given with an implied assumption that women were liberated from such oppression today.

There did however appear to be undercurrents in some groups. On two occasions, women rebuked male participants for perceived (or actual) negative attitudes towards female characters. However, on other occasions they colluded with mild condescension and used self-deprecation in doing so. A number verbalized identifying with female characters although this was by no means a majority position. Younger women were least likely to comment on gendered issues, but women were more willing than men to criticize female characters in the text. Men largely remained silent or defended them. This mixture of responses ranged from an outright feminist agenda and wholehearted support for female proactivity through to criticism and condescension towards "silly girls." This suggests a complex and often contradictory set of responses from young evangelicals, and evangelical emerging adult men appear to be highly sensitive to accusations of sexism. It would be interesting to further explore this in male-only groups to discover whether these attitudes are genuine or influenced by what they perceive as appropriate views to articulate in a mixed group.

In line with feminist critiques, the majority of groups paid minimal attention to minor female characters in the narratives. Some attention was given to Naaman's slave and Rhoda but, in all three churches Mary, the hostess of the early church and Naaman's wife, appeared to be invisible. It was not the case that minor characters were not observed at all, servants were frequently discussed in all three narratives and Peter's guards also received attention. However, these two powerful female figures were simply not seen, even by those (women) who claimed to make a point of noting women in the text.

A final note is that in some cases the wider agenda of the church was clearly evident in the ways groups engaged themes of power and gender. The congregationalist emphasis of Central Chapel was demonstrated in their repeated emphasis on God using the weak and powerless. The intentionally pro-women agenda of New Life manifested itself in awareness of wider gender issues and an engagement with strong women as real, flawed individuals used by God. The positive attitude of the Trinity church groups suggested that they saw no incongruity in the complementarian position of their church with regard to God using women, or at least none they were willing to discuss. Thus, there were similarities and divergences around issues of gender, although the general tone across all the churches was one of enthusiasm for God's use of women and an endorsement of their faith and courage.

8

Evangelical Group Dynamics: Challenging the Stereotype

THE PREVIOUS CHAPTERS CONSIDERED hermeneutical practices and theological distinctives among ordinary evangelical readings; this chapter will attend to group dynamics and interaction. Although it was beyond the remit of this research project to undertake a detailed discourse analysis, some interesting patterns did emerge that add to the wider, though still limited, body of work on Christian small groups.

Studying Small Groups

Why Small Groups?

Methodologically, the decision to use focus groups was taken because small group Bible study is a regular feature of evangelical spirituality and, it was hoped, would be a naturalistic environment for participants. Small groups in this context can be described as "[a]rtificially or intentionally created groups of less than twenty members (often significantly less) where members share regular contact and have a shared sense of purpose."[1] Usually evangelical Bible study groups are significantly smaller than twenty, but they have a long history within the Christian tradition and have seen a dramatic increase over the past century.[2]

The two most pertinent pieces of recent research are those of Wuthnow and Walton. Wuthnow undertook an extensive survey of small groups in the United States in the 1990s. These included religious, self-help and other social small groups from which he drew parallels and conclusions.[3]

1. Walton, *Disciples Together*, 73.
2. Ibid., 85–107.
3. Wuthnow, *Sharing the Journey*.

Clearly, there are cultural differences and his remit was more extensive than religious groups, but his findings are helpful in providing wider context. His further edited volume focuses on religious small groups and provides helpful ethnographic parallels, again within an American context.[4] Walton's recent work is more directly comparable since it involved small groups within British churches. Although on a smaller scale, and not particularly focussed on evangelicals or emerging adults it provides evidence of contemporary attitudes within the UK.[5]

Wuthnow reports that in the mid 1990s, 40 percent of Americans belonged to some form of small group, many affiliated to religious organizations.[6] In the UK, Kay, Walton, and Cameron all argue that currently, for the majority of New Churches as well as many older denominations, small groups are a key part of their ecclesiology and reinforce commitment to the church.[7] All of the churches selected for this project have mid-week small groups, although the groups vary from Bible study groups (Trinity Church) and "home groups" (Central Chapel) to outreach focussed "Missional communities" (New Life). These are variously oriented around Bible study, pastoral and evangelistic concerns. Most participants had been within the wider evangelical community for a considerable time, attending various churches and para-church groups, so it was considered likely that they were familiar with small group Bible study and would be relatively comfortable within that environment. Since age-related differences were a key focus, rather than undertake observations of existing groups, age-specific, one-off groups were created for the purpose of the research. These were cohorts aged eighteen to twenty-two, twenty-three to twenty-six, and twenty-seven to thirty-two.

A number of researchers have used ethnographic methods to investigate existing church small groups.[8] Although some have focussed on evangelicals, and some specifically on Bible study, none have focused on emerging adults. Nonetheless, their findings raise a number of recurring themes and traits that Christian small groups appear to demonstrate and which inform the findings of this study.

---

4. Wuthnow, "I Come Away Stronger".

5. Walton, *Disciples Together*.

6. Wuthnow, *Sharing the Journey*, 4.

7. Kay, *Apostolic Networks*, 309; Walton, *Disciples*, 104, 115; Cameron, *Resourcing Mission*, 24–37.

8. E.g., Alumkal, "Small Groups," 251–62; Searl, "Women's Bible Study," 100–112; Day, "Doing Theodicy"; Bielo, "On the Failure of Meaning"; Lehtinen, "Conversation Analysis," 233–47.

The Function of Evangelical Small Groups

Evangelical small groups perform multiple roles, including social, psychological, and spiritual functions. They provide ongoing affirmation of the belief system of participants, reinforcing plausibility structures for members who often find themselves a minority in an aggressively secular society.[9] This reassures them of the credibility of their faith and provides a means of subverting the dominant discourse.[10] They also function to socialize new members into church culture, either directly or indirectly communicating behavioural norms and expectations. Often the process of socialization is an unconscious one by which new members modify their behaviour, but Guest found evidence that small groups were intentionally used to "forge a shared Charismatic Evangelical identity."[11] Walton reports similar intentionality amongst charismatic evangelicals, and Rogers has identified intentional "apprenticing" and establishing of theological homogeneity within conservative evangelical small groups.[12]

With regard to their faith, a significant proportion those surveyed by Wuthnow reported that participation in small groups had "contributed positively to their spiritual formation,"[13] and Walton reports that similarly high numbers "believe the small group is having a profound effect on their spirituality."[14]

Groups are also shown to provide emotional support, performing a therapeutic function among the challenges of daily life.[15] This includes creating a sense of empowerment, increasing self-esteem and reducing anxiety.[16] They provide a surrogate family for those who are socially mobile or isolated from their biological one.[17] Likewise, individuals in groups may function in a mentoring role for younger believers, providing practical and emotional support as well as socializing them into the institutional norms of their faith tradition.[18] Within large and mega-churches small groups also

9. Walton, *Disciples*, 83.

10. Winston, "Answered Prayers," 11.

11. Guest, *Evangelical Identity*, 170–71.

12. Walton, *Disciples*, 105; Rogers, "Ordinary Biblical Hermeneutics," 106, 134.

13. Wuthnow, *I Come Away Stronger*, 6.

14. Walton, *Disciples*, 112.

15. Wuthnow, *I Come Away Stronger*, 355.

16. Alumkal, "Small Groups in Campus Ministry," 259; Wuthnow, *I Come Away Stronger*, 355.

17. Walton, *Disciples*, 74; Guest, *University Experience*, 115–17.

18. Searl, "The Women's Bible Study," 100–112.

function to create a sense of belonging and community.[19] Certainly, Bible study is a key component for many evangelical small groups, but rather than being an educational process *per se*, the widely reported norm for this practice is pragmatic: to apply Scripture to one's daily life and the small problems of one's existence.[20]

Consequent Group Dynamics

It has been noted that, in order to accomplish these functions, a key characteristic of evangelical small groups is that they must provide a positive experience for members. They need to be experienced as encouraging and supportive. Wuthnow argues that, "This norm added to the pressure not to offend anyone. Members were supposed to come away from meetings having their self-esteem bolstered and feeling good about themselves."[21] Consequently, an atmosphere of trust is vitally important, and conflict within such groups is rare. In line with this sense of necessary harmony, Bielo notes that even theological discussions need not be resolved but rather multiple interpretations of the biblical text were "left hanging" in the Bible study group he observed. The priority for his group was in evaluation and discussion rather than resolution and, rather than overtly disagree, it appeared normal practice to allow multiple interpretations. Rogers's work echoes this. His charismatic church actively encouraged polyvalence of reading with mutual hermeneutics being a core value.[22]

Wuthnow suggests that the "deep code" for small groups is non-judgementalism with tolerance as an underlying expectation.[23] Guest too identified this pattern among English evangelicals.[24] However, this tolerance included "gentle nudges in the 'right' direction," and functioned within certain boundaries.[25] Bielo observed that individuals who regularly expressed views outside normative interpretations *were* likely to be challenged and ultimately leave the group.[26] Small groups then appear to

19. Wellman et al., "God is Like a Drug," 663.

20. Malley, *How the Bible Works*, 73; Bielo, "On the Failure of Meaning," 5; Wuthnow, *Sharing the Journey*, 18.

21. Wuthnow, *I Come Away Stronger*," 358–59.

22. Bielo, "On the Failure of Meaning," 5; Rogers, "Ordinary Biblical Hermeneutics," 210.

23. Wuthnow, *Sharing the Journey*, 205.

24. Guest, *Evangelical Identity*, 176–77.

25. Ibid.

26. Bielo, "On the Failure of Meaning," 10.

"operate on common procedures for engaging with the text, sharing hermeneutic assumptions, interpretative strategies and performative styles."[27] Thus, according to Malley, within socially determined theological frameworks, a variety of views and opinions are tolerated, but acceptable limits exist and transgressing these causes discomfort and possibly censure from the group. "Individual interpretative creativity can create a serious problem for community," and thus "social mechanisms for constraining interpretations have developed."[28]

Boundaries on acceptable topics for group discussion and appropriate behaviours are well documented in wider sociological research.[29] Institutionalization is common to human experience, with those joining acquiring the habits and practices of a group. "Every institution has a body of transmitted knowledge, that is, knowledge that supplies the institutionally appropriate rules of conduct."[30] Evangelicals then do not have a monopoly on behavioural or interpretative boundaries, nor are they unique in enforcing them. The complications around discussion of sensitive subjects in research focus groups are well documented and, in many settings, the limits of acceptable conversational topics are often marked with silence, avoidance or awkwardness rather than overt censure.[31]

Focus group methodology emphasizes that minority voices will often self-censure in a discussion context and any "group may censor deviation from group standards, inhibiting people from talking about certain things," often by using non-verbal responses.[32] Thus conflict avoidance and compliance to a majority view is a common trait in many group settings. Becker, exploring conflict within churches, also notes, "Groups that value close emotional ties tend to suppress conflict. Actual families, especially middle-class ones, often suppress and avoid conflict or ignore it when it does happen."[33] Wuthnow and Bielo both report that, rather than address concerns, those dissatisfied with their small groups are likely to leave and find one that is more conducive to their views and needs.[34]

27. Bielo, *Words upon the Word*, 13.

28. Malley, "Understanding the Bible's Influence," 203.

29. Kitzinger, "The Methodology of Focus Groups, 109; Sim, "Qualitative Data," 348.

30. Berger and Luckmann, *The Social Construction*, 83.

31. Kitzinger and Farquhar, "Sensitive Moments," 156–57.

32. Kitzinger, "The Methodology of Focus Groups," 109.

33. Edgell-Becker, *Congregation in Conflict*, 93.

34. Wuthnow, *Sharing the Journey*, 206–7; Bielo, "On the Failure of Meaning," 4.

This conflict aversion may have theological roots in the idea of "loving one another"(John 13:34) or "turning the other cheek" (Matt 5:38), but it perhaps has more to do with socioeconomic class. Baumgartner suggests that middle-class suburban communities tend to maintain social order by avoiding conflict and ignoring individuals or divisive subjects. This, he argues, is possible because they have higher expectations of individualism, including a minimalist attitude towards commitment to community. Thus conflict need not be addressed directly because the individual is likely to move location or can diversify their social network and avoid the person or group with whom they have a problem.[35] In the case of this project, such patterns are likely to be exacerbated by peculiarities of English culture. Fox documents widespread "English inhibitions at confronting offenders" and the importance of politeness and avoidance of conflict.[36] Since, in the UK at least, the majority of evangelicals are middle class, it seems likely that the cultural norms of conflict avoidance that pervade their small groups are often the result of habitualized socioeconomic and cultural factors as much as they are theological.[37] It is likely that evangelical small groups will work hard to maintain a hospitable, non-confrontational environment, rather than risk their group dissolving. However, the growing trend of post-evangelicalism and the continual diversification of evangelical churches suggests that those who are dissatisfied, hold minority views, or are considered (or consider themselves) to be outsiders are leaving such groups and churches to start their own.[38] If this is the case then those who remain, like these participants, are likely to be in agreement with the values or theology of the church or group and thus most comfortable complying with institutionalized norms.

Added to these factors are some peculiarities of contemporary emerging adult culture. In general, Generation Y places a high emphasis on individualism, tolerance, and moral relativism; judgementalism is largely unacceptable.[39] The perception of fundamentalist religion as judgemental and a negative global force is also a powerful social norm, particularly in England, where earnestness is often mocked and religious zeal makes people uncomfortable.[40] Woodhead argues that in contemporary Britain, God is a conversational taboo and all religious conversation is highly contentious.[41]

---

35. Baumgartner, The Moral Order of a Suburb.

36. Fox, Watching the English, 84, 36.

37. Bebbington, Evangelicalism, 110–11; Ward, Growing Up Evangelical, 35–44.

38. Bielo, Emerging Evangelicals, 5–6.

39. Smith, Lost in Transition, 27.

40. Fox, Watching the English, 62, 357.

41. Woodhead, "Introduction," 25.

Fox concurs that English "benign indifference" to religion only continues as long as those with any sort of faith "stay in their place" and do not attempt to engage others in their beliefs.[42] Indeed, many British conservative evangelicals appear to be highly conscious that their values are "out of date" and that they are perceived as bigots. Strhan reports that they experience a sense of struggle and shame which creates reserve and inhibits conversation about matters of faith.[43] Thus many evangelical emerging adults are uncertain as to whether it is acceptable for them to express strong religious views and are often hesitant in doing so. Indeed, Guest's recent survey of English university students reports a reluctance to proselytize, even amongst the most highly committed Christians.[44] The fear of causing offense may also be linked with a happy midi-narrative.[45] This not only suggests that each individual should expect to be happy but also that they must not impinge on someone else's happiness or freedom, particularly by passing any form of moral judgment. This is likely to cause Generation Y to be even more reluctant to engage in conflict or risk-causing offence beyond, but also within, their faith community.

Methodological Influences on Group Dynamics

Clearly, there are methodological considerations and limits which must be taken into account with regard to findings on group dynamics within this project. Firstly, the groups were artificially created. In some, particularly the older groups, there were existing relationships and higher levels of familiarity. In other groups, individuals had never met before. Thus some groups were more "natural" while others presented how individuals functioned in an unfamiliar setting. This unfamiliarity was compounded by the intentional use of unfamiliar texts for discussion. The purpose of this was to avoid existing assumptions about the narrative. It seemed likely that unfamiliar narratives would both offset the tendency to reinforce shared assumptions or socialized interpretations and make the interpretative processes more transparent. In short, it was hoped that the hermeneutic "workings" of their reading would be demonstrated as they wrestled with unfamiliar texts. The first text was the most unfamiliar across all the groups while the third text was universally the most familiar. This probably exacerbated behaviours typical of awkwardness or uncertainty at the beginning of the sessions and

42. Fox, *Watching the English*, 257.
43. Strhan, *Discipleship and Desire*, 12, 28.
44. Guest, *University Experience*, 98.
45. Savage, *Making Sense of Generation Y*, 35.

meant that the more familiar text, discussed as the group were more relaxed, produced associated behaviours. This in itself is an interesting process to observe, but it should be noted that the familiarity of texts and their sequence may well have exerted an influence. Giving an unfamiliar text to a relaxed group might have produced different results.

Secondly, the location where the groups were held may well have influenced behaviour.[46] Seven of the groups were run in buildings associated with the respective churches. All the Trinity Church groups took place in a classroom-style setting, around a table. The New Life groups were located in a small church office with informal chairs clustered around a coffee table. One of the Central Chapel groups took place in a church lounge, while the two others were held in the home of one of the church leaders, with participants seated on sofas. The associations of typical activity for the venue and the relative formality and informality of settings may have contributed to the dynamics and behaviour of participants. However, this was unavoidable given the dependence of the researcher on participating churches to provide suitable spaces to meet.

Finally, the presence of a researcher inevitably altered dynamics and behaviour. Specific factors include gender and participation levels. Despite attempting (after initial explanation of the process) to exert low-end influence on the groups, some needed more direction than others to give meaningful data.[47] Thus, researcher participation was not entirely uniform. Similarly, it is also possible that the gender of the researcher may have influenced dynamics, encouraging women to contribute more to discussion than they might otherwise have done.[48] However, despite these factors, there were some striking patterns that emerged, and it is reasonable to assume that many of these behaviours are habitualized routines adopted from wider evangelical culture and that they therefore do provide some insight into it.

Findings on Group Dynamics

Collaboration

Perhaps the most noticeable quality of the group dynamics across the majority of the groups was their collaborative and enthusiastic nature. Even those who began tentatively were highly engaged and interactive by each

46. Stringer notes the significance of "sacred space" on the behaviour of individuals and groups in *Contemporary Western Ethnography*.

47. Morgan, *Focus Groups*, 48.

48. James and Drakich, "Understanding Gender Difference," 281–312.

session's end. Those participating had volunteered and were probably highly motivated, but all groups demonstrated high levels of collaborative discussion. Typical behaviours included asking for the views of others, requesting clarification or information on salient points, offering suggestions and demonstrating high levels of agreement.

In some groups, interaction and collaboration markedly increased over time. This suggested that as they relaxed and became familiar with each other participants were more inclined to contribute. Greater familiarity with texts also appeared to improve confidence levels. A number of groups engaged in extensive corporate research using the wider biblical text or contributed from prior knowledge, including sermons and personal experience. There was considerable evidence in support of Tannen's theory that overlapping in conversation is primarily a collaborative activity, demonstrating enthusiasm and agreement rather than attempting to subvert the speaker.[49] When groups became particularly animated, agreed strongly or found something amusing, overlapping statements dramatically increased.

Use of Humour

A second notable feature was the widespread use of humour and presence of laughter in all the groups. Fox argues that humour is omnipresent in English conversation: a pervasive undercurrent. "Most English conversations will involve at least some degree of banter, teasing, irony, understatement, humorous self-deprecation, mockery or just silliness. Humour is our default mode."[50]

The evidence of this project confirms this. Although a detailed analysis is not possible, the number of episodes of laughter ranged from twelve through to forty-eight, with the median being nineteen episodes in approximately two hours. Trinity Church groups appeared most relaxed and used humour in their discussion most, but there were no obvious patterns with regard to age or gender in terms of use of humour, it was ubiquitous.

With regard to the texts, the first discussed (1 Samuel 25) induced the most episodes of laughter, 101 in total, the final one (Acts 12) induced eighty-two, and 2 Kings 5 only forty-two. This seems odd, given that the 1 Samuel text is not obviously funny and certainly scholars have not noted humour as a literary mechanism within the narrative. One explanation is that in the initial stages of the discussion process humour was used to dispel tension, particularly in the groups that did not know each other well.

49. Tannen, *Conversational style*, 77
50. Fox, *Watching the English*, 61.

Robinson and Smith-Lovin report a similar pattern of humour used early in conversation between strangers, which then lulls but increases again later on. They attribute this to initial solidarity building and tension relief, followed later on by a more relaxed "in group" use of humour.[51]

It seems to be the case here that humour was used as a vehicle for building cohesion, creating a positive atmosphere and strengthening bonds while participants were getting to know each other and engaging an unknown text.[52] It also appeared to be tension relieving, potentially because of the anxiety of an unknown situation, being observed by a stranger and engaging with a Bible passage some had never read before. Joking may then have covered up a sense of personal insecurity and inadequacy. Jokes and the subsequent laughter were primarily aimed at details within the text. For example, among the oldest Central Chapel group:

> Caroline: "I want to know what a dressed sheep is?"
>
> Lewis: "It means prepared doesn't it?"
>
> Catherine: "Yeah, like ready to cook."
>
> Caroline: "That makes a lot more sense than T-shirt and shorts!"
>
> (Laughter)

Or the Trinity Church mid-aged group;

> James: "So Naaman comes to his house and Elisha doesn't even come out. He just sends his messenger to pass the message on."
>
> Bridget: "Oh, so he's at the front door, and he didn't even go out. [That's] a bit rude!"
>
> Chris: "Maybe he's on the toilet?"
>
> James: "I think that would add a whole new dynamic to this biblical story. Elisha was on the loo!"
>
> (Laughter)

This light-hearted humour as a response to lack of understanding dispersed any sense of it as problematic. They appeared to be side sequences occurring when a group momentarily left the task and made a remark that caused others to laugh.[53] They served the purpose of refreshing and refocussing the group. They did not distract from the task of discussing the text;

51. Robinson and Smith-Lovin, "Getting a Laugh," 139.

52. Frances, "Laughter, the Best Mediation," 147–63.

53. Sacks, "An Analysis," 337–53; Robinson, "Getting a Laugh," 127.

rather, they were interspersed with serious discussion and, in general, the groups self-moderated to return to the task at hand. It would appear that light-hearted word play and even juvenile humour was part of the process of engagement, but did not undermine or diminish the seriousness with which the groups read the text.

Laughter was also regularly used by all the groups to dispel or deflect discomfort:

- "Here Gehazi—have some leprosy!"(Laughter).

- "Is it like immediately he [Herod] dies and the worms started eating him?" "Did they eat him from the inside or the outside?" (Laughter)

- "I'm a bit confused about the worms!" (Laughter)

On these occasions, the individuals were uncertain about the actions of God. This discomfort, rather than causing conflict or being dealt with as a serious theological reflection, was acknowledged but minimized with laughter. At times it appeared to be apologetic in tone, a way of making light of a difficult theological point. Thus humour appeared to function as bonding mechanism but also covered up participants' discomfort or confusion while keeping the tone of even difficult theological issues pleasant.[54]

Humour within the Acts 12 narrative has received considerable scholarly attention.[55] The text uses farce, tension, anti-climax and irony to create a gripping narrative. The groups engaged with this narrative in an animated manner, recognizing both the humour and the seriousness of events. Despite being tired by this point, all of the groups rallied, many visibly relaxing because it was a narrative with which they were more familiar. Some focussed on the persecution of believers and had more sober discussions, but several groups were highly amused by Herod's "death by worms." In some cases, it was evident that the whole group had relaxed by this point, and those who had been relatively quiet now had the confidence to join in—making jocular comments. This was particularly true of less vocal women in the youngest groups and those who were newer converts.

Dominance, Turn-taking, and Gender

As already described, all groups demonstrated high levels of collaboration, but in the majority of groups there was also a dominant individual. On some

54. Todd found similar use of laughter around "delicate" issues such as hell and sin. "Talk and Text," 78.

55. Bruce, Acts; Witherington, Acts; Walaskay, Acts; Harrill, "Dramatic Function," 150–57; Chambers,"Knock, Knock"; Pervo, Acts.

occasions, these participants seemed unaware that they were talking more than others, but others appeared to function as a self-appointed chair-person, summarizing points, asking questions and redirecting the discussion.[56]

Among the younger groups, these individuals were predominantly male, but in the mid-aged and older groups they were both male and female. The leader of Trinity Church commented that it is typical for their groups to have a directive leader and thus this appeared to be a socialized norm.[57] However, even these dominant individuals seemed reluctant to be perceived as having superior knowledge. It was common for them after an extensive speech act to make a self-deprecatory statement such as,

- "Someone stop me, I'm just saying words now!" (Laughing)
- "I don't really know what I'm trying to say!"
- "I'm not fully formed in what I'm thinking."

Strhan found similar patterns of "subjunctive mood" among English conservative evangelicals. The linguistic use of "possibly" and "perhaps" expresses not only conversational politeness but also, without dominating, invites others to contribute.[58] She noticed a refraining from assertiveness which was also largely the pattern amongst the groups in this project.[59] Fox suggests that it a peculiarly English trait to habitually self-deprecate. She argues that people belittle their own credentials and achievements because taking oneself too seriously or appearing self-important is socially unacceptable. She also suggests that English people read such self-deprecation as a form of false modesty designed to communicate status.[60] It is possible that in some cases high status participants felt they had expertise and were self-deprecating in order to maintain an amiable reputation for collaboration. However, on other occasions it appeared that individuals were verbally processing their thoughts and were genuine in their uncertainty. Thus, their self-deprecation was sincere although they too were trying to ensure that they did not lose reputation in the group by asserting themselves too much and disrupting the collaborative environment.

It is also noteworthy that there were fewer lengthy speech acts among the older groups. Instead, there were higher levels of overlap and shorter contributions. The older participants seemed more comfortable to interrupt,

56. Barbour, *Doing Focus Groups*, 136.

57. Rogers identified trained leaders controlling discussion within conservative groups. "Ordinary Biblical Hermeneutics," 146.

58. Sennett, *Together*, 22.

59. Strhan, *Discipleship and Desire*, 135.

60. Fox, *Watching the English*, 69.

either to collaborate with or challenge a contribution, and those who took dominant roles made shorter comments than those in the mid and younger cohorts. It has been noted that, in some cultural settings, debating and even arguing are signs of engagement and even intimacy, and it is possible that this was the case among groups who had established historic relationships.[61] Alternatively, a high emphasis on turn taking was evident among the younger and mid-aged groups, with people more reluctant to interrupt each other and frequently apologizing when they did so. The result of this was that in some cases there were lengthy speech acts which became sermonic, but again individuals tended to self-deprecate after such an incident, for example, "But who knows the answer? Luke I guess!" "I'm just waffling now, so I'll stop there." Again, a desire to not be seen as pompous, or too earnest was exhibited.

Much has been written about gender and dominance in mixed group settings.[62] Much of the literature argues that men are more likely to initiate topics for discussion, are less likely to lose the floor and tend to dominate in task based and formally structured environments, while women speak more in informal ones.[63] Other research suggests that alternative factors such as volubility and expertise are as significant as gender in establishing status and dominance.[64] The long history of male domination within evangelical Christianity is also well documented and so it might have been anticipated that men would dominate the focus groups (particularly in the complementarian church). Although a detailed analysis was beyond the remit of this project, there were some notable patterns with regard to speech acts and gender.

In terms of overall contribution to the discussions (as measured by counting lines of text in transcripts) younger women spoke least, although not significantly less than their male counterparts (40/60 percent). The mid-aged cohort demonstrated an equal proportion of male and female contribution, and in the older cohort women, proportionally, spoke more than the men did (60/40 percent). Typically, women challenged comments and ideas more than men, although they were also more inclined to be concerned that the views of others were heard. In terms of using personal testimony to illustrate their point, it was primarily, although not exclusively, women who did

61. Tannen, *Gender and Discourse*, 44.

62. West and Zimmerman, "Small Insults," 103–18; Smith-Lovin and Brody, "Interruptions," 424–35; James and Drakich, "Understanding Gender Differences," 281–312; Glick and Fiske, "Gender, Power Dynamics," 365–98; Ridgeway and Smith-Lovin, "The Gender System," 191–216.

63. James and Drakich, "Understanding Gender Differences" 294–96.

64. Okamoto and Smith-Lovin, "Changing the Subject," 870.

this, supporting theories of relationality as central to women's faith.[65] Far from being silenced, young evangelical women on this occasion appeared confident to speak up, express their views and, on some occasions, be the dominant voice in the group. This is particularly noteworthy among those attending the complementarian church and supports the findings of Brasher and Griffith that evangelical women find ways of feeling empowered, even within a restrictive context.[66] It is possible that the gender of the researcher encouraged this behaviour, but there did appear to be evidence that Redfern and Aune are correct in understanding young people as unaware feminists, instinctively valuing equality, fairness, and non-discrimination.[67] It seems unlikely that many of the participants would describe themselves as feminist, but they appeared to demonstrate equal respect for the views of both genders and at times made comments asserting equality between genders. It also appeared that, for women, the confidence to contribute increased with age, but even in younger groups when quieter women spoke up they were actively encouraged by the groups as a whole; their contributions were taken seriously and often affirmed as important.

These emerging adults seemed genuinely concerned that everyone should have the chance to speak. It is perhaps significant that a number of the mid-aged women were in professional fields and that many of the older women held positions of responsibility within their churches. It may well be that they either have more assertive personalities or have developed a sense of competence in their professional lives and communities that outworks in this setting too. Nonetheless, it was clear that women in all the groups were used to contributing to theological debate in a group setting and, contradicting earlier research, were not noticeably more self-depreciating than the men.[68]

Overall then, there were dominant voices in many groups and, although some appeared unaware of their dominance, the majority of participants were self-conscious, self-deprecating and intentional in ensuring that the group ran smoothly and stayed on task. There was a high emphasis on politeness, turn taking and inclusiveness. It was rare for someone to assert their view in a non-negotiable or insistent manner. These were almost entirely polite, pleasant and affirming discussions, even on difficult or unfamiliar themes, and the position of the church on questions of gender appeared to make little difference.

65. Tubbs Tisdale, "Women's Ways," 104–14.

66. Brasher, *Godly Women*; Griffith, *God's Daughters*.

67. Redfern and Aune, *Reclaiming the F Word*, 5.

68. Campbell, *A Mind of Her Own*, 118.

Disagreement

In the light of this, and considering both Wuthow's findings and Fox's observations on English conflict avoidance, it is also pertinent to consider how participants disagreed with each other. Overall, there was remarkably little disagreement and only on one occasion was there anything approaching conflict. Groups were harmonious and members were highly supportive of each other's ideas. In line with the findings of Bielo and Rogers, the groups were inclined to accept multiple interpretations or a layering of ideas.[69] Typical phrasing used to provide an alternative idea included, "That's true, but . . ."; "Yeah, maybe, but . . ."; "I completely agree, but . . . ." These communicated agreement with the previous speaker and then presented an alternative view.[70]

Fox argues that, for the English, "Flat contradiction of a factual statement is still taboo," and that the basic etiquette for disagreeing is to begin with a statement of agreement, even if one then makes an entirely contradictory statement.[71] This appeared to be what was occurring during the focus groups. Rarely did individuals overtly disagree and, even when they did, they used a conciliatory tone and diplomatic language to do so. (E.g., "Yeah. I still don't think David thought that though." "That's true, but it's not what this is about.") Even overt disagreement was couched in conciliation and affirmative language.

Another mechanism for disagreement was personalizing, and thus relativizing opinions. This was extremely common. Rather than insisting that their view was absolute or correct, the majority of participants presented ideas as personal, thus relative and valid even if different from those of others. For example, "I see it more as . . ." or "I think though that . . . ." Alternatively, when their idea was not greeted with enthusiasm, a slightly defensive, "Well, that's just how I see it!"

There were, however, some more specific patterns within the groups. One was related to age. The older groups were far more inclined to debate an issue. This was still done within a polite linguistic framework but, in all three churches, members of the older groups were more likely to ask each other directly challenging questions or ask for clarification. Much of this was done using humour, and it never became aggressive, but they did appear more confident to directly present an alternative and at times contradictory opinion. On some occasions, individuals did modify their

69. Bielo, "On the Failure of Meaning," 1; Rogers, "Ordinary Biblical Hermeneutics," 210.

70. Gibson, "Marking the Turn," 137–43.

71. Fox, *Watching the English*, 30.

views in light of such challenges but this was usually based on direct reference to the text or some form of relevant literary or cultural information. "But the text says . . ." was the most common direct challenge, and it was universally acquiesced to. It may well be the case that members of the older groups were simply more confident and therefore prepared to question each other, that they knew each other and felt familiar enough to do so, or that they considered themselves to have some measure of expertise. However, at no point did these discussions become awkward, and there was no sense of insistence that their view was correct. They were rather contributing to a good-natured debate with collaborative pooling of ideas to be considered by the group.

A second pattern on disagreement was that it was noticeable that the groups from Trinity Church were more inclined to actively debate with each other than most groups from the other two churches. This appeared to be a normal part of the process for them; although at no point did these become sufficiently heated to cause conflict. The groups were prepared to argue their case but not directly refute someone else's view. One explanation for this is that the setting was relatively formal, seated around a table in a room where the church regularly held its Bible study discussions. It is possible that the setting caused the groups to function more like an academic seminar than an informal "home group." The majority had attended university and, in a seminar setting, debate is appropriate, even encouraged. Thus they may have been bringing an alternative socialized norm into play. Even so, debate was polite, deferential, and tolerant. It is also possibly related to the Reformed heritage of Trinity Church. Culturally, English conservative evangelical spirituality tends towards robust debate and absolute statements on issues of faith.[72] This is rooted in a self-understanding as defenders of orthodoxy, which, combined with the public school background of many of their leaders, results in a propensity to assertiveness.[73]

Fox suggests that English male bonding techniques revolve around competition and challenge, even if individuals agree with each other.[74] This practice, presumably habitualized in all male educational environments by key conservative evangelical leaders, may have had the effect of influencing communication patterns within conservative churches, trickling down to congregations, particularly since all their leaders are male. Although the leaders at Trinity Church are not themselves public school educated, it seems likely that, given its theological influences, the church has either

72. Bebbington, "Evangelical Trends," 98.

73. Ward, *Growing Up Evangelical*, 30.

74. Fox, *Watching the English*, 55.

attracted those who are similarly inclined or socialized individuals into a more assertive self-expression. Strhan observed Bible study and debate as part of the normal praxis of the conservative evangelicals in London. She does, however, comment that the highly assertive, even combative comments made by clergy did not necessarily reflect the vocabulary of members of the congregation. She reports members as more likely to speak in a deferential manner and subjunctive mood.[75] This was also the case with the Trinity focus groups. Nonetheless, there did appear to be some evidence from them that a more robust discussion was a habitualized practice with which they were comfortable.

Central Chapel, which intentionally tries to accommodate a wide spectrum of evangelicals, and New Life, with its emphasis on non-judgementalism and postmodernism, may well have church cultures that are highly tolerant and strongly conflict avoidant—as represented by the majority of their focus groups.

Boundaries

Despite the resistance towards overt disagreement, there was also evidence which supports Bielo's findings on acceptable and unacceptable ideas marked by boundaries. On a small number of occasions, individuals posited ideas which were evidently beyond the acceptable theological limits of the group. Responses to them were interesting.

On two occasions, statements that appeared to demonstrate a spirituality that was more charismatic or Pentecostal than that of the majority of the group were simply ignored. No comment was made and someone else immediately changed the subject. On two other occasions, the group responded with silence. One young woman, realizing her view was unorthodox, asked the question, "Am I reading too much into this?" Two male participants responded with, "I like it, but . . ." and, "I never even thought of that . . . ." This was followed by silence before someone changed the subject. It was clear on this occasion that the young woman realized she was crossing a boundary and gave permission for the group to address this. They did so gently, affirming her while not accepting her theory. Thus the group effectively answered "No" without saying it directly and either humiliating or alienating her.

The second boundary monitoring episode was more pronounced. An individual expressed an interpretative strategy for dealing with violent acts attributed to God. He did this by rejecting the wording of the text in

75. Strhan, "Discipleship and Desire," 135.

1 Samuel 25:38—"About ten days later the Lord struck Nabal and he died."
Marcus provided an alternative explanation:

> I think God allowed him to die but I don't think God killed him.
> Like, a different way of looking at the story of [say] Sodom and
> Gomorrah, where everyone was turned to stone. I think there
> was a volcano or something, and if people turned back they'd
> die in the volcano. I try and put it in a context that isn't just God
> raining down fire and just killing people. Maybe it was some-
> thing God allowed to happen and as a result people died.

He expressed this opinion with fervour, but it was greeted with silence.
After twelve seconds of this silence, he responded in a more muted tone
with, "That's just how I see it." Without immediate affirmation, he quickly
withdrew his assertive tone and restated his reading as a personal one. This
would have been hard to refute without direct confrontation but it was clear
that the rest of the group were not comfortable with the text being challenged in this manner. What was particularly interesting was that a female
member of the group attempted to placate him and reintroduce agreement
to the group

> Mandy: "Yeah, no, that's fine. There isn't an easy answer to this.
> You know, God is a God of love and a God of justice and some-
> how he makes it work. I don't know, I just don't get it."

> Marcus: "I don't think we'll ever fully understand."

Marcus moved from a fervent but unorthodox position, to restating
his idea as subjective. Ultimately, he accepted that the issue could not really
be understood but was a mystery. This did not undermine his view since,
in the face of a mystery it might have been correct, but he equally backed
away from crossing the interpretative boundaries held by the wider group.
Mandy, concerned that Marcus might feel unhappy or alienated, provided
the opportunity for him to modify his view, again without humiliation or
overt disagreement. These negotiations of boundaries were striking in that
they were extremely rare, which is interesting given the potentially controversial issues raised in the texts. Perhaps, in an existing group, where people
knew each other well and felt more secure, they would be more inclined to
push and explore these boundaries but, within these groups, boundaries
were rarely crossed and it was gently dealt with or met with silence when
someone did cross them.

Conflict

There was only one episode of conflict in any of the groups. This took place between a woman and a Chinese man in the mid-aged Central Chapel group. Although the original intention of the project was to look at British emerging adults, seven of the nine groups contained a non-British national. Three of these were European/Western (German, French, New Zealand) and four were Asian or African. The group was largely good natured and collaborative but had the unusual dynamic of individuals giving lengthy speeches, expressing their opinions rather than being limited to the shorter interactive speeches of other groups. It was in this context that Mary and Charles fundamentally disagreed on experience of the supernatural. Charles expressed a generalization about the lack of contemporary dramatic experience of God. Mary strongly disagreed and challenged his view. He responded by talking over her and reasserting his view. It was interesting that on previous occasions Mary had not given way to interruptions but had continued to hold the floor. On this occasion, however Charles raised his voice over her and kept talking. At this point, she acquiesced and became silent. It was also noticeable that she said virtually nothing for the rest of the discussion. Having been a highly vocal and enthusiastic contributor, being shouted down caused her to withdraw from the discussion entirely. How far this episode is the result of personality is unclear but it is noticeable that Charles did not conform to English politeness codes, and it may be that his cultural background is a causal factor in this conflict. Equally, it may be that Mary, who was used to being acquiesced to as a dominant voice, responded badly and hence withdrew. It was also interesting that the other female participant, who had been largely silent, then became engaged in the conversation. Using a gentle tone of voice and the deferential language of, "I wonder if . . . ?" she soothed the group with an alternative but non-contradictory idea. This was followed by male participant who used humour to dispel any remaining tension. It was evident that the group was uncomfortable with the interaction and used a variety of strategies to restore an amicable atmosphere.

Silence

One final issue which should be mentioned was the use of silence in groups. Although silences of over six seconds were recorded in transcripts, it must be noted that interpreting these silences is a subjective process and thus impressionistic.[76]

There appeared to be a number of uses of silence within the groups. One use was for reflection. Particularly with the more unfamiliar texts, a majority of the groups had considerable numbers of silences while participants considered the text, re-read or looked for other biblical passages to inform their discussion. Having read the text out loud, several groups requested time to re-read in silence in order to familiarise themselves further before discussing it. Thus, they used silence to give space for reflective or creative thought.[77]

A second use of silence was also positive and demonstrated in the clear pattern of turn taking, especially among younger and mid-aged groups. Essentially, it was part of a politeness formula, waiting for someone to finish before speaking.[78] Silence also marked the conclusion of discussions. Although, in some cases, time constraints meant natural discussion was interrupted, in others it became evident that participants had nothing further to add to the discussion. The discussion dried up and thus silence marked a corporate sense of completion.

Not all uses of silence were obviously positive. With the New Life youngest group, it was evident that silence was related to awkwardness and lack of confidence—it was painful silence. Initially there were extensive silences within the group and researcher prompting was frequently required, but after this early awkwardness, the group became more engaged and verbal and silences decreased. By the final narrative, they were animated, collaborative and overlapping in their conversation. Similarly, with individual participants, silence appeared, on some occasions, to demonstrate a lack of confidence or ideas to contribute. It was noticeable that three of the four individuals who were most recent converts initially made few contributions. Similarly, two black women in one younger group said very little. There might well have been cultural elements to this silence, but it was evident that these individuals spoke less than those more socialized into British evangelical culture, illustrating the high value of speech over reflective quiet in those circles.[79]

The final use of silence was to register disagreement in a conflict-avoidant manner.[80] It was noticeable when this occurred because polite and

76. Poland and Pederson, "Reading between the Lines," 194.

77. Tannen, "Silence, Anything But," 94.

78. Ibid., 96.

79. Tannen, "Silence, Anything But," 109.

80. Ibid., 97.

enthusiastic agreement were the norm. And was most pronounced around theological boundaries when whole groups became silent simultaneously. On these occasions, participants typically averted their gaze and appeared to be closely examining the text. This implied that they were reflecting on something else, or re-reading the passage rather than rejecting the proposed idea but, nonetheless, the effect was to communicate disagreement. Silence therefore was a significant part of the discussions and used in a variety of ways, primarily as a reflective space, a politeness practice or a way of disagreeing without causing conflict.

Conclusions

Background information provided by participants indicated that only four of the fifty stated their faith was less than three years old. The majority described conversion either in their early teens or early twenties (as undergraduates). These are emerging adults who have spent considerable parts of their lives within evangelical circles, and almost all of them described the influence of other churches, youth and para-church organizations on their faith. They are highly socialized into evangelical culture and thus will inevitably bring habitualized social processes into a setting like this.

Inevitably, the nature of the research process will have had some effects on group dynamics such as an initial self-consciousness at being recorded, potential inhibition at being observed by a researcher, the make-up of the group and venue. However, the homogeneity of the findings and consistency across nine groups make it possible to draw some conclusions.

Essentially the conflict avoidance described by Wuthnow, Bielo and Walton in small groups is confirmed among emerging adults. Likewise, tolerance for a multiplicity of acceptable interpretations, within certain theological boundaries, is also confirmed, silence being the main communicative tool when those boundaries are crossed.

Some elements of gendered findings are confirmed, such as women's propensity to self-disclosure, peace-making and concern for inclusion, but others are challenged. Among these emerging adults, young women were articulate, confident and in some cases dominant in discussion. This does increase with age but there is evidence of an instinctive egalitarianism in the conversation, a postfeminist assumption of equality by both men and women. There were dominant individuals but, especially in the mid-aged and older groups, they were largely self-aware and concerned to focus the groups on the task in hand without appearing controlling or self-aggrandizing. Negotiation, self-deference, and turn-taking demonstrated a polite and collaborative socialized culture. There was little evidence of judgemental-ism or conflict within the groups, and a number commented afterwards that they had enjoyed the process. Indeed, the amount of laughter suggested they found it an entertaining experience.

Certainly, the participants were highly committed, motivated volun-teers, mostly from middle-class backgrounds and all with tertiary education. They were likely to be articulate and have experienced discussion groups in a variety of social settings. They may not be universally representative of the wider cohort of evangelical emerging adults, but the consistency of behaviour across all nine groups does suggest that some patterns can be deduced. Essentially, they are egalitarian, collaborative, polite and funny, open to multiple interpretations and ideas around the biblical text within acceptable frameworks while also being largely avoidant of conflict, using silence as censure rather than direct confrontation. It is not possible to know whether, faced with those from other traditions with more diverse reading, there might have been more robust debate and conflict. But, within the interpretative norms of their congregations, the patterns were highly consistent and suggest that evangelical emerging adults do not actively en-gage in conflictual debate by choice but prefer affirmative and exploratory discussion. This represents a significantly different model of communica-tion from the stereotype of evangelicalism or even of previous generations.

9

Some Conclusions: Fresh Views on the Faith of Generation Y

As STATED IN THE introduction, this project is a study in biblical hermeneutics and the sociology of evangelicalism. It was motivated by four interlinking areas of interest: The faith development of evangelical emerging adults, their attitudes towards issues of gender, the ordinary hermeneutical processes they demonstrated, and how theological diversity influenced their Bible reading. This concluding chapter considers some of the key findings in these four areas that contribute to the fields of ordinary biblicism, the faith of Generation Y and studies in British evangelicalism.

Faith Development and Emerging Adulthood

Theories of human development since Erickson have considered the transition from late adolescence to early adulthood as particularly significant in terms of an individual's establishment of identity, worldview and belief systems.[1] The earliest models of faith development, such as that of Fowler, considered eighteen to twenty-two as particularly pertinent.[2] More recent researchers argue that, for wide-ranging socioeconomic reasons, this period of identity formation has extended among certain socioeconomic groups in post-industrial societies. Arnett states that most emerging adults do not have a fully formed worldview at the age of eighteen but few reach thirty without one.[3] Furstenberg extends this age to thirty-four and Wuthnow notes the influence of global travel and technology in altering developmental

1. Erikson, *Childhood and Society*; E.g., Levinson, *Seasons of a Man's Life*.
2. Fowler, *Stages of Faith*, 241–45.
3. Arnett, *Emerging Adulthood*, 165.

patterns.[4] This exploratory life stage is extended for Generation Y and many undertake the traditional tasks of establishing themselves as adults much later than previous generations.[5] Indeed, many identify adulthood as being based on qualities of character, such as self-sufficiency, rather than on marrying, establishing a home or career.[6] This project indicates how this extended period affects the formation of coherent theological frameworks and consequent worldviews.

Generation Y, Spiritual Eclecticism, and Evangelical Orthodoxy

Much of the literature focussing on faith within this transitional life stage suggests that Generation Y are spiritually eclectic and non-committal with regards to established religions, showing a decrease in religious practice.[7] It is argued that they prioritize personal autonomy, experience, happiness and non-judgementalism and are resistant to orthodox beliefs and religious structures.[8] However, evangelical, charismatic, and Pentecostal churches are among the most effective in maintaining emerging adult commitment and orthodoxy.[9]

The beliefs and ideas expressed by participants in this project were largely orthodox. Their views were varied but most of them articulated opinions within a normative range for their type of evangelical congregation.[10] On the rare occasion when an individual approached doctrinal boundaries, the groups monitored this by ignoring it, changing the subject, responding with silence or by asking for clarification, which typically led the individual to modify their view. However, this policing of acceptable boundaries was done in a self-effacing, somewhat hesitant manner. Participants appeared reluctant to be perceived as judgemental or critical of another's views, but nonetheless reinforced theological boundaries.

---

4. Furstenberg et al., "On the Frontier of Adulthood," 18; Wuthnow, *After the Baby Boomers*, 10–11.

5. Shanahan et al., "Subjective Age Identity," 225–26.

6. Arnett, "Emerging Adulthood," 473.

7. Koening et al., "Stability and change," 532–43; Stopp and Lefkowitz, "Changes in Religiosity," 23–38.

8. Florey and Miller, "Expressive Communalism," 10; Mason, "Spirituality of Young Australians," 55; Tacey, "Young Adults," 67; Nash et al., *The Faith of Generation Y*, 18; Smith, " Moralistic Therapeutic Deism," 44.

9. Guest, *University Experience*, 92; Hill, "Faith and Understanding," 543; Smith, *Souls in Transition*, 281.

10. Warner, *Reinventing Evangelicalism*, 229–30.

When presented with an example of an unorthodox reading by the researcher, eight of the nine groups were confident in defending their established position. These groups are far from the stereotype of aggressive evangelicals, who are insistent on doctrinal orthodoxy as proof of one's salvation, but there were normative, orthodox boundaries which they defended when they felt it necessary.[11]

With regard to theories of spiritual eclecticism, background surveys provided evidence of a measure of trans-denominationalism and the accessing of a wide range of evangelical resources. 24 percent of Trinity Church participants had been part of charismatic or Pentecostal communities and 18 percent of New Life participants had come from Reformed, Orthodox or Catholic backgrounds. Thus, although the majority had remained consistently within a given evangelical "tribe," between one fifth and one quarter had made a significant transition across denominations.[12] Nevertheless, most of their *current* theological input fell within their existing tradition; they read books, listened to podcasts, and attended conferences associated with their current choice of evangelicalism. Central Chapel showed the greatest diversity, with 28 percent of their participants reporting a pattern of heterogeneity in their current theological influences. They were eclectic, drawing on Reformed, mainstream evangelical, and charismatic resources.[13] Overall, these emerging adults did show a measure of diversity in their spirituality, but almost exclusively from *within* evangelicalism. Transfer across, and breadth of input from within the evangelical subculture occurred, but engagement with other Christian and religious traditions after conversion was negligible. They were not widely eclectic or engaged in creating their own spiritual "bricolage" but instead accessed resources from a range limited to Anglo-American evangelicalism.[14]

Evangelical Worldview Formation and Faith Development

In terms of faith development, these findings provide further nuance to existing models. Two patterns emerged demonstrating notable differences across the age range. The clearest example related to confidence in handling the Bible.

11. Concurs with Strhan's findings, "Discipleship and Desire," 135.

12. Ward, "The Tribes of Evangelicalism," 20–22.

13. Some cited listening to Driscoll, Johnson, and HTB podcasts, plus attending New Word Alive and New Wine or Momentum.

14. Beckford, "Forward," xxiv.

Unsurprisingly, the older the group the more self-assured they appeared in engaging unfamiliar biblical passages. They had greater biblical knowledge and background resources to draw from, were most confident to situate texts within the biblical metanarrative and were most inclined to consider authorial and literary questions (although this was still minimal). These habits seem likely to be the result of greater exposure to such practices and longer socialization within their tradition. This conclusion was further supported by the contrasting lack of such knowledge among newer believers within the older groups. They clearly had not yet developed the same experience or hermeneutical skill set.

However, the most significant age related pattern was that the oldest groups typically asked fewer theological questions than other cohorts did; their questions predominantly focussed on cultural or historical context. By contrast, the youngest cohort asked more theological questions and appeared least equipped to answer them. The youngest groups often drew, inconclusively, on an eclectic selection of ideas from a diverse range of backgrounds. These were typically suggested in a fairly unreflective manner, thrown into a pool of possible solutions and, although rarely dismissed, often left unresolved. This reflects arguments that many emerging adults of this age are exposed to a variety of new ideas and that exploration of worldview questions is particularly intense.[15] It may also be the case that their ongoing cognitive development still limits their ability to resolve the tensions.[16] This is a genuine period of exploration; simple answers are no longer satisfactory, but complex answers are as yet unconsolidated.

The oldest groups might have briefly acknowledged the theological questions the youngest cohort wrestled with, but typically did not engage in exploration. There are a number of possible explanations for this. One is that such dilemmas were resolved for them and either they were resigned to the mystery of the question (it was unknowable and they were unwilling to spend energy speculating), or they had a satisfactory theological resolution and did not feel the need for discussion. This is supported by the fact that the newer believers within this oldest cohort *did* ask the same theological questions as the youngest group. These (legitimate) questions were typically left unengaged where, in younger groups, they provoked discussion. It is possible therefore that such questions are more related to formation of a coherent evangelical belief than to age and are particularly pressing in the early days of faith.

15. Parks, *Critical Years*, xii; Levenson, "Religious Development," 144; Arnett, *Emerging Adulthood*, 165.

16. Luna et al., "Maturation of Cognitive Processes," 1357–65.

An alternative explanation is that life stage modifies priorities for theological exploration. Undergraduates often find themselves in a particularly intense period of development. The "rising thirties" may simply have had other concerns. Their interests, for example, in ethical behaviour within marriage or the ability to maintain faith in a strongly secular culture may be indicative of the personal pressures they face rather than them having resolved all their theological uncertainties. The response of the oldest New Life group to questions of divine violence demonstrated that they, at least, did not have answers to all their questions.

Without further data it is hard to conclusively prove why older participants did not engage the theological questions which so interested younger and new believers. It is possible that Arnett is correct: by thirty, many emerging adults (particularly those who have grown up within a faith tradition or converted at a young age) have established a coherent worldview and theological framework. Alternatively, they may be more pragmatic, less concerned by theological questions and more with the reality of lived faith. However, those in the early stages of their faith journey (regardless of age) appear to wrestle with larger theological dilemmas, while also being concerned about personal application.

To understand this developmental process, the behaviour of the mid-aged cohorts is particularly significant. If Fowler and earlier models are correct, by their mid-twenties these individuals might be expected to have resolved many of their questions or be in a different life stage and thus behave as the older cohort did. If, however, emerging adult models are more accurate and the transition to a coherent worldview takes longer, then this may not be the case.

Demographically, mid-aged participants had more in common with the younger group. Few were married and none had children. They were typically postgraduate students or in the early stages of professional careers. In terms of their discussion, they also had more in common with the younger cohorts. They often asked theological questions and explored a variety of ideas to attempt a resolution, expressing uncertainty and confusion. Mid-aged groups were, however, more likely to question each other's suggestions than to leave them unexplored as younger groups had. This suggests an increased capacity to critically reflect and confidence to articulate and challenge ideas. However, on two occasions (Central Chapel and Trinity Church) discussions were resolved by an individual who used penal substitution as a default answer. This answer did not always cohere with the question under discussion but appeared to draw a line under it. If no satisfactory resolution was found, then Christ's death would suffice. An individual from the Trinity Church youngest group also undertook the same action, which suggests that this is a strongly socialized convention among conservative evangelicals. It may well prevent exploration of other theological concepts but appears to bring a sense of resolution.

Overall, these findings suggest that the process of forming a coherent theological framework is not complete in many ordinary evangelicals by their mid-twenties but that development is ongoing. The ability to critique theological ideas seems to be more advanced than in the late teens, but uncertainty appears to persist. A contributory factor may be the ongoing exposure to a wide range of theological positions as they continue to be geographically mobile, accessing various sources of religious input.[17] Such diversity may inhibit or delay the resolution of an orthodox evangelical framework, as emerging adults regularly read and listen to conflicting resources. However, as their lives become less transient, it seems likely that emerging adults will settle within a particular church tradition whose worldview they find most credible.[18]

It seems probable that emerging adults exposed to more consistent teaching will adopt a related theological framework in their later twenties and become rooted in a "Network of belonging which is congruent with [their view of] god."[19] Significant exploration and faith formation appears to be taking place in the early twenties, but this evidence suggests that it continues well into the second half of the decade and longer for newer believers.

Evangelical Emerging Adults and Postfeminism

Contemporary Evangelicalism and Women's Leadership

A second field in which this project makes a contribution concerns the relationship between evangelicalism and feminism. The two have often regarded each other with hostility and, despite the evangelical faith which informed the activities of first wave feminists, much of the feminist-evangelical heritage has been lost.[20] However, alongside wider cultural changes, "biblical feminism" has made a significant impact through the reinterpretation of key

---

17. Mid-aged participants reported an average attendance of three and a half years within their congregation.

18. Oldest participants reported an average attendance of seven years.

19. Parks, *Critical Years*, 89.

20. Redfern and Aune, *Reclaiming The F Word*, 154; Merrill-Groothuis, *Women Caught in the Conflict*, 31.

biblical passages.[21] A large majority of British evangelicals are now reported to support women's preaching and leadership.[22] Similarly, the 2015 appointment of the first woman bishops in the Church of England, approved of by many Anglican evangelicals, indicates a clear shift in attitudes within that tradition.[23]

The findings of this study demonstrate that some historically complementarian congregations are becoming egalitarian and, even in churches which maintain a complementarian position, there are active attempts to increase the visibility of women's ministry. The doctrinal tide appears to be turning in favour of evangelical women's leadership, although actual numbers of women leaders are still small.[24]

Attitudes towards Feminism

These findings provide evidence of an ambivalence between evangelicalism and overt feminism.[25] Only one individual articulated a strongly feminist agenda, and her contributions were met with silence and a sense of awkwardness; she had apparently been too assertive for comfort. Her opinions on gender were neither challenged nor affirmed but simply ignored by the other participants. Ultimately, she was shouted down by a male participant; her assertiveness was quashed though, interestingly, not over questions of gender. Nonetheless, as a feminist she was part of a mainstream evangelical community and, according to the leader, not alone in it.

Despite this ambivalence towards assertive feminism, positive attitudes towards assertive women in the biblical text were expressed across groups from all three churches. However, the New Life groups more frequently articulated general comments about gender. These were primarily conversational asides. One referred to the belief that Luke's gospel promoted the faith of women; another drew attention to God using a woman (Abigail) to minister to men. In a church with high egalitarian priorities, there appeared to be a greater consciousness of gender as a contemporary issue. It seems likely that evangelicals from churches intentionally promoting women's ministry have experienced regular Bible teaching explicitly justifying such policies.[26]

---

21. Redfern and Aune, *Reclaiming The F Word*, 155; Ingersoll, *War Stories*, 19.

22. www.eauk.org/women-should-lead, Accessed April 4, 2014.

23. www.eauk.org/women-bishops, Accessed May 1, 2015.

24. www.eauk.org/women-should-lead, Accessed April 4, 2014.

25. E.g., Gallagher, "Antifeminist Evangelicals?" 458, 470; Guest, *University Experience*, 186; Aune, "Singleness," 66.

26. Sarah reported that regular teaching on women's leadership is undertaken since new student cohorts are often confused on the subject.

Thus they demonstrated a higher awareness and engagement with issues of sexism; whereas, for the majority, it was not a pressing subject.

Had the groups been presented with the so-called "difficult texts," (1 Cor 14:34–36; Eph 5:22–23; 1 Tim 2:11–15) their views on gender would undoubtedly have been more overt. However, when presented with narratives, most groups engaged the subject in an indirect manner, discussing female characters and their behaviour but not extrapolating it significantly.

Evidence of "Both and Neither" Postfeminism

Overall, there was a general criticism of sexism within the ancient world described in the text. However, it appeared that participants understood themselves to be living in an egalitarian society where such issues were a thing of the past. Thus it seems that many young evangelicals demonstrate a particular form of post-feminism. As described in chapter 7, post-feminism can be understood in various ways, but these groups demonstrated an ambiguous "both and neither" form.[27] This embraces equality and a nostalgic idealization of a pre-feminist social order, simultaneously endorsing and rejecting feminist values. Under this model, women have high expectations of self-actualization but are strongly individualistic, typically ignoring wider sociopolitical oppression.[28] Reflecting Redfern and Aune's findings there seemed to be an assumption of equality between the genders as common sense but also that sexism was archaic.[29] On no occasion was contemporary inequality addressed, and there was no reflection on the policies of participants' churches.

Discussions showed little evidence of male dominance, even in the complementarian church. Women of all ages voiced opinions, challenged ideas and, on some occasions, functioned as unofficial group leaders. The confidence to contribute *did* increase with age for women, and the youngest female participants were the lowest average contributors, but there was no significant evidence of female passivity. If anything, the reverse was true. When discussing issues of gender (such as polygamous marriage, women as political pawns or female testimony being disbelieved) it was evident that participants considered these injustices. However, on some occasions when men spoke up (even in support of women) female participants rebuked them. These young women appeared confident to challenge what

27. Budgeon, "Emergent Feminist (?) Identities," 12; Llewellyn, "Across Generations," 181–85.

28. Genz and Brabon, *Postfeminism*, 3.

29. Redfern and Aune, *The F Word*, 5.

they perceived as minor acts of sexism and were sometimes sensitive to benign comments. This concurs with findings on the assertiveness of young women to defend themselves.[30] It appeared that the younger men, despite their largely pro-women opinions, were nervous to comment, apparently uncertain that they had a right to speak on the subject or perhaps anxious that they might be accused of sexism.

The argument for "both and neither" postfeminism is also supported by evidence that suggested participant egalitarianism was not entirely consistent. Opinions on marriage illustrate this. Some groups articulated a view of marriage as a reward from God for faithful behaviour and had a romantic or idealized perspective on it. The subject of female submission, or at least deference to their husbands, was raised on a number of occasions (usually by women) and reflected traditional, pre-feminist views on relationships. On other occasions, there was a greater sense of cynicism or pragmatism towards marriage. Overriding one's husband (if he behaved badly enough) appeared to be considered appropriate by both sexes—including in the complementarian groups. Equally, one New Life (egalitarian) group was antagonistic towards Abigail's behaviour. Both women and men insisted that she should have submitted to Nabal's foolish leadership, since he was her husband.

At times women belittled themselves and females in the text as being "silly girls" and there were occasional hints of condescension from some male participants. However, on other occasions, men (as well as women) identified with and were inspired by the female characters, and older men were universally positive towards female characters.[31]

In Central Chapel and New Life groups, there was a frequent endorsement of God's empowering of the weak to bring about his plans. However, in the same groups, where male minor characters were discussed, female characters were ignored, confirming arguments regarding female invisibility in textual readings.[32]

It would appear then that there is a complex attitude towards gender among young British evangelicals. Generation Y appears to believe itself to be egalitarian, beyond archaic sexism and embracing equality, but at the same time it demonstrates a curious mixture of responses towards women and girls. This includes challenging alleged sexism on some occasions but, on others, ignoring condescension and the inconsistencies of the views they

30. Budgeon, "Emergent Feminist (?) Identities," 12; Ingersoll, *War Stories*, 133.

31. Women often identify with female biblical characters. Perrin, "Discipleship and Empowerment," 16.

32. Schussler Fiorenza, *Bread Not Stone*, 16.

articulated and the policies of their churches. This ambivalence appears to reflect the tensions in wider British society as well as within the evangelical church: a theoretical assumption of equality but relatively unreflective attitudes towards patriarchal systems and existing injustices.[33]

Faced with overt discrimination or sexism, young evangelicals express their disapproval. Those who had experienced gender-related criticism (such as New Life members) sometimes indicated an awareness of wider issues, but the majority did not engage with the structures and systems which perpetuate ongoing discrimination in either their churches or wider society. There is clearly a need for further exploration of these issues, a more focussed study of attitudes towards gender, and perhaps other marginalized groups. Many evangelicals pride themselves on their concern for social justice and are prolific activists but these findings raise questions about how far difficult subjects such as sexism are addressed directly within churches and how far young evangelical understanding is merely a largely non-reflective representation of the secular contemporary culture which they inhabit?

Evangelical Emerging Adults and the Negotiation of Biblical Authority

Introduction

Much has been written about evangelical attitudes towards the Bible. However, there is relatively little nuanced data about how British evangelicals negotiate Scriptural authority. Bielo explores the idea of textual ideologies as being formed and negotiated among communities of practice. His observations that for evangelicals the text is "true" and has absolute authority are largely echoed, but also nuanced by the findings of this study.[34]

The variation in understanding scriptural authority within British evangelicalism is demonstrated by the doctrinal statements of the participating churches. Trinity Church states, "As originally given [the Bible] is true in its entirety," and it is the "supreme authority" by which to test human behaviour and belief. Central Chapel describes it as "fully trustworthy in matters of faith and conduct," and New Life considers it an "inspired narrative" which believers should meditate upon in order to inform their daily life. These represent a spectrum of attitudes but do not necessarily indicate the beliefs of individual participants, which were not directly explored. However, the discussions provided convincing evidence that negotiation of

33. Bugdeon, "Emergent Feminist (?) Identities," 16.

34. Bielo, Words upon the Word, 52–53.

biblical authority is not simple for British evangelical emerging adults and they use a variety of strategies to do this.

A Schema of Interpretative Strategies

It is well documented that most evangelicals adopt a plain-sense reading of Scripture, assuming it to be accurate and authoritative until they identify a text which creates a problem of some sort.[35] At this point, they often engage in "remote" reading.[36]

The dominant problem for a significant number was acts of violence attributed to God. Chapter 6 describes this in detail, but there were a variety of ways in which participants negotiated textual authority with these uncomfortable events. These form a schema of five categories which relate to their varying levels of discomfort. They are: *unquestioning acceptance, reader limitation, uncomfortable resignation, explicable misrepresentation,* and *partial resistance.* Broadly speaking they correlate to the age and church background of the groups.

Clearly, for some participants (Older Central Chapel and Trinity Church groups), violent acts attributed to God were of limited theological or ethical concern and so their responses to these accounts were straightforward. This does not necessarily mean that their response to every event described in Scripture would be the same. It may well be the case that they would have used different strategies in engaging an issue that was of greater concern to them. However, on this occasion, these groups and individuals *unquestioningly accepted* the text as authoritative and accurate, a straightforward reporting of historical events.

A second category included those who expressed mild concern at the textual account. Their conversations often included cross-canonical quotation, i.e., the use of other scriptural examples and themes to support the validity of the textual account. Alternatively, they explored cultural and historical context in order to legitimise what, from their late modern perspective, appeared confusing. They assumed that they must be missing significant information that would ultimately explain why God had acted in such a manner. Thus, the problem was with their understanding rather than the textual account, and they believed further information would provide some form of acceptable theodicy, allowing God's actions to be understood in a more favourable light. The text remained authoritative but *reader*

---

35. Harris, *Fundamentalism,* 281; Barton, *Biblical Criticism,* 89; Malley, *How the Bible Works,* 100; Barr, *Fundamentalism,* 50; Crapanzano, *Serving the Word,* 2.

36. Barton, *Biblical Criticism,* 95–96.

limitations on understanding meant they were in need of further expertise to fully comprehend the trustworthy textual account.

A third category were those with significant concern about the text's account. These were typically in the younger cohort, and they often followed similar strategies to the second group: cross-referencing, engaging wider theological themes and expressing a need for contextual information. However, despite their confusion, they often defaulted to a position that ultimately, because it was in Scripture, the account must be historically accurate. Unlike the first category who accepted the text's authority unquestioningly, this appeared to be an *uncomfortable resignation*. They were not comfortable with the text's version but their high view of Scripture meant that somehow it must be correct, although they were uncertain and often left concerns unresolved.

Explicable misrepresentation describes the attitude of a fourth group towards the text. These readers were typically from New Life or mid-aged groups, and demonstrated major concerns with the version of events describing divine violence. They exhibited a variety of strategies to negotiate this problem, allowing for scriptural authority while challenging the exact wording of the text. As with other groups, they discussed the need for further cultural and historical information but also included the idea of ancient primitivism. Groups speculated as to whether ancient peoples had lacked sufficient scientific understanding to accurately describe events. Thus, the inexplicable death of an individual was described as divine action when in fact it had been a medical or "natural" event. Violence ascribed to God was not really his direct action, but merely represented a naïve understanding of the universe. God, therefore, was not culpable for the action, and the text described an ancient understanding rather than an entirely accurate account.

A second hermeneutical procedure was to explore alternative versions or possibly errors in translation. Groups checked a variety of English translations to see if they provided a more palatable description and, in one group, frequently consulted Bible study-notes. This information was particularly endorsed when it provided explanations which concurred with their contemporary (rather than primitive) explanation for events.[37] Occasionally it was suggested that perhaps the original language (if only they could read it) might provide a more acceptable version of events and that the confusion lay in the translation rather than the text itself. Participants had no way of verifying this theory but it confirms observations about evangelical belief

37. Bielo found similar regard for Bible footnotes, *Words upon the Word*, 84.

in the supremacy of the original version.[38] Unlike the third category, these discussions were usually resolved at some level, since participants were sure that the text didn't mean what it appeared to say at first glance; it was a misrepresentation, but this was legitimate and explicable and the account was still trustworthy.

The final category was rare, being observed on only two occasions, both within New Life contexts. It is best described as a *partially resistant* reading by those with overwhelming concern about the biblical account. These episodes showed an overt rejection of the text, "I don't believe God acts like that." As described in chapter 6 on one occasion (a sermon) there was no justification, a statement in the text was simply rejected within an exegesis that otherwise presented the passage as authoritative. The other example involved the proposal of an alternative explanation to the biblical account. This denied God's participation as ascribed to Him. The participant extended his thesis to include another biblical episode he was similarly uncomfortable with. The reading was not fully resistant. He did not identify an authorial agenda which he rejected or denounce scripture's authority, but it was a partial rejection of the text. It was, in his view, an inaccurate description of divine action. That this view was greeted with an extensive silence made it evident that it was a minority opinion and that the rest of the group were unwilling to describe the biblical text as wrong. However, it does provide support for there being a willingness among charismatics to sometimes challenge the textual account.[39]

These categories were fluid. Individuals who articulated *reader limitation* or *explicable misrepresentation* on some occasions also used "but the text says . . ." to reassert a plain reading on other topics. The negotiation of textual authority was complex and variable. For a majority of the time, participants were prepared to accept the text as authoritative and truthful, it was only when anxieties emerged about the theological or ethical message of the narrative that participants engaged these negotiations, demonstrating varying levels of willingness to challenge it or strategies to engage it.

One other question to ask is how young evangelicals negotiate such texts in a different setting, for example when reading alone? It seems likely that a sixth category is needed within this schema; that of *avoidant acquiescence*, when a reader simply skips over or ignores a difficult passage and moves on to a more palatable or encouraging text. It seems likely that these strategies are what individuals have witnessed within their church settings, in particular within sermons and Bible studies from where they reported

38. Malley, *How the Bible Works*, 51; Bielo, "On the Failure of Meaning," 13.

39. Rogers, "Ordinary Biblical Hermeneutics," 208.

most of their biblical understanding originated. Clearly, the theological perspective on Scripture itself has an influence on how such complications are handled but it is interesting to note the patterns and the fact that young evangelicals are thoughtful and nuanced in how they negotiate these challenges.

Theological Diversity in Managing Rationalist-Supernaturalist Tensions

Introduction

A final reflection from these findings is on the tensions young evangelicals evidently feel about some of the supernatural dimensions of Christian faith. It highlights the dichotomous framework in which many are modern Christians are caught. This often presents the world as largely running under rationally explicable "natural law" with occasional divine involvement in the form of the miraculous.[40] The biblical account, however, presents God as being intimately involved in all aspects of his creation and sometimes demonstrating dramatic acts of power.[41]

Despite demonstrating considerable similarities, it is evident from chapter 5 that diversity of theological position and underlying worldview create a range of responses to supernatural biblical accounts and expectations of lived faith. While participants accepted biblical accounts as accurate descriptions of historical events, there were mixed views as to whether such things might be expected in contemporary Christian discipleship. Parks comments, "Faith must stand up under the test of the truth of lived human experience."[42] It was evident that participants experienced considerable tension between their own experience of the numinous, the rationalist western culture around them and their religious belief system.

Clearly, secular education and wider western cultural norms have a powerful influence on young evangelicals. The conflicts they experience are not only in the countercultural lifestyle their faith inspires.[43] They are well aware that other people consider their beliefs implausible and many (including some participants) report having been ridiculed for their faith.[44]

---

40. Del Colle, *Miracles*, 248.

41. Moberly, "Miracles in the Hebrew Bible," 58–60.

42. Parks, *Critical Years*, 19.

43. Irby, "Dating in Light of Christ," 260–83; Strhan, *Discipleship and Desire,* 16; Guest, *University Experience,* 119.

44. Savage, *Making Sense of Generation Y*, 14.

These discussions showed that participants also experience internal conflict in embracing some supernatural aspects of Christian faith. Their high view of Scriptural authority encouraged the acceptance of miraculous biblical events and no one expressed overtly cessationist views.[45] However, as leaders at Central Chapel and Trinity Church had anticipated, experience and expectation of the numinous appeared limited to *miracular interior,* and God acting in "mundane" ways, or "little, gentle things." Some participants expressed frustration at their lack of dramatic divine encounter and even members of New Life were resistant to describing events they are reported to have experienced.

It is clear that holding rationalism and supernaturalism together is not an easy task, but these findings show that members of different evangelical traditions use various strategies to resolve this tension and resist the influence of secular rationalism, with mixed results.

Strategies for Managing the Tension

Trinity Church considers itself to be a "left-leaning," "continuist," Reformed evangelical community. Will was adamant that they were not cessationist in their doctrine and was disparaging of those who were. However, participants from within the wider Reformed tradition are likely to have sceptical and non-expectant attitudes towards supernatural experience. One service I attended included discussion about depression and while compassion was expressed towards sufferers and medical treatment advised, there was virtually no reference to the possibility of divine healing nor was prayer for it offered. Will described supernatural healing as "mysterious" and was highly critical of "shallow answers from the worst sort of parts of the healing movement," adding, "If you work in healthcare you just know that's nonsense." Trinity Church, then, demonstrated high rationalism in its teaching but was unwilling to entirely rule out the possibility of supernatural events and its participants showed a mixture of confusion and reluctance to discuss the subject.

Ultimately, some groups made a cognitive decision to believe that God was still active in non-rational ways, based on the biblical account; if God had done it before, he was capable of doing it again. However, as well as being critical of those whom they considered had made false promises about divine healing, some were self-critical at the doubts their own rationalism created. They were frustrated by their uncertainty in the existence of contemporary miracles and confused over the mechanics of prayer. It seems

45. Ruthven, *Cessation,* 191.

likely that the experience of bereavement as a community, combined with their high view of God's sovereignty and their Reformed background, had reinforced doubts about contemporary miracles. Some, however, wished they had greater faith in God's supernatural activity and their main defence against overwhelming rationalism appeared to be the Bible itself. The complete avoidance of the subject by one group and overt curiosity about numinous experience by younger members and newer believers suggests a mixture of attitudes, but fundamentally the Bible and submission to its authority was their primary response.

Central Chapel members undertook a different method of resistance to rationalism. Ken had, somewhat apologetically, described his own lack of expectation of supernatural experience, and he considered conversion to be the primary divine miraculous activity today. Like the Trinity groups, Central Chapel participants accepted the biblical account as an accurate historical episode but linked supernatural events to conversion. Their personal expectation of numinous encounter appeared limited to *miracular interior*, but they did believe that dramatic divine events occurred in other locations, particularly where evangelization or persecution of believers were prolific. Miracles were proof of the veracity of the gospel message. One individual was overt in describing the New Testament as sufficient evidence for the gospel and thus believed that for contemporary believers—who had access to a Bible, miracles were unnecessary. Others considered that if their own prayer or evangelistic activities were more daring then they might have supernatural experiences. This was generally accompanied by a measure of self-criticism; their own lack of faith or courage was the reason for their lack of divine encounter.[46] The mechanism for managing the tension appeared to be a limitation of divine activity primarily to *miracular interior*—the processes of conversion and sanctification of the believer. However, in extreme situations they believed miracles might occur to further proselytization.

New Life groups appeared to feel the rationalist-supernaturalist tension least. It would appear that their romantic worldview, practise of charismatic gifts and experience of the numinous in worship and prayer provided the strongest resistance to secular rationalism. The New Life groups were the most confident that supernatural activity was going on all around them. Their primary point of reference was experience; they or someone they knew had encountered God or another supernatural entity in a remarkable way. Certainly, they considered that biblical events were reliable and remarkable, but they also cited non-biblical episodes as proof that supernaturalism was

---

46. This argument was also used by a member of Hope Community in the pilot study, clearly some charismatic evangelicals also have this understanding.

real. As Hopewell suggests, "The world in which the charismatic lives is fundamentally equivocal and dangerous, challenging the believer to seek its blessings amid the peril of evil forces and events. God's steady providence accompanies the self who launches out towards God in an exciting, romantic adventure."[47]

An understanding of spiritual activity all around them appeared to allow New Life participants to interpret experiences others might consider coincidences, as divine acts. Encounters with God did not have to be astonishing, they could be found in everyday events. They distinguished between "ordinary miracles," which were undramatic in process but might have a remarkable outcome (which a number cited experienced of), and "proper miracles," which occurred by obviously astonishing means. This normalcy of divine action was expressed in a different manner to the "mundane" actions of God described in Central Chapel. Rather they had learnt to interpret the ordinary as exciting, and celebrate daily events as divine interventions. Similarly, understanding their actions as participation with God appeared to have added a deeper significance to daily life. Prayer, worship, and community service were spiritually powerful activities undertaken with a conviction that believers have cosmic significance. They were not preoccupied with demonic activity or spiritual warfare (as previous generations of Charismatics have been accused), but this understanding of spiritual significance and divine encounter in the small details of life appeared to give the New Life groups the greatest resistance to rationalism of all three churches.[48]

However, few of the dramatic experiences described were personal, they were largely anecdotal and, like other churches, participants were self-critical of the paucity of their prayer lives. There appeared to be a reluctance to share stories of healing or other "proper miracles" despite their reported occurrence at New Life. It seems plausible that New Life members know their testimonies are received with scepticism by outsiders and were unwilling to have them scrutinized and potentially criticized by an unknown researcher. These participants appear to feel the rationalist-supernaturalist tension in a different way. They are confident of their beliefs but reluctant to expose them to ridicule by those they suspected may be sceptics.

It is also interesting that the youngest Trinity Church group expressed considerable curiosity about numinous experience, and some members of the mid-aged Central Chapel group were adamant that supernatural experiences did occur in other countries. It is possible that, among a generation

47. Hopewell, *Congregations*, 76.

48. Hollenweger, "Critical Issues for Pentecostals," 180; Walker, "Demonology," 53–72.

which prioritizes experiential knowledge there is a desire for experience of the numinous.[49] This may explain the success of charismatic evangelical churches within British university towns, since they provide opportunity for supernatural experience *and* biblical engagement.[50] Charismatic spirituality and its romantic worldview also tend to emphasize a Christian form of self-actualization, the idea of individual believers having God-given gifts and a personal calling to participate in divine plans. This may well appeal to a generation of altruistic individualists who are at an exploratory life-stage, attempting to establish their identity and a meaning for their lives.[51] Whether it risks indulging narcissism and self-absorption within "Generation Me" is a legitimate question.[52] Likewise, if numinous experiences are not forthcoming, or long-term Christian discipleship fails to be a romantic adventure, whether this form of evangelicalism can provide believers with resources to maintain their faith throughout adulthood is unclear.

These findings raise questions for all types of evangelicals about biblical literacy and the effects of selectivity in their Scriptural engagement. This includes whether a strong focus on God as benign and the resultant avoidance of significant parts of the Bible will encourage functional Marcionism among portions of the evangelical church.[53] Likewise, consistently presenting God as congenial risks the development of Moralistic Therapeutic Deism among young British evangelicals.[54] However, it should be stressed that there was no evidence of "MTD"' among the data gathered in this study. Despite Smith's assertion that American emerging adults view God as a "divine butler and cosmic therapist," the participants in this project focussed on the service of God as significant for their faith.[55] New Life were most overt about this participation in "kingdom plans," but comments were made in several groups about the responsibility to evangelize and pray for the persecuted. Suffering for the Christian faith and being mocked or misrepresented by non-believers was presented as something to be expected. Certainly, they might expect divine help, but participants did not presume an easy life was

---

49. Although resistant to the excesses of charismatic and Pentecostal spirituality, the leaders of both Trinity Church and Central Chapel expressed a desire to encourage use of some of the charismata, particularly prophecy, but felt uncertain about how to instigate this and aware that portions of their congregations were resistant to such activities.

50. Guest, *University Experience*, 98.

51. Ibid., 27.

52. Twenge, *Generation Me.*

53. Seibert, *Disturbing Divine Behavior*, 67.

54. Smith, "Moralistic Therapeutic Deism," 41.

55. Ibid.

their due. God did not appear to exist for their comfort and convenience; rather, they expressed an understanding of themselves as being subservient to, or in partnership with, his cosmic plans.

These findings are significant in terms of challenging simplistic assumptions that British and American emerging adults hold the same worldview. It suggests a somewhat less individualistic and consumeristic attitude among young British evangelicals, perhaps rooted in them being a distinct minority within a widely secular culture. Whether, in reality, young British evangelicals expect God to give them everything they desire needs further investigation, but what was articulated in these discussions was more in line with traditional understandings of Christian discipleship than with "MTD."

Final Word

This research uncovered a large amount of detailed data about the Bible reading and ordinary hermeneutics of young British evangelicals including how they negotiate the tensions between being members of a post-Christian contemporary society and followers of evangelical Christian faith. It has provided evidence of the nuances within British evangelical belief and praxis, highlighted some differences with American evangelicals, and challenged some of the stereotypes too often made about evangelicalism more widely. However, it is clearly only the beginning of exploring the beliefs and practises of this under-researched demographic group. There is considerable scope for further work in many of the areas explored within this book, both among emerging adults and beyond. A wide range of potential comparative studies would provide fascinating data, as would more directly exploring many of the themes considered. It is also hoped that this study might provide a workable methodology for further explorations of ordinary Bible reading and function as a stimuli for research which will be useful in influencing understanding and praxis within both church and academy. It does not claim to be definitive, but rather lifts the lid on some assumptions, challenges generalizations, and illustrates the sincere faith of those living in a time and place where their beliefs often make them a disregarded or misunderstood minority.

Bibliography

24/7 Prayer. Online: http://www.24-7prayer.com/about/what/.

Acute. *The Nature of Hell*. Edited by David Hilborn. Carlisle, UK: Paternoster, 2000.

Alpha. Online: http://www.alphafriends.org/facts-figures.

Alumkal, A. "Small Groups in Campus Ministry." In *I Come Away Stronger, How Small Groups are Shaping American Religion*, edited by Robert Wuthnow, 251–62. Grand Rapids: Eerdmans, 1994.

Ammerman, Nancy Tatom. *Bible Believers: Fundamentalists in the Modern World*. New Brunswick, NJ: Rutgers, 1987.

———. "Operationalizing Evangelicalism: An Amendment." *Sociological Analysis* 43.2 (1982) 170–71.

Arnett, Jeffrey Jensen. "The Dangers of Generational Myth Making: A Rejoinder to Twenge." *Emerging Adulthood* 1.1 (2013) 17–20.

———. "Emerging Adulthood: A Theory of Development from the Late Teens through the Twenties." *American Psychologist* 55.5 (2000) 469–80.

———. *Emerging Adulthood: The Winding Road from the Late Teens through the Twenties*. Oxford: Oxford University Press, 2004.

Astin, A. W., and H. S. Astin. *Spirituality in College Students: Preliminary Findings from a National Study*. Los Angeles: UCLA, 2003.

Astley, Jeff. "Insights from Faith Development Theory and Research." In *Learning in the Way*, edited by Jeff Astley, 124–42. Leominster, UK: Gracewing, 2000.

———. *Ordinary Theology: Looking, Listening, and Learning in Theology*. Aldershot, UK: Ashgate, 2002.

Aulén, Gustav. *Christus Victor: An Historical Study of the Three Main Types of the Idea of Atonement*. Translated by A. G. Herber. New York: Macmillan, 1969

Aune, Kristen. "Evangelical Christianity and Women's Changing Lives." *The European Journal of Women's Studies* 15.3 (2008) 277–94.

———. "Marriage in a British Evangelical Congregation: Practising Postfeminist Partnership?" *Sociological Review* 54.4 (2006) 638–57.

———. "Singleness and Secularization: British Evangelical Women and Church Disaffiliation." In *Women and Religion in the West: Challenging Secularization*, edited by Kristen Aune et al., 57–70. Aldershot, UK: Ashgate, 2008.

Bach, Alice, ed. *The Pleasure of Her Text: Feminist Readings of Biblical and Historical Texts*. Philadelphia: Trinity, 1990.

Barbour, R. S., and J. Kitzinger, eds. *Developing Focus Group Research: Politics, Theory and Practise*. London: Sage, 1999.

Barclay, Oliver R. *Evangelicalism in Britain 1935–1995: A Personal Sketch.* Leicester, UK: IVP, 1997.

Barr, James. *Fundamentalism.* London: SCM, 1997.

Barrett, C. K. *Acts: A Shorter Commentary.* London: Continuum, 2002.

Bartkowski, John P. "Beyond Biblical Literalism and Inerrancy: Conservative Protestants and Hermeneutic Interpretation of Scripture." *Sociology of Religion* 57 (1996) 259–72.

———. *Remaking the Godly Marriage: Gender Negotiation in Evangelical Families.* New Brunswick, NJ: Rutgers, 2001.

Barton, John. *The Nature of Biblical Criticism.* Louisville: Westminster John Knox, 2007.

Basinger, David. "What Is a Miracle?" In *Miracles,* edited by Graham Twelftree, 19–35. Cambridge: Cambridge University Press, 2011.

Bauerlein, Mark. *The Dumbest Generation: How the Digital Age Stupefies Young Americans and Jeopardizes Our Future. Don't Trust Anyone under 30.* New York: Tercher, 2008.

Bauckham, Richard. *Gospel Women.* Grand Rapids: Eerdmans, 2002.

Baumgartner, M. P. *The Moral Order of a Suburb.* New York: Oxford University Press, 1988.

Beaujouan, Eva, and Máire Ní Bhrolcháin. "Cohabitation and Marriage in Britain since the 1970s." Online: http://www.ons.gov.uk/ons/taxonomy/ index.html? nscl=Age+ at+.

Bebbington, D. W. *Evangelicalism in Modern Britain: A History from the 1730s to the 1980s.* London: Unwin Hyman, 1989.

———. "Evangelical Trends 1959–2009." *Anvil* 26.2 (2009) 93–101.

Beck, Ulrich, and Elisabeth Beck-Gernsheim. *Individualization: Institutionalized Individualism and Its Social and Political Consequences.* London: Sage, 2002.

Beckford, James A. "Forward." In *Religion and Youth,* edited by Sylvia Collins-Mayo and Pink Dandelion, xxiii–xxiv. Farnham, UK: Ashgate, 2010.

Bell, Rob. *Love Wins.* London: Harper Collins, 2011.

———. "Nooma." Online: http://nooma.com.

———. *Sex God.* Grand Rapids: Zondervan, 2011.

———. *Velvet Elvis.* Grand Rapids: Zondervan, 2007.

Bergen, Wesley J. *Elisha and the End of Prophetism.* JSOTSS 286. Sheffield, UK: Sheffield Academic Press, 1999.

Berger, Peter L. *The Sacred Canopy: Elements of a Sociological Theory of Religion.* New York: Random House, 1967.

Berger, Peter L., and Thomas Luckmann. *The Social Construction of Reality.* London: Penguin, 1975.

Berger, Yitzhak. "Ruth and Inner-Biblical Allusion: The Case of 1 Samuel 25." *Journal of Biblical Literature* 128 (2009) 253–72.

Berlin, Adele. "Characterization in Biblical Narrative: David's Wives." *Journal for the Study of Old Testament* 23 (1982) 69–85.

Bethel Church Redding. Online: http://www.ibethel.org/offering-readings.

———. Online: http://bssm.net/about/mission.

Bialecki, Jon. "The Bones Restored to Life: Dialogue and Dissemination in the Vineyard's Dialectic of Text and Presence." In *The Social life of Scriptures,* edited by James Bielo, 136–56. New Brunswick, NJ: Rutgers, 2006.

Bible Society. "H+ Making Good Sense of the Bible." Online: http://www.biblesociety. org.uk /about-bible-society/our-work/h-mgsotb/.

———. "Our Work." Online: http://www.biblesociety.org.uk/about-bible-society/our-work/lectio-divina.

———. "Taking the Pulse: Is the Bible Alive and Well in the Church Today?" Online: www.eauk.org/church/research-and-statistics/attitudes-to-the-bible.cfm.

———. "You've Got Time." Online: http://www.biblesociety.org.uk/news/youve-got-the-time-hits-the-number-one-spot.

Bickle, Mike. "The Father Heart of God." Online: http://mikebickle.org/resources/category/intimacy/father-heart-of-god.

Bielo, James S. *Emerging Evangelicals: Faith, Modernity and the Desire for Authenticity.* New York: New York University Press, 2011.

———. "On the Failure of Meaning: Bible Reading in the Anthropology of Christianity." *Culture and Religion* 9.1 (2008) 1–21.

———, ed. *The Social Life of Scriptures: Cross Cultural Perspectives on Biblicism.* New Brunswick, NJ: Rutgers, 2009.

———. *Words upon the Word: An Ethnography of Evangelical Group Bible Study.* New York: New York University Press, 2009.

Bilezikian, Gilbert. *Beyond Sex Roles: What the Bible Says about a Woman's Place in Church and Family.* Grand Rapids: Baker, 2001.

Birch, Ian. "Baptists and Biblical Interpretation: Reading the Bible with Christ." In *The "Plainly Revealed" Word of God? Baptist Hermeneutics in Theory and Practise,* edited by Helen Dare and Simon Woodman, 153–71. Macon, GA: Mercer University Press, 2011.

Blume, Fred. H. "Justinian." Online: www.uwyo.edu/lawlib/blume-justinian/_files/docs/book9-4.pdf.

Bogle, Kathleen A. *Hooking Up: Sex, Dating, and Relationships on Campus.* New York: New York University Press, 2008.

Bonner, Fred A. et al., eds. *Diverse Millennial Students in College: Implications for Faculty and Student Affairs.* Sterling, VA: Stylus, 2011.

Bonnington, Mark. "Patterns in Charismatic Spirituality." *Anglicans for Renewal* 83 (2001) 29–35.

Boone, Kathleen C. *The Bible Tells Them So: The Discourse of Protestant Fundamentalism.* London: SCM, 1989.

Bosworth, David A. *The Story within the Biblical Hebrew Narrative.* Washington, DC: Imprint, 2008.

Boyd, Gregory A. *Satan and the Problem of Evil: Constructing a Trinitarian Warfare Theodicy.* Downers Grove, IL: IVP, 2001.

Boyle, Marjorie Rourke. "The Law of the Heart: The Death of a Fool 1 Samuel 25." *Journal of Biblical Literature* 120 (2001) 401–27.

Brasher, Brenda. *Godly Women: Fundamentalism and Female Power.* New Brunswick, NJ: Rutgers, 1998.

Brierley, Peter. *Pulling Out of the Nose Dive: A Contemporary Picture of Churchgoing.* London: Christian Research, 2006.

———. *Quantitative Study: Bible Reading Today: Report of the 2003 Survey.* London: Christian Research, 2004.

———. *UKCH Religious Trends, No. 7: British Religion in the 21st Century.* Swindon, UK: Christian Research, 2008.

Briggs, Richard. "The Bible before Us: Evangelical Possibilities for Taking Scripture Seriously." In *New Perspectives for Evangelical Theology*, edited by Tom Greggs, 15–25. London: Routledge, 2010.

———. *Reading the Bible Wisely: An Introduction to Taking Scripture Seriously*. Eugene, OR: Cascade, 2011.

———. "These are the Days of Elijah? The Hermeneutical Move from 'Applying the Text' to 'Living in Its World.'" *Journal of Theological Interpretation* 8.2 (2014) 157–74.

———. *The Virtuous Reader*. Grand Rapids: Baker Academic, 2010.

Brodie, Thomas L. *The Crucial Bridge*. Collegeville, MN: Glazier, 2000.

Brogan, John J. "Can I Have Your Autograph? Uses and Abuses of Textual Criticism in Formulating an Evangelical Doctrine of Scripture." In *Evangelicals and Scripture: Tradition, Authority and Hermeneutics*, edited by Vincent Bacote et al, 93–111. Downers Grove, IL: IVP, 2004.

Brown, Colin. "Issues in the History of the Debates on Miracles." In *Miracles*, edited by Graham Twelftree, 273–90. Cambridge: Cambridge University Press, 2011.

Bruce, F. F. *The Book of Acts*. Grand Rapids: Eerdmans, 1988.

Brueggemann, Walter. *1 & 2 Kings*. Macon, GA: Smyth & Helwys, 2000.

———. *Testimony to Otherwise: The Witness of Elijah and Elisha*. St. Louis, MO: Chalice, 2001.

Bryant, Alyssa N., and Helen Astin. "The Correlates of Spiritual Struggle during the College Years." *Journal of Higher Education* 79.1 (2008) 1–27.

Buckler, G., and J. Astley. "Learning and Believing in an Urban Parish." In *The Contours of Christian Education*, edited by Jeff Astley and David Day, 396–416. Great Wakering, UK: McCrimmons, 1992.

Budgeon, S. "Emergent Feminist? Identities; Young Women, and the Practise of Micro Politics." *The European Journal of Women's Studies* 8.1 (2001) 7–28.

Burgess, J. "Focussing on Fear." *Area* 28.2 (1996) 130–36.

Calver, Clive, and Rob Warner. *Together We Stand*. London: Hodder & Stoughton, 1996.

Calvin, J. *Commentaries on the Book of Joshua*. Grand Rapids: Eerdmans, 1949.

Cameron, H. *Resourcing Mission: Practical Theology for Changing Churches*. London: SCM, 2010.

Campbell, Anne. *A Mind of Her Own: The Evolutionary Psychology of Women*. Oxford: Oxford University Press, 2002.

Campbell, Anthony F. *1 Samuel*. Grand Rapids: Eerdmans, 2003.

Capon, John. *Evangelicals Tomorrow*. Glasgow: Fount, 1977.

Carelton-Paget, James. "Miracles in Early Christianity." In *Miracles*, edited by Graham Twelftree, 131–48. Cambridge: Cambridge University Press, 2011.

Cartledge, Mark J. *Testimony in the Spirit: Rescripting Ordinary Pentecostal Theology*. Farnham, UK: Ashgate, 2010.

Cartedge, Tony W. *1 & 2 Samuel*. Macon, GA: Smyth & Helwys, 2001.

Chalke, Steve, and Alan Mann. *The Lost Message of Jesus*. Grand Rapids: Zondervan, 2003.

Chambers, K. "Knock, Knock—Who's There? Acts 12.6–17 as a Comedy of Errors." In *A Feminist Companion to the Acts of the Apostles*, edited by A. Levine, 89–97. London: Continuum, 2004.

Chambers, Paul. "The Effects of Evangelical Renewal on Mainstream Congregational Identities: A Welsh Case Study." In *Congregational Studies in the UK*, edited by M. Guest et al., 57–70. Aldershot, UK: Ashgate, 2004.

Cherlin, Andrew J. "The Deinstitutionalisation of American Marriage." *Journal of Marriage and Family* 66 (Nov 2004) 848–61.

Christianity Explored. Online: http://www.christianityexplored.org.

Christians for Biblical Equality. "Statement of Faith." Online: http://www.cbe international. org/content/statement-faith.

Christianity Today. "Goodbye Mars Hill." Online: http://www.christianitytoday.com/ gleanings/2014/october/goodbye-mars-hill.

———. "Love Wins." Online: http://www.christianitytoday.com/ct/2011/april/love wins.html.

Christus Victor Ministries. Online: http://www.gregboyd.org.

Claibourne, Shane. *The Irresistible Revolution: Living as an Ordinary Radical*. Grand Rapids: Zondervan, 2006.

———. *Red Letter Revolution: What If Jesus Really Meant What He Said?* Nashville: Thomas Nelson, 2012.

Clark, Andrew C. *Parallel Lives: The Relation of Paul to the Apostles in the Lucan Perspective*. Carlisle, UK: Paternoster, 2001.

Clines, David J. A. *The Bible and the Modern World*. Sheffield, UK: Sheffield Academic Press, 1997.

Coakley, Sarah. *God, Sexuality and the Self*. Cambridge: Cambridge University Press, 2013.

Cocksworth, Christopher. "Holding Together: Catholic Evangelical Worship in the Spirit." In *Remembering our Future*, edited by Andrew Walker and Luke Bretherton, 131–49. Milton Keynes, UK: Paternoster, 2007.

Cohn, Robert. *2 Kings*. Collegeville, MN: Glazier, 2000.

———. "Form and Perspective in 2 Kings V." *Vetus Testamentum* 33.2 (1983) 171–84.

Coleman, Simon. "When Silence Isn't Golden: Charismatic Speech and the Limits of Literalism." In *The limits of Meaning: Case Studies in the Anthropology of Christianity*, edited by Matthew Engelke and Matt Tomlinson, 39–61. New York: Bergham, 2006.

Collins-Mayo, Sylvia. "Evangelicalism and Gender." In *21st Century Evangelicals*, edited by Greg Smith, 102–17. Watford, UK: Instant Apostle, 2015.

——— et al. *The Faith of Generation Y*. London: Church House, 2010.

Collins-Mayo, Sylvia, and Pink Dandelion, eds. *Religion and Youth*. Farnham, UK: Ashgate, 2010.

Conzelmann, Hans. *Acts of the Apostles: A Commentary on the Acts of the Apostles*. Translated by James Limburg. Hermeneia. Philadelphia: Fortress, 1987.

Coupland, Douglas. *Generation X: Tales for an Accelerated Culture*. London: St. Martin's, 1991.

Crapanzano, Vincent. *Serving the Word: Literalism in America from the Pulpit to the Bench*. New York: Free, 2000.

Dare, Helen. "In the Fray: Reading the Bible in Relationship." In *The Plainly Revealed Word of God? Baptist Hermeneutics in Theory and Practice*, edited by Helen Dare and Simon Woodman, 230–52. Macon, GA: Mercer University Press, 2011.

Dawson, John. Online: http://www.lastdaysministries.org.

Day, Abby. "Doing Theodicy: An Empirical Study of a Women's Prayer Group." *Journal of Contemporary Religion* 20.3 (2005) 343–56.

Del Colle, Ralph. "Miracles in Christianity." In *Miracles,* edited by Graham Twelftree, 235–43. Cambridge: Cambridge University Press, 2011.

De Wit, Hans, ed. *Through the Eyes of Another: Intercultural Reading of the Bible.* Indiana: Institute of Mennonite Studies, 2004.

Deyoung, K., "Rob Bell Love Wins Review." Online: http://thegospelcoalition.org/blogs/ kevindeyoung/2011/03/14.

Dickson, Ian. "The Use of the Bible in Pastoral Practice 2002–3." Online: http://www.cardiff.ac.uk/share/research/projectreports/previousprojects/biblepastoral pratice/the-use-of-the-bible-in-pastoral-practice.html.

Douglas, C. E. "From Duty to Desire, Emerging Adulthood in Europe and its Consequences." *Child Development Perspectives* 1.2 (2007) 101–8.

Douglas, S. *Where the Girls Are: Growing Up Female with the Mass Media.* London: Penguin, 1995.

Driscoll, Mark. "Complementarianism." Online: https://theresurgence.com/2009/03 /29/complementarianism.

———."God Works Our Witness." Online: http://marshill.com/media/gods-work-our-witness/ where-are-you.

Dube, M. W., and G. O. West. "Reading With: An Exploration of the Interface between Critical and Ordinary Readings of the Bible: African Overtures." *Semeia* 73 (1996) 1–284.

Dunn, James D. G. *The Acts of the Apostles.* Peterborough, UK: Epworth, 1996.

Earl, Douglas. *The Joshua Delusion: Rethinking Genocide in the Bible.* Eugene, OR: Cascade, 2010.

Edgell Becker, Penny. *Congregation in Conflict: Cultural Models of Local Religious Life.* Cambridge: Cambridge University Press, 1999.

Ekblad, B. *Reading the Bible with the Damned.* Louisville: Westminster John Knox, 2005.

Eldredge, John. *Wild at Heart: Discovering the Secret of a Man's Soul.* Nashville: Thomas Nelson, 2001.

Eldredge, John, and Stasi. *Captivating: Unveiling the Mysteries of a Woman's Soul.* Nashville: Thomas Nelson, 2005.

Ellul, Jacques. *The Politics of God and the Politics of Man.* Grand Rapids: Eerdmans, 1972.

Erikson, Eric, H. *Childhood and Society.* New York: Norton, 1993.

Esler, A. *Generations in History: An Introduction to the Concept.* Williamsburg, VA: Esler, 1982.

Evangelical Alliance. "2010 Report." Online: http://www.eauk.org/snapshot/read.cfm.

———. "Basis of Faith." Online: http://www.eauk.org/about/basis-of-faith.cfm.

———. "Soul Survivor." Online: www.eauk.org/church/stories/soul-survivor.

———. "Women Bishops." Online: http://www.eauk.org/culture/friday-night theology /women-bishops-disagreement-and-division.cfm.

———. "Women Should Lead." Online: http://www.eauk.org/current-affairs/media/press-releases/women-should-lead-in-every-church.cfm.

Faithworks. Online: http://www.faithworks.info/Standard.asp?id=4257.

Fee, Gordon D. "Hermeneutics and Common Sense: An Explanatory Essay on the Hermeneutics of the Epistles." In *Inerrancy and Common Sense,* edited by Roger Nicole and J. Ramsey Michaels, 161–86. Grand Rapids: Baker, 1980.

Fee, Gordon D., and Douglas Stuart. *How to Read the Bible for All It's Worth.* Grand Rapids: Zondervan, 2003.

Fellowship of Independent Evangelical Churches. Online: http://www.fiec.org.uk.

Field, Clive D. "Is the Bible Becoming a Closed Book? British Opinion Poll Evidence." *Journal of Contemporary Religion* 29.3 (2014) 503–28.

Field-Belenky, Mary, et al. *Women's Ways of Knowing.* New York: Basic, 1986.

Firth, David G. *1 & 2 Samuel.* Nottingham, UK: Apollos, 2009.

Finlay, Linda. "Negotiating the Swamp: The Opportunity and Challenge of Reflexivity in Research Practice." *Qualitative Research* 2.2 (2002) 209–30.

Fish, Stanley. *Is There a Text in this Class?* Cambridge: Harvard University Press, 1980.

Fisher, E., et al. "A Survey of Bible Reading Practice and Attitudes to the Bible among Anglican Congregations." In *The Contours of Christian Education,* edited by Jeff Astley and David Day, 387–96. Great Wakering, UK: McCrimmons, 1992.

Florey, Richard, and Donald E. Miller. "The Expressive Communalism of Post-Boomer Religion in the USA." In *Religion and Youth,* edited by Sylvia Collins-Mayo and Pink Dandelion, 9–15. Farnham, UK: Ashgate, 2010.

Flyvbjerg, Bent. "Five Misunderstandings about Case-study Research." In *Qualitative Research Practice,* edited by Clive Seale et al., 420–34. London: Sage, 2004.

Forster, Faith, and Roger Forster. *Women and the Kingdom.* London: PUSH, 2010.

Fowler, James. *Stages of Faith: The Psychology of Human Development and the Quest for Meaning.* San Francisco: Harper Collins, 1995.

Fox, K. *Watching the English.* London: Hodder & Stoughton, 2004.

Frances, L. "Laughter, the Best Mediation: Humour as Emotion Management in Interaction." *Symbolic Interaction* 17 (1994) 147–63.

Francis, Leslie. J. "The Pews Talk Back: The Church Congregation Survey." In *Learning in the Way: Research and Reflection on Adult Christian Education,* edited by Jeff Astley, 161–86. Leominster, UK: Gracewing, 2000.

Friend-Harding, Susan. *The Book of Jerry Falwell: Fundamentalist Language and Politics.* Princeton, NJ: Princeton University Press, 2000.

Fritz, Volkmar. *1 & 2 Kings.* Minneapolis: Fortress, 2003.

Fulcrum. "Evangelical Centre." Online: http://www.fulcrum-anglican.org.uk/about/what-is-the-evangelical-centre.

———. "News." http://www.fulcrumanglican.org.uk/news/2007/20070423wright.Cfm?doc =205.

Fusion. Online: http://www.fusion.uk.com.

Gallagher, Sally. "Defining Spiritual Growth: Congregations, Community and Connectedness." *Sociology of Religion* 70.3 (2009) 232–61.

———. *Evangelical Identity & Gendered Family Life.* New Brunswick, NJ: Rutgers, 2003.

———. "Where Are the Antifeminist Evangelicals? Evangelical Identity, Subcultural Location, and Attitudes toward Feminism." *Gender and Society* 18.4 (2004) 451–72.

Gallagher, Sally, and Sabrina L. Wood. "Godly Manhood Going Wild: Transformations in Conservative Protestant Masculinity." *Sociology of Religion* 66.2 (2005) 135–59.

Gasque, W. *A History of the Interpretation of the Acts of the Apostles.* Peabody, MA: Hendrickson, 1989.

Genz, S., and B. Brabon, eds. *Postfeminism, Cultural Texts and Theories.* Edinburgh: Edinburgh University Press, 2009.

Gibson, D. "Marking the Turn: Obligation, Engagement and Alienation in Group Discussion." *Social Psychology Quarterly* 73.2 (2010) 137–43.

Gilligan, C. "Remapping Development: The Power of Divergent Data." In *Value Presuppositions in Theories of Human Development,* edited by L. Cirillo and S. Wapner, 37–53. Hillsdale, NJ: Earlbaum, 1987.

Gillham, Bill. *The Research Interview.* London: Continuum, 2000.

Glancey, Jennifer A. *Slavery in Early Christianity.* Minneapolis: Fortress, 2006.

Glick, P., and S. Fiske. "Gender, Power Dynamics and Social Interaction." In *Revisioning Gender,* edited by M. Ferree, et al., 365–98. Thousand Oaks, CA: Sage, 1999.

Glick, P., et al. "Beyond Prejudice as Simple Antipathy: Hostile and Benevolent Sexism across Cultures." *Journal of Personality and Social Psychology* 79.5 (2000) 763–75.

Goldingay, John. "Charismatic Spirituality." *Theology* 99 (1996) 179–86.

———. "James Barr on Fundamentalism." *Churchman* 91.4 (1977) 295–308.

Gordon, Robert P. *1 & 2 Samuel: A Commentary.* Library of Biblical Interpretation. Grand Rapids: Zondervan, 1986.

———. "David's Rise and Saul's Demise: Narrative Analogy in 1 Samuel 24–6." *Tyndale Bulletins* 31 (1980) 37–64.

Goss, J. D., and T. R. Leinbach. "Focus Groups as Alternative Research Practice." *Area* 28.2 (1996) 115–23.

Gray, J. *I & II Kings: A Commentary.* London: SCM, 1970.

Green, Barbara. "Enacting Imaginatively the Unthinkable: 1 Samuel 25 and the Story of Saul." *Biblical Interpretation* 11 (2003) 1–23.

Green, Joel B. and Mark D. Baker. *Recovering the Scandal of the Cross: Atonement in New Testament and Contemporary Contexts.* Downers Grove, IL: IVP, 2000.

Greenbelt. Online: http://www.greenbelt.org.uk/about/organisation/values.

Greggs, Tom. *New Perspectives for Evangelical Theology.* London: Routledge, 2010.

Grenz, Stanley. "Introduction." In *Evangelicals and Scripture,* edited by Vincent Bacote et al., 11–12. Downers Grove, IL: IVP, 2004.

Grenz, Stanley, and Roger E. Olsen, *Who Needs Theology? An Invitation to the Study of God.* Downers Grove, IL: IVP, 1996.

Griffith, Marie. *God's Daughters: Evangelical Women and the Power of Submission.* Berkeley: University of California Press, 2000.

Grudem, Wayne. "Continuism and Cessationism." Online: http://www.challies.com/ interviews/continuationism-and-cessationism-an-interview-with-dr-wayne-grudem.

———. *Systematic Theology: An Introduction to Biblical Doctrine.* Leicester, UK: IVP, 2000.

———. "Women Pastors." Online: http://www.beliefnet.com/Faiths/Christianity/ 2006/10/Women-Pastors-Not-The-Path-To-Blessing.aspx?p=1.

Guest, Mathew, et al., *Christianity and the University Experience: Understanding Student Faith.* London: Bloomsbury Academic, 2013.

———. *Evangelical Identity and Contemporary Culture: A Congregational Study in Innovation.* Evangelical History and Thought. Milton Keynes, UK: Paternoster, 2007.

————. "Evangelicalism and Politics." In *21st Century Evangelicals*, edited by Greg Smith, 82–99. Watford, UK: Instant Apostle, 2015.

————. "Friendship, Fellowship and Acceptance: Public Discourse of an Evangelical Church." In *Congregational Studies in the UK*, edited by Mathew Guest et al., 71–83. Aldershot, UK: Ashgate, 2004.

Guest, Mathew, et al., eds. *Congregational Studies in the UK*. Aldershot, UK: Ashgate, 2004.

Gundry, Patricia. *Heirs Together: Applying the Biblical Principle of Mutual Submission in Your Marriage*. Grand Rapids: Suitcase, 1999.

Gunn, David M. *The Fate of King Saul: An Interpretation of a Biblical Story*. JSOTSupp Sheffield, UK: Sheffield Academic Press, 1980.

Halpern, Baruch. *David's Secret Demons: Messiah, Murderer, Traitor, King*. Grand Rapids: Eerdmans, 2001.

Hanson, R. P. C. *The Acts in the Revised Standard Version*. Oxford: Oxford University Press, 1967.

Harrill, J. "The Dramatic Function of the Running Slave Rhoda in Acts 12.13–16: A Piece of Greco-Roman Comedy." *New Testament Studies* 46.1 (2000) 150–57.

Harris, Harriet A. *Fundamentalism and Evangelicals*. Oxford: Clarendon, 2007.

Harris, M. "Completion and Faith Development." In *Faith Development and Fowler*, edited by C. Dykstra and S. Parks, 15–33. Birmingham: Religious Education, 1986.

Hattaway, B. Y. P. *The Heavenly Man: The Remarkable True Story of Chinese Christian Brother Yun*. Oxford: Monarch, 2002.

Hays, Richard B. *The Moral Vision of the New Testament: Community, Cross, New Creation: A Contemporary Introduction*. Edinburgh: T. & T. Clark, 1997.

Hendry, Leo N., and Marion Kloep. "Redressing the Emperor! A rejoinder to Arnett." *Child Development Perspectives* 1.2 (2007) 74–79.

Hennink, M. *International Focus Group Research: A Handbook for the Health and Social Sciences*. Cambridge: Cambridge University Press, 2007.

Henry, Carl. "Those Incomprehensible British Fundamentalists." *Christianity Today*, June 2, 1978, 22–26.

Hens-Piazza, Gina. *1–2 Kings*. Nashville: Abingdon, 2006.

Hilborn, David ed. *Toronto in Perspective: Papers on the New Charismatic Wave of the Mid-1990s*. Carlisle, UK: Paternoster, 2001.

Hilborn, David, and Matt Bird, eds. *God and the Generations: Youth Age, and the Church Today*. Carlisle, UK: Paternoster, 2002.

Hill, Jonathan. "Faith and Understanding: Specifying the Impact of Higher Education on Religious Belief." *Journal for the Scientific Study of Religion* 50.3 (2011) 543–46.

Hobbs, T. R. *2 Kings*. Word Biblical Commentaries. Waco, TX: Word, 1985.

Hollenweger, Walter J. *Critical Issues for Pentecostals*. JJPTSS 15. Sheffield, UK: Sheffield Academic Press, 1999.

————. "Crucial Issues for Pentecostals." In *Pentecostals after a Century: Global Perspectives on a Movement in Transition*, edited by Allan H. Anderson and Walter J. Hollenweger, 164–72. Sheffield, UK: Sheffield Academic Press, 1999.

Holmes, Stephen R. "Evangelical Theology and Identity." In *21st Century Evangelicals*, edited by Greg Smith, 23–36. Watford, UK: Instant Apostle, 2015.

Holy Trinity Brompton. Online: http://www.htb.org.uk.

Hoover, Eric. "The Millennial Muddle." Online: http://www.Chronicle.com/article/the-Millenial-Muddle-How/48772/Oct.11.

Hopewell, J. F. *Congregation: Stories and Structure*. London: SCM, 1998.

Howe, Neil, and William Strauss. *Generations: The History of America's Future, 1584 to 2069*. New York: Morrow, 1991.

Hunt, Stephen. "Magical Moments: An Intellectualist Approach to the Neo-Pentecostal Faith Ministries." *Religion* 28.1 (1998) 271–80.

Ingersoll, Julie. *Evangelical Christian Women: War Stories in the Gender Battles*. New York: New York University Press, 2003.

Irby, Courtney Ann. "Dating in Light of Christ: Young Evangelicals Negotiating Gender in the Context of Religious and Secular American Culture." *Sociology of Religion* 75.2 (2014) 260–83.

James, D., and J. Drakich. "Understanding Gender Differences in Amount of Talk: A Critical Review of Research." In *Gender and Conversational Interaction*, edited by D. Tannen, 281–312. Oxford: Oxford University Press, 1993.

James, William. *The Varieties of Religious Experience: A Study in Human Nature, Centenary Edition*. London: Routledge, 2004.

Jobling, David. *1 Samuel*. Collegeville, MN: Liturgical, 1998.

Johnson, Bill, *Face to Face with God*. Lake Mary, FL: Charisma House, 2007.

———. *When Heaven Invades Earth: A Practical Guide to a Life of Miracles*. Shippensburg, PA: Treasure House, 2003.

Josephus, Flavius. *The Genuine Works of Flavius Josephus*. Translated by William Whiston. Newcastle upon Tyne, UK: Dinsdale & Angys, 1784.

Kay, William K. *Apostolic Networks in Britain: New Ways of Being Church*. Studies in Evangelical History and Thought. Milton Keynes, UK: Paternoster, 2007.

Kaye, Bruce N. *The Supernatural in the New Testament*. Guildford, UK: Lutterworth, 1977.

Keener, Craig S. *Miracles: The Credibility of the New Testament Accounts, Vol. 1*. Grand Rapids: Baker Academic, 2011.

Keller, Timothy. *The Prodigal God: Recovering the Heart of the Christian Faith*. New York: Penguin, 2008.

———. *The Reason for God: Belief in an Age of Scepticism*. London: Hodder & Stoughton, 2008.

Kertzer, David I. "Generation as a Sociological Problem." *Annual Review of Sociology* 9 (1983) 125–49.

Keswick Convention. Online: www.keswickministries.org.

Kim, Jean Kyoung. "Reading and Retelling Naaman's Story 2 Kings 5." *Journal for the Study of the Old Testament* 30 (2005) 49–61.

Kimball, Dan. *They Like Jesus But Not the Church*. Grand Rapids: Zondervan, 2007.

Kitzinger, J., and C. Farquhar. "The Analytical Potential of 'Sensitive Moments' in Focus Group Discussions." In *Developing Focus Group Research*, edited by R. Barbour and J. Kitzinger, 156–57. London: Sage, 1999.

———. "Introducing Focus Groups." *British Medical Journal* 311 (1995) 299–302.

———. "Introduction." In *Developing Focus Group Research; Politics, Theory and Practise*, edited by R. S. Barbour and J. Kitzinger, 1–6. London: Sage, 1999.

———. "The Methodology of Focus Groups: The Importance of Interaction between Research Participants." *Sociology of Health and Illness* 16.1 (1994) 4–19.

Klein, Ralph W. *1 Samuel*. Word Biblical Commentary. Nashville: Thomas Nelson, 1983.

Koening, L. B., et al. "Stability and Change in Religiousness during Emerging Adulthood." *Developmental Psychology* 44 (2008) 532–43.

Kraft, Charles H. *Defeating Dark Angels: Breaking Demonic Oppression in the Believer's Life.* Tonbridge, UK: Sovereign World, 1993.

Krueger, Richard A. *Focus Groups.* London: Sage, 1994.

———. *Focus Groups: A Practical Guide for Applied Research.* London: Sage, 1988.

Larkin, William J. *Acts.* Downers Grove, IL: IVP, 1995.

Larmer, Robert A. "The Meaning of Miracles." In *Miracles,* edited by Graham Twelftree, 36–54. Cambridge: Cambridge University Press, 2011.

Larsen, Timothy. "Defining and Locating Evangelicalism." In *Cambridge Companion to Evangelical Theology,* edited by Timothy Larsen and Daniel Trier, 1–14. Cambridge: Cambridge University Press, 2007.

Lash, Nicholas. *The Beginning and the End of Religion.* Cambridge: Cambridge University Press, 1996.

Lawrence, Louise. J. *The Word in Place: Reading the New Testament in Contemporary Contexts.* London: SPCK, 2009.

Lawrence, James. "Engaging Gen Y: Leading Well across the Generations." *Grove Leadership Series* L8. Cambridge: Grove, 2012.

Lefkowitz, E. S. "Things Have Gotten Better: Developmental Changes among Emerging Adults after the Transition to University." *Journal of Adolescent Research* 20 (2005) 40–63.

Lehtinen, Esa. "Conversation Analysis and Religion: Practices of Talking about Bible Texts in Seventh Day Adventist Bible Study." *Religion* 39 (2009) 233–47.

Leithart, Peter. *1 & 2 Kings.* Grand Rapids: Baker, 2006.

Levinson, Daniel J. *Seasons of a Man's Life.* New York: Knopf, 1978.

Levenson, Jon D. "1 Samuel 25 as Literature and as History." *Catholic Biblical Quarterly* 40 (1978) 11–28.

Levenson, Jon D., and Baruch Halpern. "The Political Import of David's Marriages." *Journal of Biblical Literature* 99 (1980) 507–18.

Levenson, Michael R., et al. "Religious Development from Adolescence to Middle Adulthood." In *Handbook of the Psychology of Religion and Spirituality,* edited by R. F. Paloutzian and C. L. Park, 144–61. New York: Guildford, 2005.

Liebert, Elizabeth. "Seasons and Stages." In *In Her Own Time,* edited by Jeanne Stephenson-Moessner, 19–44. Minneapolis: Fortress, 2000.

Llewellyn, Dawn. "Across Generations: Women's Spiritualties, Literary Texts, and Third Wave Feminism." In *Feminist Spirituality: The Next Generation,* edited by C. Klassen, 179–200. Lanham, MD: Lexington , 2009.

Loevinger, Jane. *Ego Development.* San Francisco: Jossey-Bass, 1976.

London Institute for Contemporary Christianity. "Life on the Frontline." Online: http://www.licc.org. uk/imagine-church/resources/life-on-the-frontline.

Longnecker, Richard N. *Acts.* The Expositors Bible Commentary. Grand Rapids: Zondervan, 1995.

Lüdemann, Gerd. *Early Christianity according to the Traditions in Acts: A Commentary.* Minneapolis: Fortress, 1989.

Luhrmann, T. M. *When God Talks Back: Understanding the American Evangelical Relationship with God.* New York: Vintage, 2012.

Luna, B. et al. "Maturation of Cognitive Processes from Late Childhood to Adulthood." *Child Development* 15.5 (2004) 1357–72.

Maddox, M. "Rise Up Warrior Princess Daughters: Is Evangelical Women's Submission a Mere Fairy Tale?" *Journal of Feminist Studies in Religion* 29.1 (2013) 9–26.

Malley, Brian. *How the Bible Works: An Anthropological Study of Evangelical Biblicism.* Walnut Creek, CA: Altamira, 2004.

———. "Understanding the Bible's Influence." In *The Social Life of Scriptures: Cross Cultural Perspectives on Biblicism,* edited by James Bielo, 194–204. New Brunswick: Rutgers, 2009.

Mannheim, Karl. "The Problem of Generations." In *Essays on the Sociology of Knowledge,* 276–320. New York: Oxford University Press, 1952.

Marcus, D. *From Baalam to Jonah: Anti Prophetic Satire in the Hebrew Bible.* Atlanta: Scholars, 1995.

Markova, I., et al. *Dialogue in Focus Groups: Exploring Socially Shared Knowledge.* London: Equinox, 2007.

Marsden, George, M. *Understanding Fundamentalism and Evangelicalism.* Grand Rapids: Eerdmans, 1991.

Marsden, Paul, and Roger Forster. *God's Strategy in Human History.* Eugene, OR: Wipf & Stock, 2000.

Marshall, I. Howard. *The Acts of the Apostles: An Introduction and Commentary.* Leicester, UK: IVP, 1980.

———. *Beyond the Bible: Moving from Scripture to Theology.* Grand Rapids: Baker Academic, 2004.

Martin, Lee Roy. "Introduction to Pentecostal Hermeneutics." In *Pentecostal Hermeneutics: A Reader,* edited by R. D. Moore, 1–9. Leiden: Brill, 2013.

Mayrl, Damon, and Freeden Oeur. "Religion and Higher Education: Current Knowledge and Directions for Future Research." *Journal for the Scientific Study of Religion* 48.2 (2009) 260–75.

Mason, Michael. "The Spirituality of Young Australians." In *Religion and Youth,* edited by Sylvia Collins-Mayo and Pink Dandelion, 55–62. Farnham, UK: Ashgate, 2010.

MacArthur, John F. Online: http://johnmacarthur.org/.

McClaren, Brian. "Will Love Wins Win?" Online: http://brianmclaren.net/archives/blog/challenging-three-cherished-evan.html.

McClung, Floyd. *The Father Heart of God.* London: Kingsway, 1985.

McGrath, Alister E. *Evangelicalism and the Future of Christianity.* London: Hodder & Stoughton, 1995.

McGuire, Meredith B. *The Social Context.* Long Grove, IL: Waveland, 2002.

McKenzie, Steven L. *King David: A Biography.* Oxford: Oxford University Press, 2000.

McMullin, J., et al. "Generational Affinities and Discourses of Difference: A Case Study of Highly Skilled Information Technology Workers." *British Journal of Sociology* 58.2 (2007) 297–316.

McNamara Barry, Carolyn, et al. "Religiosity and Spirituality during the Transition to Adulthood." *International Journal of Behavioural Development* 34.4 (2010) 311–24.

Meadors, Gary T., ed. *Four Views on Moving beyond the Bible to Theology.* Grand Rapids: Zondervan, 2009.

Merrill-Groothuis, R. *Women Caught in the Conflict.* Grand Rapids: Baker, 1994.

Miles, A. "Overcoming the Challenges of Pastoral Work? Peer Support Groups and Psychological Distress among United Methodist Church Clergy." *Sociology of Religion* 74.2 (2013) 199–226.

Miscal, Peter D. *1 Samuel: A Literary Reading*. Bloomington: Indiana University Press, 1986.

Missional Communities. Online: http://missionalcommunities.co.uk.

Moberly, Walter. "Miracles in the Hebrew Bible." In *Miracles*, edited by Graham Twelftree, 57–74. Cambridge: Cambridge University Press, 2011.

———."Is Monotheism Bad for You? Some Reflections on God, the Bible, and Life in the Light of Regina Schwartz's 'The Curse of Cain." In *The God of Israel*, 94–112. Cambridge: Cambridge University Press, 2007.

Momentum. Online: http://momentum.co.uk.

Montgomery, D. *Sing a New Song*. Edinburgh: Rutherford House, 2000.

Moore, Rick D. *God Saves: Lessons from the Elisha Stories*. Sheffield, UK: Sheffield Academic Press, 1990.

———. "A Pentecostal Approach to Scripture." In *Pentecostal Hermeneutics*, edited by Lee Roy Martin, 11–14. Boston: Brill, 2013.

Morgan, David L. *Focus Groups as Qualitative Research*. London: Sage, 1988.

Morgan, David L., and R. A. Krueger. "When to Use Focus Groups and Why." In *Successful Focus Groups*, edited by David L. Morgan, 15–16. London: Sage, 1993.

Murphy, Francesca Aran. *1 Samuel*. Grand Rapids: Brazos, 2010.

Murphy, Liam D. "The Trouble with Good News; Scripture and Charisma in Northern Ireland." In *The Social Life of Scriptures, Cross Cultural Perspective on Biblicism*, edited by James S. Bielo, 10–29. New Brunswick, NJ: Rutgers, 2009.

Myers, Ched. *Binding the Strong Man: A Political Reading of Mark's Story of Jesus*. Maryknoll, NY: Orbis, 1998.

Myers, Greg. "Enabling Talk: How the Facilitator Shapes a Focus Group." *Talk & Text* 27 (2007) 79–106.

Nash, Sally, et al. *The Faith of Generation Y*. London: Church House, 2010.

Nelson, Richard. *First and Second Kings*. Louisville: Westminster John Knox, 1987.

New Calvinist.com. "Tim Keller's False Gospel." http://www.newcalvinist.com/tim-kellers-false-gospel.

New Frontiers. Online: http://www.newfrontierstogether.org/.

New Wine. Online: http://www.new-wine.org.

———. "Vision and Values." Online: http://www.new-wine.org/home/vision-a-values.

New Word Alive. "Declaration of Belief." Online: http://newwordalive.org/about-us/declaration-of-belief.

Nicol, George G. "David, Abigail and Bathsheba, Nab Al and Uriah: Transformations within a Triangle." *Scandinavian Journal of the Old Testament* 12 (1998) 133–40.

North West Training Partnership. Online: http://northwestpartnership.com.

Okamoto, D., and L. Smith-Lovin. "Changing the Subject: Gender, Status and the Dynamics of Topic Change." *American Sociological Review* 66.6 (2001) 852–73.

Osgood, D. Wayne, et al. "Six Paths to Adulthood; Fast Starters, Parents without Careers, Educated Partners, Educated Singles, Working Singles and Slow Starters." In *On the frontier of Adulthood; Theory, Research and Public Policy*, edited by R. A. Settersten Jr., et al, 320–47. Chicago: University of Chicago Press, 2005.

Osiek, Carol. *Families in the New Testament World: Households and House Churches*. Louisville: Westminster John Knox, 1997.

Packer, J. I. "Infallible Scripture and the Role of Hermeneutics." In *Scripture and Truth*, edited by D. A. Carson and J. D. Woodbridge, 325–56. Grand Rapids: Zondervan, 1983.

————. "Understanding the Bible: Evangelical Hermeneutics." In *Restoring the Vision*, edited by M. Tinker, 27–35. Eastbourne, UK: Monarch, 1990.

Pally, Marcia. *The New Evangelicals: Expanding the Vision of the Common Good*. Grand Rapids: Eerdmans, 2011.

Parks, Sharon. *The Critical Years: The Young Adult Search for a Faith to Live by*. San Francisco: Harper & Row, 1986.

Pascarella, Ernest T., and Patrick T. Terenzini. *How College Affects Students: A Third Decade of Research*. San Francisco: Jossey-Bass, 2005.

Peden, A. "Contextual Bible Study at Cornton Vale Women's Prison, Stirling." *The Expository Times* 117 (2005) 15–18.

Pelikan, Jaroslav. *Acts*. Grand Rapids: Brazos, 2006.

Penchansky, D. *What Rough Beast? Images of God in the Hebrew Bible*. Louisville, KY: Westminster John Knox, 1999.

Peppiatt, Lucy. "Response to Stephen Holmes, 'Evangelical Theology and Identity.'" In *21st Century Evangelicals*, edited by Greg Smith, 37–38. Watford, UK: Instant Apostle, 2015.

Percy, Martin. *The Toronto Blessing*. Oxford: Latimer House, 1996.

Perriman, Andrew. *Faith, Health and Prosperity: A Report on 'Word of Faith' and 'Positive Confession' Theologies*. Carlisle, UK: Paternoster, 2003.

Perrin, Ruth. "How Might the Evangelical Church Use Neglected, Female, Biblical Role Models as a Method of Discipleship and Empowerment amongst Young Women?" MATM diss., Durham University, 2007.

————. "Inspiring Women: Discovering Biblical Role Models." *Grove Biblical Series* B52, Cambridge: Grove, 2009.

————. "Searching For Sisters: The Influence of Biblical Role Models on Young Women from Mainstream and Charismatic Evangelical Traditions." In *The Faith Lives of Women and Girls*, edited by Nicola Slee et al., 111–20. Farnham, UK: Ashgate, 2013.

Pervo, R. I. *Acts: A Commentary*. Minneapolis: Fortress, 2009.

————. *Profit with Delight: The Literary Genre of the Acts of the Apostles*. Philadelphia: Fortress, 1987.

Peterson, David G. *The Acts of the Apostles*. Grand Rapids: Eerdmans, 2009.

Pilch, John J. *Flights of the Soul: Visions, Heavenly Journey, and Peak Experiences in the Biblical World*. Grand Rapids: Eerdmans, 2011.

Pinnock, Clark H. "The Work of the Spirit in the Interpretation of Holy Scripture from the Perspective of a Charismatic Biblical Theologian." In *Pentecostal Hermeneutics: A Reader*, edited by R. D. Moore, 233–48. Leiden: Brill, 2013.

Piper, John. *Countering the Claims of Evangelical Feminism: Biblical Responses to Key Questions*. Colorado Springs: Multnomah, 2006.

————. "The Supremacy of Christ." Online: http://www.desiringgod.org/conference-messages/the-supremacy-of-christ-and-joy-in a-postmodern-world.

Poland, B., and A. Pederson. "Reading between the Lines: Interpreting Silences in Qualitative Research." *Qualitative Enquiry* 293.4 (1998) 194–308.

Porter, Stanley E. "Hermeneutics, Biblical Interpretation, and Theology: Hunch, Holy Spirit, or Hard Work?" In *Beyond the Bible: Moving from Scripture to Theology*, edited by Howard I. Marshall, 97–128. Grand Rapids: Baker Academic, 2004.

Powell, Mark Allen. *Chasing the Eastern Star*. Louisville: Westminster John Knox, 2001.

————. *What Do They Hear?* Nashville: Abingdon, 2007.

Powell, R. A., and H. M Single. "Focus Groups." *International Journal of Quality in Health Care* 8.5 (1996) 499–504.

Prince, Derek. *They Shall Expel Demons*. Grand Rapids: Chosen, 1998.

Proclamation Trust. Online. http://www.proctrust.org.uk.

———. "Women's Conference." Online: http://www.proctrust.org.uk/conferences/women-in-ministry.

Provan, Iain W. *1 and 2 Kings*. NIBCOT. Peabody, MA: Hendrickson, 1995.

Race, K. E. et al. "Rehabilitation Program Evaluation: Use of Focus Groups to Empower Clients." *Evaluation Review* 18.6 (1994) 730–40.

Rainer, T., and J. Rainer. *The Millennials*. Nashville: B. & H., 2011.

Randall, Ian. *Educating Evangelicalism: The Origins, Development and IMpact of London Bible College*. Carlisle, UK: Paternoster, 2000.

Redfern, Catherine, and Kristin Aune. *Reclaiming the F Word*. London: Zed, 2010.

Reform. "Covenant." Online: http://reform.org.uk/about/reform-covenant.

Reimer, Sam. "Higher Education and Theological Liberalism: Revisiting the Old Issue." *Sociology of Religion* 71.4 (2010) 403–8.

Reynolds, T. "Friendship Networks, Social Capital and Ethnic Identity." *Journal of Youth Studies* 10.4 (2007) 383–398.

Richter, Philip. "Denominational Cultures: The Cinderella of Congregational Studies?" In *Congregational Studies in the UK*, edited by Mathew Guest et al., 169–84. Aldershot, UK: Ashgate, 2004.

Richter Reimer, Ivoni. *Women in the Acts of the Apostles: A Feminist Liberation Perspective*. Translated by Linda M. Maloney. Minneapolis: Fortress, 1995.

Ridgeway C., and L. Smith-Lovin. "The Gender System and Interaction." *Annual Review of Sociology* 25 (1999) 191–216.

Ritchie J., and J. Lewis. *Qualitative Research Practice: A Guide for Social Science Students and Researchers*. London: Sage, 2003.

Robbins, Joel. "The Globalization of Pentecostal and Charismatic Christianity." *Annual Review of Anthropology* 33 (2004) 117–43.

Robbins, Mandy, and William K. Kay. "Evangelicals and the Charismatic Movement." In *21st Century Evangelicals*, edited by Greg Smith, 137–53. Watford, UK: Instant Apostle, 2015.

Robinson, D., and L. Smith-Lovin. "Getting a Laugh: Gender, Status and Humor in Task Discussions." *Social Forces* 80.1 (2001) 123–58.

Rogers, Andrew P. "Ordinary Biblical Hermeneutics and the Transformation of Congregational Horizons within English Evangelicalism: A Theological Ethnographic Study." PhD diss., King's College, London, 2009.

Roland, Emily K. "More Than Alone with the Bible: Reconceptualising Religious Reading." *Sociology of Religion* 73.3 (2012) 323–44.

Ruthven, Jon. *On the Cessation of the Charismata: The Protestant Polemic on Postbiblical Miracles*. Sheffield, UK: Sheffield Academic Press, 1993.

Ryan L. "Islam Does Not Change: Young People Narrating Negotiations of Religion and Identity." *Journal of Youth Studies* 17.4 (2014) 446–60.

Ryder, Norman B. "The Cohort as a Concept in the Study of Social Change." *American Sociological Review* 30 (1965) 843–61.

Sacks, H. "An Analysis of the Course of a Joke's Telling in Conversation." In *Explorations in the Ethnography of Speaking*, edited by R. Bauman and J. Sherzer, 337–53. Cambridge: Cambridge University Press, 1974.

Sanders, J. "Divine Suffering in an Openness of God Perspective." In *The Sovereignty of God Debate*, edited by G. Stephen Long and G. Kalantzis, 112–37. Cambridge: Clark, 2010.

Savage, Sara, et al. *Making Sense of Generation Y: The Worldview of 15–25 year olds.* London: Church House, 2011.

Scotland, Nigel. *Charismatics and the Next Millennium.* London: Hodder & Stoughton, 1995.

———. "Evangelicalism and the Charismatic Movement." In *The Futures of Evangelicalism: Issues and Prospects*, edited by Craig Bartholomew et al., 271–301. Leicester, UK: IVP, 2003.

Schüssler Fiorenza, Elizabeth. *Bread Not Stone: Challenge of Feminist Biblical Interpretation.* Edinburgh: T. & T. Clark, 1984.

———. *Searching the Scriptures.* New York: Crossroad, 1993.

Searl, N. "The Women's Bible Study: A Thriving Evangelical Support Group." In *"I Come Away Stronger" How Small Groups are Shaping American Religion*, edited by R. Wuthnow, 100–112. Grand Rapids: Eerdmans, 1994.

Sears, James T., and J. Dan Marshall. "Generational Influences on Contemporary Curriculum Thought." *Journal of Curriculum Studies* 32.2 (2000) 199–214.

Segovia, F., and M. A. Tolbert, eds. *Reading from this Place, Vols. 1 & 2.* Minneapolis: Fortress, 1995.

Seibert, E. A. *Disturbing Divine Behavior: Troubling Old Testament Images of God.* Minneapolis: Fortress, 2009.

Seim, Turid Karlsen. *The Double Message: Patterns of Gender in Luke-Acts.* Edinburgh: T. & T. Clark, 1994.

Sennett, R. *Together: The Rituals, Pleasures and Politics of Cooperation.* London: Penguin, 2012.

Shanahan, M., et al. "Subjective Age Identity and the Transition to Adulthood: When to Adolescents become Adults?" In *On the Frontier of Adulthood: Theory, Research and Public Policy*, edited by R. A. Settersten et al., 225–55. Chicago: University of Chicago Press, 2005.

Shields, Mary. "A Feast Fit for a King: Food and Drink in the Abigail Story." In *The Fate of King David: The Past and Present of a Biblical Icon*, edited by Tod Linafelt et al., 38–54. London: T. & T. Clark, 2010.

Sim, J. "Collecting and Analysing Qualitative Data, Issues Raised by the Focus Group." *Journal of Advance Nursing* 92 (1998) 345–52.

Slee, Nicola. *Faith and Feminism: An Introduction to Christian Feminist Theology.* London: Darton, Longman & Todd, 2003.

Smail, Tom, et al. *The Love of Power of the Power of Love; A Careful Assessment of the Problems within the Charismatic and Word-of-Faith Movements.* Minneapolis: Bethany House, 1994.

Smith, Christian, et al. *Lost in Transition: The Dark Side of Emerging Adulthood.* Oxford: Oxford University Press, 2011.

———. "On 'Moralistic Therapeutic Deism' as US Teenagers' Actual, Tacit, *De facto* Religious Faith." In *Religion and Youth*, edited by Sylvia Collins Mayo and Pink Dandelion, 41–46. Farnham, UK: Ashgate, 2010.

———. *Souls in Transition: The Religious and Spiritual Lives of Emerging Adults.* Oxford: Oxford University Press, 2009.

————. *Soul Searching: The Religious and Spiritual Lives of American Teenagers.* Oxford: Oxford University Press, 2005.

Smith, Mark. "This Is That Hermeneutics." In *The Mark of the Spirit? A Charismatic Critique of the 'Blessing' Phenomenon,* edited by Lloyd Pieterson, 33–62. Carlisle, UK: Paternoster, 1998.

Smith, Greg, ed. *21st Century Evangelicals.* Watford, UK: Instant Apostle, 2015.

Smith-Lovin, L., and C. Brody. "Interruptions in Group Discussions: The Effects of Gender and Group Composition." *American Sociological Review* 54.3 (1989) 424–35.

Sophia Network. Online: http://blog.sophianetwork.org.uk.

————. "Is Jesus a Feminist?" Online: http://blog.sophianetwork.org.uk/2014/03/is-jesus-a-feminist-an-introduction.html.

Soul Survivor. Online: http://soulsurvivor.co.uk

Sparks, Kenton L. *God's Word in Human Words.* Grand Rapids: Baker Academic, 2008.

Spencer, F. Scott. *Acts.* Sheffield, UK: Sheffield Academic Press, 1997.

Spring Harvest. "Our Beliefs." Online: http://www.springharvest.org/about-us/our-beliefs/.

Stacey, J., and S. Gerard. "We Are Not Doormats: The Influence of Feminism on Contemporary Evangelicals in the United States." In *Uncertain Terms: Negotiating Gender in American Culture,* edited by F. Ginsburgh and A. Lowenhaupt Tsing, 98–117 Boston: Beacon, 1990.

Steussy, Marti J. *David: Biblical Portraits of Power.* Columbia: University of South Carolina Press, 1999.

Steven, James H. S. *Worship in the Spirit.* Studies in Evangelical History and Thought. Carlisle, UK: Paternoster, 2002.

Stevenson-Moessner, Jeanne. *In Her Own Time.* Minneapolis: Fortress, 2000.

Stibbe, Mark. "This Is That: Some Thoughts concerning Charismatic Hermeneutics." *Anvil* 15.3 (1998) 181–93.

Stopp, Tara L., and E. Lefkowitz. "Longitudinal Changes in Religiosity among Emerging Adult College Students." *Journal of Research on Adolescence* 20.1 (2010) 23–38.

Storkey, Elaine. *What's Right with Feminism?* London: SPCK, 1985.

Stott, John R. W. "Are Evangelicals Fundamentalists?" *Christianity Today,* Sept. 8, 1978, 44–46.

————. *Between Two Worlds: The Art of Preaching in the Twentieth Century.* Grand Rapids; Eerdmans, 1982.

————. *Evangelical Truth: A Personal Plea for Unity, Integrity and Faithfulness.* Leicester, UK: IVP, 2003.

————. *I Believe in Preaching.* London: Hodder & Stoughton, 1983.

————. *The Message of Acts: The Spirit, the Church & the World* Leicester, UK: IVP, 1990.

Strhan, Anna. "Discipleship and Desire: Conservative Evangelicals, Coherence and the Moral Lives of the Metropolis." PhD diss, University of Kent, 2012.

————. "Practising the Space Between: Embodying Belief as an Evangelical Anglican Student." *Journal of Contemporary Religion* 28.2 (2013) 225–39.

Stringer, M. D. *Contemporary Western Ethnography and the Definition of Religion.* London: Continuum, 2008.

Tacey, David. "What Spirituality Means to Young Adults." In *Religion and Youth,* edited by Sylvia Collins-Mayo and Pink Dandelion, 67–71. Farnham, UK: Ashgate, 2010.

Tannen, D. *Conversational Style: Analyzing Talk among Friends.* New York: Ablex, 1984.

————. *Gender and Discourse.* Oxford: Oxford University Press, 1994.

————. "Silence, Anything But." In *Perspectives on Silence*, edited by D. Tannen and M. Saville-Troike, 93–112. New York: Ablex, 1995.

Thiselton, Anthony C. *The Holy Spirit in Biblical Teaching, through the Centuries and Today.* London: SPCK, 2013.

————. *The Two Horizons: New Testament Hermeneutics and Philosophical Description.* Exeter, UK: Paternoster, 1980.

————. "Understanding God's Word Today." In *Obeying Christ in a Changing World*, edited by John Stott, 90–122. Glasgow: Fountain, 1977.

Thomson, John B. "Phronesis and Sophia: Church and Academy Practising Theology in Concert?" *Journal of Adult Theological Education* 1.2 (2004) 133–46.

Todd, Andrew J. "The Interactions of Talk and Text: Re-contextualizing Biblical Interpretation." *Practical Theology* 6.1 (2013) 69–85.

————. "The Talk, Dynamics and Theological Practice of Bible-study Groups: A Qualitative Empirical Investigation." PhD diss, Cardiff University, 2009.

Trible Phyllis, *Texts of Terror: Literary-Feminist Readings of Biblical Narratives.* Philadelphia: Fortress, 1984.

Tubbs Tisdale, L. "Women's Ways of Communicating." In *Women, Gender and Christian Community* edited by J. Dempsey Douglas and J. F. Kay, 104–14. Louisville: Westminster/John Knox, 1997.

Twelftree, Graham, ed. *Miracles.* Cambridge: Cambridge University Press, 2011.

Twenge, Jean M. *Generation Me: Why Today's Young Americans Are More Confident, Assertive, Entitled—and More Miserable Than Ever Before.* New York: Free, 2006.

Uecker, Jeremy E., et al. "Losing My Religion: The Social Sources of Religious Decline in Early Adulthood." *Social Forces* 85.4 (2007) 667–92.

Universities and Colleges Christian Fellowship (UCCF). "Vision and Values." Online: http:// www.uccf. org.uk/about/mission-vision-values.htm.

Vanhoozer, Kevin J. *Remythologizing Theology.* Cambridge: Cambridge University Press, 2010.

Vaidhyanathan, Siva. "Generational Myth: Not All Young People Are Tech-savy." Online: http://www.itma.vt.edu/modules/spring11/efund/lesson3/Vaidhyanathan 2008MyhOfDigialNatives.pdf.

Village, Andrew. *The Bible and Lay People.* Aldershot, UK: Ashgate, 2007.

————. "Biblical Interpretative Horizons and Ordinary Readers: An Empirical Study." *Research in the Social Scientific Study of Religion* 17 (2007) 157–76.

Vincent, John. *Acts in Practise.* Practise Interpretation 2. Blandford Forum, UK: Deo, 2012.

————, ed. *Stilling the Storm: Contemporary Responses to Mark 4.35—5.1.* Practise Interpretation 1. Blandford Forum, UK: Deo, 2012.

Vineyard. "Statement of Faith." Online: http://www.vineyardchurches.org.uk/about-vineyard-churches/statement-of-faith.html.

Volf, M. *Exclusion and Embrace: A Theological Exploration of Identity, Otherness, and Reconciliation.* Nashville: Abingdon, 1996.

Wagner, C. Peter. *Confronting the Powers.* Venture, CA: Regal, 1996.

Walaskay, Paul W. *Acts.* Louisvillem KY: Westminster/John Knox, 1988.

Walker, Andrew G. "Demonology and the Charismatic Movement." In *The Love of Power of The Power of Love: A Careful Assessment of the Problems within the*

Charismatic and Word-of-Faith Movements, edited by Tom Smail et al., 53–72. Minneapolis: Bethany House, 1994.

Walton, R. *Disciples Together: Discipleship, Formation, and Small Groups.* London: SCM, 2014.

————. "Using the Bible and Christian Tradition in Theological Reflection." *British Journal of Theological Education* 13.2 (2003) 133–51.

Ward, Keith. *Divine Action: Examining God's Role in an Open and Emergent Universe.* Philadelphia: Templeton Foundation, 1990.

Ward, Pete. *Growing Up Evangelical: Youth Work and the Making of a Subculture.* London: SPCK, 1997.

————. "The Tribes of Evangelicalism." In *The Post-Evangelical Debate,* edited by G. Cray et al, 19–34. London: Triangle, 1997.

Ward, Peter, and Heidi Campbell. "Ordinary Theology as Narratives: An Empirical Study of Young People's Charismatic Worship in Scotland." *International Journal of Practical Theology* 15 (2001) 226–42.

Warner, Rob. *Reinventing English Evangelicalism 1996–2001: A Theological and Sociological Study.* Studies in Evangelical History and Thought. Milton Keynes, UK: Paternoster, 2007.

Warnock, A. "Grudem Retracts." Online: http://www.patheos.com/blogs/adrianwarnock /2006/12/wayne-grudem-retracts-his-agreement-to-the-use-of-the-word-blasphemy-in-regard-to-Steve-Chalke.

Warrior, R. A. "A Native American Perspective: Canaanites, Cowboys, and Indians." In *Voices from the Margin; Interpreting the Bible in the Third World,* edited by R. S. Sugirtharajah, 287–96. London: SPCK, 1991.

Weber, Katherine. "Rob Bell Tells How *Love Wins* Led to Mars Hill Departure." *Christian Post,* Dec 3, 2012. Online: http://www.christianpost.com/news/rob-bell-tells-how-love-wins-led-to-mars-hill-departure-85995.

Wellman, J. K., et al. "God Is Like a Drug . . . : Explaining Interaction Ritual Chains in American Megachurches." *Sociological Forum* 29.3 (2014) 650–73.

Wengraf, Tom. *Qualitative Research Interviewing.* London: Sage, 2001.

West, C., and D Zimmerman. "Small Insults: A Study of Interruptions in Cross-Sex Conversations between Unacquainted Persons." In *Language, Gender and Society,* edited by B. Thorne et al, 103–18. Cambridge, MA: Newbury House, 1983.

West, Gerald. *The Academy of the Poor: Towards a Dialogical Reading of the Bible.* Sheffield, UK: Sheffield Academic Press, 1999.

Whitney, Donald S. "Teaching Scripture Intake." In *The Christian Educators Handbook on Spiritual Formation,* edited by Kenneth O. Gangel and James C. Wilhoit, 164–73. Grand Rapids: Baker, 1997.

Wilcox, W. Bradford. *Soft Patriarchs: New Men.* Chicago: University of Chicago Press, 2004.

Wilkinson, Bruce. *The Prayer of Jabez: Breaking through to the Blessed Life.* Colorado Springs: Multnomah, 2000.

Wilson, Bryan. *Social Dimensions in Sectarianism.* Oxford: Oxford University Press, 2004.

Wimber, John, and Kevin Springer. *Power Evangelism: Signs and Wonders Today.* London: Hodder & Stoughton, 1985.

Wink, Walter. *Transforming Bible Study.* Nashville: Abingdon, 1980.

Winston, D. "Answered Prayers: The Rock Haven House Fellowship." In *I Come Away Stronger, How Small Groups are Shaping American Religion,* edited by R. Wuthnow, 7–36. Grand Rapids: Eerdmans, 1994.

Wiseman, Donald J. *1 and 2 Kings.* Tyndale. Leicester, UK: IVP, 1993.

Witherington III, Ben. *The Acts of the Apostles: A Socio-Rhetorical Commentary.* Grand Rapids: Eerdmans, 1998.

———. *Women in the Earliest Churches.* Cambridge: Cambridge University Press, 1988.

Wood, M. T. "Penal Substitution in the Construction of British Evangelical Identity: Controversies in the Doctrine of the Atonement in the Mid-2000s." PhD diss, Durham University, 2011.

Woodhead, Linda. "Epilogue." In *Religion and Youth,* edited by Sylvia Collins-Mayo and Pink Dandelion, 239. Farnham, UK: Ashgate, 2010.

———. "Gender Differences in Religious Practise and Significance." In *The Sage Handbook of the Sociology of Religion,* edited by J. Beckford and N. J. Demerath, 566–86. Los Angeles: Sage, 2007.

———. "Introduction." In *Religion and Change in Modern Britain,* edited by Linda Woodhead and Rebecca Catto, 1–3. London: Routledge, 2012.

Wolffe, John. *The Expansion of Evangelicalism.* Nottingham, UK: IVP, 2006.

Wright, Nigel. *The Radical Evangelical: Seeking a Place to Stand.* London: SPCK, 1996.

———. "The Theology of Signs and Wonders." In *The Love of Power or the Power of Love,* edited by Tom Smail et al., 37–52. Minneapolis: Bethany House, 1994.

Wright, N. T. *Scripture and the Authority of God.* London: SPCK, 2005.

Wuthnow, Robert, ed. *After the Baby Boomers: How Twenty and Thirty Somethings are Shaping the Future of American Religion.* Princeton: Princeton University Press, 2007.

———. *I Come Away Stronger, How Small Groups are Shaping American Religion.* Grand Rapids: Eerdmans, 1994.

———. *Sharing the Journey: Support Groups and America's New Quest for Community.* New York: Free, 1994.

Lightning Source UK Ltd.
Milton Keynes UK
UKOW05f1952211116
288210UK00002B/2/P

9 781498 293426